BELFAST IN THE THIRTIES

AN ORAL HISTORY

RONNIE MUNCK & BILL ROLSTON

WITH GERRY MOORE

THE
BLACKSTAFF
PRESS

First published in 1987 by
The Blackstaff Press Limited
3 Galway Park, Dundonald, Belfast BT16 0AN, Northern Ireland

Printed in Northern Ireland by
The Universities Press Limited

British Library Cataloguing in Publication Data
Munck, Ronnie
Belfast in the thirties : an oral history.
1. Belfast (Northern Ireland) — Social
life and customs
I. Title II. Rolston, Bill
941.6'70822 DA995.B5

ISBN 0 85640 374 1

Contents

Preface

There is a standard view of Belfast, and one which has been exacerbated in this past generation of 'troubles', that if there is one word which sums up the city it is 'sectarianism'. Now, while it is true that every aspect of life is pervaded to some extent, whether consciously or unconsciously, by sectarian division, sectarianism is not the totality of the Belfast experience. This is especially true when one considers political activity and consciousness in Belfast. If normal Belfast politics is about sectarianism, then the appearance of any other political form, for example, socialism, is seen as abnormal. The abnormal requires an explanation. By analogy, the explanation is of non-sectarian politics as a seed which tries to break through, but is constantly smothered by the dead weight of sectarianism and the machinations of sectarian politicians. Sectarianism and non-sectarianism are portrayed as two sides of the one coin; the fate of one is seen to be totally dependent on the fate of the other.

We reject that explanation and argue instead that as Ireland's main industrial city, Belfast also has another history and another politics, which can be loosely termed 'socialist'. There are numerous examples of labour militancy, strikes, unemployment marches, etc. Sometimes socialism is totally over-shadowed by sectarianism, but the crucial point is that it has never been non-existent. So, the history of Belfast is that of at least two major forces, and of the relationship between them.

That relationship is far from simple. There is, of course, an endemic intertwining of the two forces, an interplay which at times frustrates the analyst attempting to examine each strand in turn. But it is one of the central points of this book that the two strands are, at least analytically, relatively autonomous from each other. The metaphor of them being two sides of the same coin is therefore an inadequate one; they are more realistically comparable to two ends of the one spectrum, or two tides lapping on the same shore.

Our task is to examine each of the forces and the interplay between them in one specific period, the 1930s. More specifically, we focus on the years between 1932 (when the Outdoor Relief strike, a high point of what we have termed socialist politics, occurred) and 1935 (when there were bloody sectarian riots). We attempt to portray these events not as starkly isolated ones, but within the context of the complexity of real politics and consciousness. In short, we seek to look as much at the nuances as at the extremes. These nuances are often well known to people who experienced the thirties directly. So, it was to such people that we turned in compiling our story. The reminiscences of approximately fifty people (see Appendix 1) are the base of this book.

When it comes to acknowledgements we must of course begin by thanking these respondents for their time, patience, openness and above all trust. We can only hope that in transcribing what they had to say and in choosing excerpts for this book we have not betrayed that trust.

We wish to thank also Tony Gallagher for his help in the tedious task of transcription, his newspaper research and his interviewing, and Marie Quierry for transcription and for ploughing through the records of the Belfast Trades Council in the Public Record Office of Northern Ireland. Thanks are due to the Trades Council for permission to examine these records. Thanks too to the staffs of various libraries, in particular Belfast Central and Ulster Polytechnic but above all to John Gray and John Killen of the Linen Hall Library. Philip Johnston of the Ulster Polytechnic was our main link to the often frustrating world of audio taping. And numerous people gave us names, addresses, advice and other leads which proved invaluable in the pursuit of respondents and written and photographic sources; our thanks to them all.

The research was made possible by the generosity of two institutions: the Ulster Polytechnic, now the University of Ulster at Jordanstown, which provided six months salary for a Research Assistant, and the Nuffield Foundation which provided a further five months salary. Without both of these grants we doubt if we could have produced this book.

Finally, we would like to thank our Research Assistant. Gerry Moore combined all the skills of academic researcher, door-to-door salesperson, private detective and confidante. It perhaps sounds too much of a cliche to say that the project would not have succeeded without him. But we can think of no other way of stating the obvious truth; he conducted most of the interviews, having in the first place tracked down most of the respondents, and he did large amounts of the transcribing. Without him we would have had no data on which to base what follows.

This book has thus resulted from a collective effort. However, as in all such endeavours, there is ultimately a division of labour. Thus, when it came to the actual writing, Bill Rolston was responsible for Part One, and Ronnie Munck for Part Two and the Afterword on Ideology.

Introduction

In Northern Ireland oral history is in its infancy, at least as regards the treatment of politics and social conflict. For several years this method has been used to collect folklore material, especially in a rural setting, and this tradition has recently coalesced in the Ulster Society for Oral History. Our own project – Belfast in the 1930s – was explicitly concerned with social, political and even armed conflict so we knew our difficulties were going to be considerable. Here we describe some of these difficulties and the lessons we learned in the course of our research. We had no experience of oral history. The project sprang in fact from our political commitment. In 1982 it was to be the 50th Anniversary of the 1932 Outdoor Relief (ODR) strike when Protestant and Catholic unemployed workers for once fought together against the state in a short but sharp battle. Our idea was simply to "do something" to commemorate these events which were an important element in the tradition of the local labour movement. Interviews with participants seemed the obvious way to reconstruct the sequence of events and their significance. Our theoretical underpinning was Marxism, but its orthodox version did not prepare us well to understand the complexity of social and sectarian conflict and, above all, the contradictory nature of ideology.

Riots and pogroms

We began our project with only some very general research hypotheses. We knew, largely from the Communist Party literature[1], that in 1932 Protestant and Catholic unemployed workers had "crossed the sectarian divide" to take militant class action against the state. The supposed class unity of this period was often referred to in labour or socialist circles as a "golden era" which we should strive to recreate. Yet, we also knew that in 1935 some of the worst sectarian riots since the creation of the Northern Ireland state in 1920-22 had taken place in Belfast. What had happened between the ODR strike in 1932 and the riots of 1935 which many referred to as a "pogrom"? Our working hypothesis was that the "class unity" of 1932 had been exaggerated and that events of 1935 were not a break in the historical pattern but an eruption of a relatively autonomous "sectarian politics". We believed, in short, that class and religion generated two forms of political practice with independent rhythms and were not mutually exclusive.

As our interviews were proceeding local trade union official Paddy Devlin published his account of outdoor relief in Belfast between 1920 and 1939 which also focused on the 1932 events.[2] Extracts of the book appeared in *The Irish Times* and these elicited a letter from John McWade, a participant in the early unemployed marches. McWade made the point that 1932 was not the first move to unite Protestant and Catholic unemployed workers and cited a number of marches in the 1920s. He also questioned the role allotted to Betty Sinclair and Tommy Geehan of the Communist Party (or Revolutionary Workers' Group as it was known then) in the 1932 events. He concluded that "if history has to be written, let it be written accurately – from first hand sources" (*The Irish Times*, 30 September 1981). What McWade had done in this letter, and in subsequent interviews we held with him, was place 1932 in some kind of context. It was not a one-off affair and many others had been active on unemployment before the Communist Party came on the scene. This was already sowing doubts in our minds about the traditional account of 1932 as a unique event in Belfast's labour history. A number of our interviews also failed to confirm the "romantic" view of 1932 as expressed in the Revolutionary Workers' Group' statement:

> "The working class of the North is razing to the ground the disunity barriers erected by generations of imperialist deception and intrigue. A new era is opening up in the Irish working class movement."
>
> (*Irish Workers' Voice*, 15.10.32)

The next point on which our own "demystification" occurred was over the 1935 riots. These were usually accounted for by socialists as a result of a number of sectarian initiatives and declarations of Unionist politicians after 1932 – "beating the Orange drum" in short.[3] Paddy Devlin faithfully reflects this image when he writes of the Prime Minister's

> " . . . attempts to drive the Protestant working class away from their fellow workers. He had concluded that the only way to do it was to blow apart the newly forged unity between Catholic and Protestant unemployed . . . By 1935, the Unionist Party had recovered its position in the working-class areas, and was again able to influence events in ways that suited their strategy. Riots returned to inner Belfast, and before they were finished, 500 Catholic families had been driven from their homes, hundreds of people suffered gunshot wounds or injuries and thirteen people were killed."[4]

As we began to delve into the events after 1932 – through interviews and conventional historical research – we could see many problems with this interpretation. Firstly, sectarian speeches by politicians could certainly influence public opinion but they could hardly have caused the 1935 riots on their own. This view was far too conspiratorial. Secondly, even given the class militancy of 1932, as sectarianism had never died out it was futile to call for the "real" class struggle to replace it as the Communist Party did in 1935 (and Devlin does by implication). Sectarian divisions had a dynamic of their own and sectarian struggles were as "normal" as class struggles, so that it was pointless to call for a "restoration" of some "pure" working-class unity which had never existed.

Class and sectarian divisions and struggles could operate together – one did not cancel out the other. As we point out in Chapter One, in 1932 itself, trains and buses were attacked in various areas as they made their way to an international Catholic religious festival in Dublin. In 1933, the still strong movement against unemployment continued but also the first sectarian killing since 1922 occurred. In 1934, the most important strike since the 1920s which paralysed the railways (with the help of the IRA) was matched by renewed sectarian agitation by the Ulster Protestant League. So, in 1935 while socialism appeared to be on the rise in Belfast, the other standard element of life in the city, sectarianism, was daily growing in strength. The "romantic" account of 1932 needed an outside factor (manipulation) to explain why the unity of class action was tainted by the sectarian riots of 1935. Our account shows a much more complex trajectory of class and "religious" divisions.

In conclusion, we believe that existing accounts of the 1930s have, by concentrating on October 1932, ignored the extent of working-class agitation on issues such as unemployment throughout the 1920s and 1930s. Secondly, they overestimate the importance of the actions of Unionist politicians in the continuance of sectarian divisions in the working class. Thirdly, they exaggerate the extent of working-class unity in October 1932 and the extent that 1935 represents a break in this pattern. Our original aim – to study the "transition" from 1932 to 1935 – had thus become redefined as we broke with the simplistic accounts we had started with.

Interviews and life stories

The first step in our research design was to make a choice of research technique. We saw the oral history approach – interviews with key participants and "ordinary people" – as providing us both with factual information and the subjective element, "their truth" as Ronald Fraser[5] called it. As a slight variant of this we decided to collect "life histories" or "life stories"[6] of people we took to be representative of socialists, republicans and our composite picture of the Protestant shipyard worker (the "labour aristocrat"). Our second step was the choice of population and we decided against random sampling in favour of theoretical sampling, i.e. looking for people who were likely to be most fruitful and revealing for the questions we were interested in. In the prevalent political situation we had to reject newspaper advertisements as a means of finding respondents – a certain level of trust had to be built up which the impersonal medium of advertising precluded. Instead we sought out "gatekeepers" to the various milieus we were interested in: the shipyard, the linen-mills, the trade unions, the socialist movement and the IRA. From then on we proceeded by what is somewhat grandly known as the "snowball strategy"[7] – gradually accumulating respondents and knowledge and refining our questions.

We did not elaborate a formal interview schedule which we thought would freeze what was after all a two-way process. What we had instead was a set of questions in the back of our minds (or on scraps of paper) to guide the interview or revive it when it was flagging. Absolutely clear, well researched questioning was essential but from then on we allowed considerable flexibility in our interview procedure. With shipyard and linen-mill workers we wished to clarify the nature of the work process, the internal social relations of the enterprise, and so on. With socialists and republicans we geared our questioning to their participation in major events of the 1930s on the one hand, and engaged in what amounted to a political debate with their outlook on the other. This is where some of the most revealing material emerged, when we could challenge, probe and debate in a constructive spirit. Other people we interviewed had no particular political role in the 1930s but were well versed in the history and outlook of their communities. We were seeking a reconstruction of everyday life in the working-class communities of Belfast and the effects of unemployment, which had been the mainspring of the 1932 riots. This "social history" side of our research was to prove the most well documented part of the project as there were many parliamentary and medical reports we could call on to build up a picture of social conditions which would frame our interview schedule.

As the research was being completed we became concerned about the representativeness of our respondents. We had 50 interviews in hand: 14 with workers (mainly from the shipyard and the linen mills) and 12 each with republicans, socialists and, for want of a better word, "ordinary people". The interviews were on average 1½ hours long, and we had followed up "good" respondents with a second, more directed, interview. We were worried that what we had was a "self-selected sample" – the most articulate and politicized having come forward, or worse, just those from certain circles or cliques. At one level we could remedy this by casting our nets wider and pursuing even the most unlikely leads. By now incidentally any notion of "sampling" (representative, theoretical or otherwise) was becoming meaningless. Our "interview selection process" depended fundamentally on the skills and methods of the detective, developed by our research assistant. At another level, as we proceeded to the transcription of our tapes, we became reassured as to the representativeness of our interviews. Our understanding of local history, our theory of social conflict, of the labour process and so on "told us" we were on the right tracks. As Bertaux notes in another case, "we may say that our sample is representative, not at the morphological level (at the level of superficial description), but at the sociological level, at the level of sociostructural relations."[8] This view, of course, represents a break with empiricist social science, and the canons of its methodology text books.

A considerably more serious problem in the end was that of gaps in our data collection process. We first noted an under-representation of women in our sample but this we remedied with the help of a temporary female research assistant. Though we filled the gap to a certain extent we would feel now that we neglected the area of gender relations and the sexual division of labour. Our overriding concern with the historical questions mentioned above kept us from focusing on this theme vital for any full reconstruction of Belfast life in the 1930s. The other major divide in Belfast society was of course between Protestants and Catholics and here we found that our initial contacts were mainly in the second community. Through our trade union contacts we were led to the shipyard workers, an almost exclusively Protestant group, but we still lacked a Protestant equivalent of an "IRA man". Various historical accounts referred to the Ulster Protestant League (UPL), an extremist Protestant grouping, which became active after the 1932 struggle and was supposedly instrumental in creating the sectarian atmosphere which led to the 1935 "pogrom".[9] Despite considerable efforts we could find no-one who had been a member of it. Our provisional conclusions are that the group was much smaller and more fluid than we supposed and that present day official condemnation of sectarianism made it more difficult for someone to admit membership of an openly sectarian organisation. Nevertheless, the gap is a serious one.

As the last interview was completed we had begun to appreciate to what an extent oral history was a *social* process. Various incidents helped highlight what we were beginning to realise theoretically. In one case an interview with a female linen mill worker fell through because her husband did not wish her to talk about the period when *he* (by rights the bread winner) had been unemployed. Another time we had set up an interview in the City Hall with a prominent Unionist politician (who had been active in labour politics in the 1930s) but in the interim a Unionist MP had been shot dead by the IRA. Early one morning our unfortunate research assistant was visited by heavily armed forces of the state who thought his interest in this politician might have been more than scholarly. In different ways we saw to what extent oral history was more than just about the past, but was really concerned with the relation between the past and the present. There was no escaping the conflicts of the present – both personal and political – in our study of the past. In fact, we could understand why the authors of another Irish oral history, which appeared as we were completing our research, could say that "the purpose of [their] book has been to somehow find the present through the past".[10]

History and oral evidence

The historical establishment tends to frown on oral evidence, clinging still to the apparent security of the archive and the public records office. Eminent British historian A.J.P. Taylor states the traditional position on the interview method: "In this matter I am an almost total sceptic . . . Old men drooling about their youth – No".[11] In the chapters which follow readers can judge for themselves the value of the oral history method. In this introduction we want to confront some of the methodological problems which arise in this relatively new area of historical research.

As newcomers to oral history we were struck by the lack of explicit theoretical underpinnings in some of the work we had seen. It is somehow as though the method is "obvious" (pick up a tape-recorder and go out and interview) so that theory is not necessary. We feel that theoretical assumptions should be made explicit in oral history work or we will fall into the positivist trap of thinking our method is neutral and not dictated by our theory. Before we went "into the field" we had clear ideas about the Belfast class structure, the question of sectarianism, the labour process, gender oppression and so on. No one could even approach Irish history without some kind of theory of nationalism for example. It was only based on this prior work[12] that we thought the issues raised in our oral history project were worthwhile; it helped us frame our questions, it largely dictated how we interpreted our answers. The interplay of theory and observation is a complex one but we cannot pretend that oral history is the naive method that its detractors, and some of its earlier supporters, portrayed.

Some practitioners of oral history, such as Jan Vansina, tend to judge the "truth" value of each testimony on largely internal grounds without cross-checking testimonies or using other kinds of evidence.[13] Whatever the value of this approach in an anthropological context we adopted a fairly meticulous policy of triangulation.[14] In the first place we carried out what may be called "investigator triangulation". That is, each transcript was checked by two or three researchers to ensure that it said what people had meant to say. In the second place we systematically did a cross-method triangulation in that every piece of oral evidence that could be was checked against a range of written sources: newspapers, parliamentary reports, documents, etc. Finally, there was a considerable amount of data triangulation possible within the oral sources themselves. One case was that of a socialist who told us:

> "The meeting was to be held in Templemore Avenue with banners like 'give us bread or we'll turn red'. Then the lambeg drummers

came out and a riot ensued. The police charged the marchers and the lambeg drummers were well protected. Many a sore head was felt by the marchers and their supporters."

By a happy coincidence we came across a loyalist who remembered:

"Not far from our house there was a field on Templemore Avenue where a Labour man would come to have his meeting. We'd take out the wee window in the kitchen to get the (lambeg) drums out and go round beside the Labour man and nobody could hear him, they drummed the whole time until the Labour man went away, he never got staying."

It is also widely acknowledged that oral history becomes more difficult when we pass from social history to political history, from the micro to the macro. Henige says that one of the major challenges of oral history is to persuade our informants "to go beyond the personal and idiosyncratic by making connections, discussing issues, and providing wider perspectives".[15] This seems somewhat of a false problem because surely the job of "providing wider perspectives" belongs to the oral historian. In Belfast, where people are generally very "political", in a local sense at least, this problem did not arise. There were of course cases of people who took no part in the 1932 events or who hardly knew they had taken place. The real problem for us was that of creating a "bridge" between the personal and political. There seems to be a lack of mediation between theories of the social structure and social change, and the experiences and recollections of the individual. The Popular Memory Group correctly stresses the need to find "some way of bridging the large-scale social processes which are the usual objects of historical accounts and the small-scale 'private' narratives which are the very stuff of personal memories".[16] We believe in the social determination of the individual so that our respondents would be part of a broader social flow whatever personal characteristics might be displayed. Furthermore, the life stories are part of a larger general history, be it that of class formation or national divisions.

Finally, in "doing" oral history one inevitably tends to reflect on the politics of this method precisely because it is so much closer to social reality than the experiment or the survey. The exponents of oral history have made important claims on its behalf. For Paul Thompson it "can be a means for transforming both the content and the purpose of history . . . it can give back to the people who made and experienced history, through their own words, a central place".[17] For Gary Okihiro "it has a potential for raising social consciousness and can provide strategies for social change".[18] We would not wish to detract from these aims and objectives – if we did not share them we would not be doing oral history – but we think some *caveats* are in order. Firstly, there is nothing in any method which is inherently democratic or radical – to believe otherwise would be a form of positivism – and oral history could equally become reactionary and antiquarian. Secondly, there seem to be a number of methodological weaknesses still which means that much of oral history is merely descriptive, not to mention the problem of memory, consciousness, etc.[19] The third, and most important, objection is raised by Luisa Passerini who sees the danger of oral history falling into "complacent populism", and a "facile democratisation" arguing that "such an approach runs the risk of constructing oral history as merely an alternative ghetto, where at last the oppressed may be allowed to speak".[20] Being aware of these dangers we can strive to avoid them.

FOOTNOTES

1. See Communist Party of Ireland, n.d.
2. Devlin, P. 1981
3. See Farrell, M. 1980: chapter 6
4. Devlin, P. 1981: 32
5. Fraser, R. 1981: 32
6. Bertaux, D. 1982
7. Ibid: 37
8. Ibid: 39
9. Farrell, M. 1980: 136
10. Griffith, K; O'Grady, T. 1982: 357
11. Cited in B. Harrison, 1976: 46
12. See for example, Rolston, B. 1980 (a) and (b), and Munck, R. 1985 and 1986
13. Rosaldo, R. 1980: 93
14. See Denzin, N. 1970: chapter 10
15. Henige, D. 1982: 110
16. Popular Memory Group, 1982: 234
17. Thompson, P. 1978: 2
18. Okihiro, G. 1981: 43
19. A critique of traditional oral history is developed in Munck, R., and Rolston, B. 1985 and 1986
20. Passerini, L. 1979: 84

PART ONE

Part One paints the backdrop against which the actions of our fifty respondents were played out. In Chapter 1 we consider in detail the history of the thirties in Belfast, and in particular those two main elements of Belfast politics and consciousness, socialism and sectarianism. The chapter concentrates especially on the high points of each element – the Outdoor Relief strike of 1932 and the sectarian riots of 1935. In Chapter 2 the social conditions experienced by Belfast's working class are examined. We do not consider the experience of paid employment until Chapter 3; here we concentrate on unemployment, health, housing, poverty, etc. using both official reports and the reminiscences of our respondents.

1. From 1932 to 1935: Socialism and Sectarianism in Belfast

When, after days of rioting in October 1932, the Outdoor Relief strike reached a successful conclusion, Tommy Geehan, the most public of its organisers told the strikers:

> "We have achieved a glorious victory. What we have achieved gives a direct lie to all who said that the workers here could not be united and would not fight. We have taken part in a glorious struggle which will be for ever remembered in the working-class history of Northern Ireland."

Yet, in 1973, when Budge and O'Leary published their comprehensive and lengthy study of Belfast politics from 1613 to 1970, they allocated only one small paragraph to the mention of the "almost forgotten riot" of October 1932[1]. While it may be possible to attribute their dismissal to a typical blindness on the part of mainstream historians to the history of working-class struggle, this would not account for the fact that Belfast's working class would seem to have defeated Geehan's prediction. For many years there were no annual commemorations and no glowing references in trade union leaders' speeches to the ODR riots. The "glorious struggle", it would seem, was remembered by few.

The exception was the CPI, not surprisingly, given its central role in the organisation of the strike. Yet, the task of salvaging the history of that important event in Belfast working-class history is not made easier by the CPI's romantic interpretation of it. October 1932 was eulogised by them as *the* unique example since the formation of the NI state of the working class casting aside its sectarianism and engaging in unadulterated class action. The romantic account needed to explain why such purity was so quickly tainted, as evidenced by the ferocity of the 1935 sectarian riots. The re-emergence of sectarianism was seen to result from the actions of Unionist politicians who, scared by the surge of unity, waved the flag and beat the Orange drum, thus dividing the working class once more. There are a number of flaws in this account. Firstly, by concentrating on October 1932, it ignores the extent of working-class agitation on issues such as unemployment throughout the twenties and thirties, as we shall see in Chapter 2.

Secondly, it over-estimates the importance of the actions of Unionist politicians and the continuance of sectarian division in the working class. And thirdly, it exaggerates the extent of working-class "unity" in October 1932.

To publicise one's own contribution to an historical occurrence is a valid endeavour. But it cannot be confused with the attempt to write a full history. An account of October 1932 which is both historically valid and perhaps even politically prescriptive must not only break the silence of mainstream historians, but also cut behind the romantic myth which has been built around the ODR strike.

Unemployment in the thirties

As the ODR strike was primarily an event in the politics of unemployment, it is necessary to begin by charting the extent of unemployment during the period.

As the twenties gave way to the thirties, the likelihood of having a job decreased for working-class people in Belfast. We recount in Chapter 3 the experiences of those who had jobs. But, bad as the experience may have been for those in work, it was better than the alternative of no job. For, in the thirties, to have no job meant often to have no income, or at most to have less money than was needed to survive. Either way, the experience of unemployment was a devastating one.

It was an experience shared by many, as the graph opposite shows. What must be remembered is that the figures presented here are for those *officially* unemployed. There were many able and willing to work who were not classed as unemployed by the state. Unemployment insurance schemes were widened in 1936 to include agricultural workers,[2] and from 1939 insured and unemployed agricultural workers were thus included in the statistics; prior to that they were not. Also excluded were uninsured workers, and, prior to 1940, workers under the age of sixteen. Consequently, a more accurate measure of the numbers of unemployed would have to include those actually unemployed people not judged statistically relevant. Such a measure is impossible to obtain, but it is possible that it would raise the official number of unemployed in any of these years by perhaps another one third or one half.

But, even the official figures are horrifying enough. The unemployment rate averaged around 15% in the few years before the Wall Street Crash, but within two years it had almost doubled, to 28%. In fact, in the period recalled by those people we interviewed, at least one in four was out of work. For some trades it was worse than others. J. Campbell of the Sheet Metal Workers' Union reported that 50% of his members were unemployed in

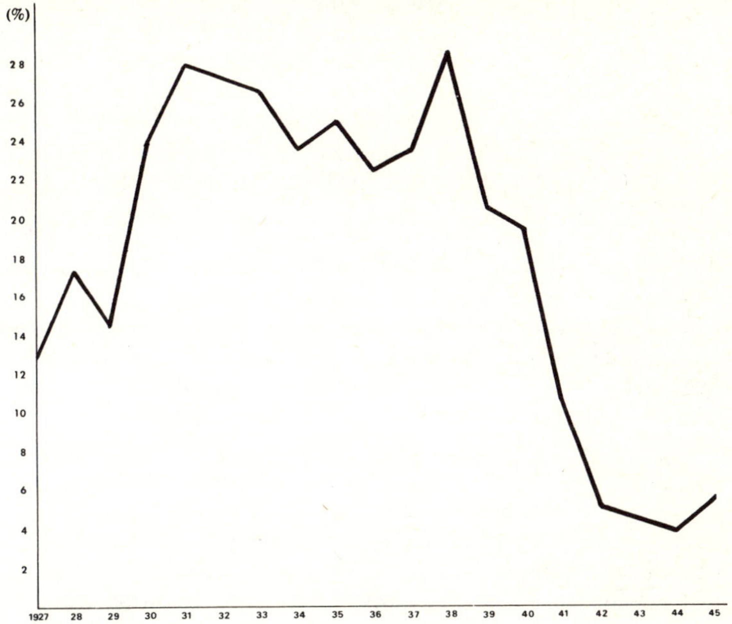

Unemployment rates in NI, 1927/45

December 1931.[3] And in March 1932, the Shipwrights' representative to the Belfast Trades Council, Atkinson, announced that out of a membership of 700 in his union only 40 were employed.[4] Throughout 1932 the worst-hit trades were shipbuilding and the building industry, as the following figures show.

INDUSTRY	UNEMPLOYMENT
Building	39.2%
Distributive Trades	17.6%
Flax and Linen	23.5%
Food and Drink	14.7%
Shipbuilding	57.0%
Tailoring/Dressmaking	26.9%

(Unemployment rates in specific industries, 1932; source: *Ulster Yearbook*).

The two central planks of the Northern Ireland local economy were collapsing. In 1932 no ships were launched in Harland and Wolff's, and only a skeleton workforce remained in the yard. "The grass grew on the slips", as anyone who lived through the period can recall. Over in the "wee yard", Workman Clark's, things proved to be even worse. W.J. Lovett, the director, had, perhaps unwittingly, accurately foretold the future when he stated in February 1930:

> "At present 50% of their building slips would suffice for the required output, and expensively-equipped yards working at 50% capacity in the face of fierce competition could not hope to be commercially sound."[5]

In 1934 Workman Clark's launched the *Acavus,* the 536th ship built there since the yard opened in 1879. In January 1935 the 'wee yard' closed, never to reopen.

In the other main industry, textiles, where many women had found employment, things looked quite bleak too. In January 1930 F. J. MacLean of the Whiteabbey Flax Company had told a meeting of the Carrick Unionist Association that:

> "there was no use trying to make the public believe that things were improving, because they were not. That is the stuff we are fed by professional politicians year in and year out. Unless the question is seriously taken up, I really wonder what the end of the whole thing is going to be."[6]

The textile industry as a whole survived during the following years, but many individual firms, especially the smaller ones, closed, laying off numerous workers. As the world-wide demand for linen was shrinking, many of these workers would never again be employed in the linen industry. There had been almost 87,000 employed in 1924; by 1935 the number was down to 61,000.[7]

As the number of unemployed increased and the time they were unemployed lengthened, the issue of unemployment became important to the working class, not only socially and emotionally, but also politically.

The politics of unemployment in Ireland and Britain

In organising on the issue of unemployment in 1932, the working class of Belfast was not unique in Irish terms. Taking just the one month of October 1932, even a cursory perusal of the newspapers reveals the extent of militancy throughout Ireland. In that one month the unemployed marched, sent delegations to councils, and even invaded council meetings in places as dispersed as Derry, Armagh, Kilkenny, Dublin, Cork, Larne, Clonmel, Drogheda, Leitrim, Carlow, New Ross, Portlaoise, Waterford, Cobh and Newry.

In short, Belfast in October 1932 was not out of step. Indeed, what would have been unusual would have been the *lack* of agitation on unemployment in the largest industrial city in Ireland.

There was one sense, however, in which Belfast's agitation was unique in an Irish context, namely, that it was violent. But even that uniqueness disappears when we take a look at Belfast in a United Kingdom context. In the months of September and October 1932 there were large marches of 10,000 or more unemployed in many British cities. Many of these were attacked by police leading to hours and sometimes days of rioting. Birkenhead, Liverpool, Westham, Clydeside, Croydon, North Shields, Paisley, Bristol, and central London were among the places where major riots occurred during that nine-week period. It was during the same period, on 11 October 1932, that Belfast erupted.

The politics of unemployment in Belfast

As a political event, the ODR strike in Belfast is noteworthy in a number of ways. It is not, however, unique, even in Belfast terms. In Chapter 5 we will look at the activities of socialists in Belfast in the 1920s. The one issue which predominated in the politics of these socialists in the period was, not surprisingly, that of unemployment. With very few resources and little support from the official trade union movement, they agitated and organised on the issue, sometimes with remarkable success.

It is in this context that the activities of the Communist Party on the issue of unemployment in the thirties must be seen. The party was able to build on the activities of the socialists of the twenties. Because the other groups had been active throughout the twenties, the CP was not in the position of trying to plough uncultivated land. Moreover, even the CP's contribution to the events of October 1932 itself must not be exaggerated. The issue of unemployment came to a head at that point. The acumen of the CP was to seek to channel the groundswell of militancy such as had not been seen in Belfast for some years – since the 44-hour strike of 1919.

There had been an embryonic CP in Ireland in the twenties, the Worker's Party of Ireland. After its collapse, the national leadership began to organise towards the establishment of a new CP. In January 1930, one branch of what was later to become that new party was established in Belfast. Originally titled the Workers' Revolutionary Party, its name was changed in 1931; the local branches were referred to as Revolutionary Workers' Groups. The Belfast district committee included Loftus Johnston (of the Woodworkers' Society), Jimmy Kater (also of the Woodworkers') and Tommy Geehan (an unemployed textile worker). Yet, despite their trade union credentials, Belfast's RWG, in line with the dominant CP philosophy at the time, was bitterly opposed to official trade union leaders. Thus, William Boyd of the RWG, invited to address the NILP conference in April 1930, rewarded his hosts by condemning them as "traitors and social fascists". Not surprisingly, the official trade union movement was wary of the RWG , and any valid criticisms the Group may have had of the movement were easily ignored because of the ferocity of the criticisms. For their part, the RWG decided to organise on that one issue which, apart from being the most politically pressing, was the one on which the official trade union movement had proved unable and/or reluctant to act – namely, unemployment[8].

The RWG used two broad tactics in their strategy on unemployment. The first was putting up RWG, or supporting non-RWG, but sympathetic, candidates for elections to Belfast Corporation and the Poor Law Guardians. In this tactic they were decidedly unsuccessful. No RWG candidates were elected. Moreover, Phil Wilson, who had been on the Board of Guardians since 1927 as a NILP member, lost his seat when he stood for re-election in May 1930 on an Irish National Unemployment Movement ticket. The INUM was an RWG-inspired movement, and it represented the cutting edge of the Group's second main tactic, building a political organisation of the unemployed. In this the RWG was much more successful. They were helped by cuts in the unemployment benefit forced upon Ramsay MacDonald's coalition government in 1931 as a condition of international loans. Many unemployed were suddenly cut off from benefits. They were thus open to the RWG message and attended meetings and marches organised by the Group throughout 1931. For a while daily meetings were held outside the unemployment exchange in Frederick Street, and the RWG managed to form active branches not only on the Falls Road, but in largely Protestant areas such as Sandy Row, Shankill Road, Antrim and Ballymena.

In the summer of 1932 agitation increased, for reasons that we shall explore shortly. The RWG put its greatest efforts into organising the ODR workers, people who worked on task work schemes in return for ODR benefit. The work was hard, the number of places on the schemes too few and the means test for getting task work was demeaning. It was around these grievances and others that the RWG built its campaign. On 17 July 1932, 1000 unemployed gathered at the Custom House steps to hear Geehan and Scottish communist Willie Gallacher speak. On 18 August 5000 marched in Belfast and a rally at the end of the march drew twice that number. On 31 August the number marching was estimated at 20,000. Dawson Bates, for one, was worried, perhaps more so than he had been since the early activities of the Unemployed Workers' committee in 1925. In a memorandum to the Cabinet in July 1932, he stated:

> "I do not desire to take an unduly alarmist view, but there can be no doubt that unless some ameliorative measures are adopted there will be a large body of the population driven to desperation by poverty and hunger, and the only alternative to relief measures is to keep order by force, and for this purpose, in the face of widespread discontent, the existing force is not adequate . . . the

situation is rapidly approaching a crisis."[9]

The organisation of the ODR workers was in the hands of a relief workers' committee formed in the summer of 1932. The RWG was firmly in control of this committee, and Geehan was its secretary. It was this relief committee that called for and organised the strike of the ODR workers in 1932. In doing so, it worked almost completely on its own. The Trades Council had been concerned about ODR rates during the summer of 1932, but had done no more than ask for meetings with the Minister of Finance, only to be refused, and the Board of Guardians, but with no success. When the ODR strike got under way, Murtagh Morgan urged the Trades Council to call a general strike; the Council declined this invitation, and instead voted to donate £5 to the ODR strike fund and to call a conference of all unions to discuss the ODR strike.[10] This conference was eventually held, and resolved to move towards a general strike only if the ODR strike failed. Their resolution was never put to the test.

The relief committee was not quite alone in publicly agitating on ODR. On 30 September the northern parliament met after a four-month recess and agreed to adjourn for a further two months. Jack Beattie protested, and demanded some discussion of unemployment. He was ruled out of order and twice lifted the mace and threw it on the floor. "I refuse to sit in a House where such hypocrisy is indulged in while thousands are starving," he shouted as he walked out. When the cry of "God Save the King" went up towards the end of the meeting, Tommy Henderson, Independent Unionist for Shankill, replied: "God save the people", and left also. As the Nationalists had withdrawn some months previously, this left Independent Unionist for Woodvale and ex-District Inspector J.W. Nixon in the ridiculous position of being the sole opposition MP!

Reasons for the strike

By the summer of 1932 the full force of the British economy measures (referred to below) hit NI. Unemployment benefit was now limited to a maximum of 156 days a year. After that, the unemployed had to seek transitional benefit. In the previous summer the administration of these transitional payments in NI had been transferred to the Board of Guardians, despite objections from the trade union movement. The Trades Council, for example, had sent delegations to the Prime Minister on the matter and had held a number of protest meetings. Their justified fear was that the Board of Guardians would administer transitional benefit with the same sensitivity they had shown in administering indoor and outdoor relief, namely, none. In particular their objection was the rigorous and demeaning means tests applied by the Board of Guardians.

The rules for transitional benefit required a set number of stamps before any payment could be made; without this number, no payment was made. Moreover, no benefit was available to people under eighteen, or married women, or to a person from a household in which another person was working. As a result of all these measures, many unemployed were not deemed eligible for transitional benefit, and had only the last resort of outdoor relief as a possible source of payment.

As unemployment grew in 1932, these measures meant that many working-class people had no source of income at all. In September 1932 there were 72,000 registered unemployed in NI; it is estimated that there were a further 30,000 unregistered. In Belfast alone there were 48,000 unemployed, 48% of whom were not receiving unemployment benefit; 14,500 of these did not have transitional benefit either.[11] The only outlet for these last people was to seek "exceptional distress relief" from the Guardians. Consequently, the numbers seeking this relief rose rapidly. Technically, the unemployed could apply for indoor or outdoor relief, both of which were administered by the Guardians. For the former, the unemployed had to enter the workhouse. Few unemployed sought this option; no matter how poor, their preference was to be free rather than a workhouse pauper. Furthermore, the workhouse only had a limited number of places, nowhere near enough for Belfast's growing army of unemployed. So, in effect the growth of unemployment led to an increased demand for outdoor relief. It was a demand to which the Board of Guardians had to respond. Farrell[12] notes that whereas on 31 January 1931 outdoor relief was given to 272 cases, affecting 1137 people, by 2 January 1932 it was given to 884 cases, affecting 4008 people. Eight months later, on 10 September, the number of cases was up to 2612, and the number of people affected to 11,983.

While this did little to assuage the needs of the army of unemployed it was, however, as far as the Board of Guardians was prepared to go. In acting thus – or, more precisely, in not acting – it was displaying the ideology of the class to which it belonged. The Guardians were, as Harry Diamond, one of the few non-unionists on the Board, recalls, for the most part shopkeepers, small businessmen and estate agents. Devlin[13] sums them up thus:

> "The Guardians were mainly drawn from the petit bourgeoisie and reflected strongly the prejudices associated with that class. They were mainly Calvinistic in religious belief and believed paupers, destitute as well as able-bodied unemployed, were being punished by God for some sin they had committed. They also believed that the destitute were scheming constantly to steal money from the Belfast ratepayers . . . ."

Appearing before them to apply for ODR was like being brought into the Star Chamber, according to James Kelly, a journalist, who never had to appear himself. But Tommy Fitzpatrick did, and confirms the inquisition-like nature of proceedings:

"When I appeared in front of the Board, the Guardians were all sitting round. Mrs Coleman asked me if my wife was working or was she signing for work. I told her: 'No'. She was a housewife and I had a daughter with brain damage. And she said that she thought I wouldn't be entitled to it except my wife would sign for work. I could put my daughter in an institution, and I said: 'No'. Mr McCabe interfered and said he had a dispensary doctor who was looking into this case and that he would give information from him. He pleaded for me to get the grant. I got the princely sum of sixteen shillings."

The Guardians seemed anxious to conclude that the unemployed were "not genuinely seeking work". In addition, some Guardians bent over backwards to be insulting and dismissive. Everyone remembers the infamous remark of Lily Coleman that if the poor worked as hard at looking for a job as they did under the blankets there would be less of a problem. John Nicholl still smarts when he remembers that statement:

"I took that personally and I think a lot of people took that personally, because there was three years and three and a half years between my youngsters."

The Board also employed ironically-named relieving officers, who visited the homes of the poor and seemed more intent to relieve them of any possessions they had than to provide relief. Harold Binks recalls:

"I heard of people having to sell the piano, having to get rid of furniture in the sitting room or parlour. I have been in houses during the last war and after the war was over where they had neither carpet nor lino on the floors of the sitting room or hall because they had to get rid of that in the thirties or thereabouts and hadn't been able to replace it. They were told they didn't need these things, they could get rid of them and raise some money on them."

Of course, all of these activities were not just exercises in nastiness for its own sake. The fewer claimants, the less strain there was on the rates. Keeping down the rates seems to have been the over-riding concern of the Guardians. In this they were successful. In a letter to the *Belfast News-Letter* the day before the ODR riots, Methodist minister J. Spence pointed out that:

"in seventeen large British cities chosen at random, the average rate per head is £4.3.0d, and in Belfast rather less than £2.10.0d per head . . . Belfast has a smaller rate per head of population than any British city of comparable size." (10.10.32.)

Keeping down the numbers on ODR was an essential element in this strategy. Another essential element was keeping the levels of relief low. Eight shillings was the rate for a married couple with no children, twelve shillings if they had one child, sixteen shillings if they had two. The maximum, no matter how many children, was 24 shillings a week. These rates were the lowest in the UK, as even the antagonistic *Belfast News-Letter* pointed out on 4 October. Taking as a measure a family of a man, woman and one child, the ODR rate in Manchester was 21 shillings a week, in Liverpool 23/-, in Glasgow 25/3d., in Bradford 26/-, and in Northampton 27/-. In Belfast it was 12/-.

Nor was this all. To qualify for payment the unemployed were required to work on task work schemes for two and a half days a week. There were not enough places on these schemes for all the unemployed, so that not every ODR claimant actually worked each week. Those who did were paid in cash. Those who did not were paid in kind, that is, chits for food; thus, in that week they had no money for the gas, the rent, and least of all "luxuries" such as clothes, drink or cigarettes.

The task work was mainly road construction. It involved lifting the "pavers" and resurfacing the streets with concrete. Jack Brady saw the work in progress:

> "Now the streets of Ballymacarrett then were all kidney-pavers; they were actually small wee rocks from the sea shores and the street was sanded and they knocked and lined them in with a hammer. The government of the time decided on an unemployed relief scheme to change all the streets, take up the pavers and laying down long reams of barbed wire as foundations for it, and putting the sand and concrete with a big plank with one man on either side of the street."

Barney Boswell was one of those men in North Belfast:

> "There was a big plank right across, an eleven by three plank, and there was a big iron bar on that with two handles, and that went right across the road. That was to take the damp out of the concrete and level it. That was brought along it, and you'd use hand trowels for round gratings. It was hard work."

Tommy Cochrane also remembers that it was hard work:

> "I've seen men was digging trenches in North Howard Street and it was raining and there was three inches of water in the trenches. There was no protective clothing, boots or wellies then. And those men was standing digging clay under them conditions."

The worst off of the unemployed were the single people. Single women were not eligible for ODR. Single men were, if they could get some task work. But with so many married men with dependents competing for that work the single man's chances were slight. For the few lucky ones the reward for two and a half days hard work was 3/6d.

ODR task work, for all that it was experienced at any one time by only a minority of the unemployed, thus became the symbol and focus of many of the grievances and frustrations of all the unemployed. Consequently, the

RWG move to call an ODR workers strike met with wide support among the working class, employed and unemployed.

The Outdoor Relief strike

The decision to strike was taken by the ODR workers on 29 September 1932 at a meeting in St Mary's Hall. The strike, to begin on 3 October, centred on five demands:

1. the abolition of all task work;
2. an increase in the scale of outdoor relief to 15/3d per week for a man, 8/- a week for his wife and 2/- for each child;
3. the replacement of payment in kind by payment in cash;
4. the payment of any street improvement work under ODR schemes at trade union rates;
5. the extension of ODR to unemployed single people.

On the first day of the strike, 3 October, there was a tremendous surge of militancy which probably surprised both organisers and authorities alike. The approximately 2,000 ODR workers downed tools and picketed sites. A massive march of workers was staged and passed off peacefully. The organisers estimated that there were 60,000 marchers, and even the *Belfast News-Letter*, opposed to the strike, put the number at 15,000. Betty Sinclair recalls that the crowd was so vast that when it reached Custom House Square eight separate platforms had to be arranged from which the various speakers could address its different sections. Geehan sounded the battle cry in his speech:

> "We have got to win. We must have more of the spirit of Birkenhead and Invergordon, and no matter what the costs or the sacrifices may be, we will win."

This same spirit of unity and determination was caught by the banner carried by the Ballymacarrett contingent at the march. It read: "Your fight is our fight – Ballymacarrett stands firm".

On the following day, Tuesday, 4 October, another march took place, this time to the workhouse where the Board of Guardians was meeting. The police lined the route of the march and blocked the entrance to the workhouse. So the marchers sat down blocking the Lisburn Road completely and chanting: "We want grub, we want work". The Board of Guardians received a deputation and told them that no increase in the rates could be conceded. Harry Diamond warned the Guardians:

> "I ask you here today to try to realise the temper of these poor people . . . and I say that if you do not meet your responsibilities at a time of distress, you are courting disaster."

Despite Diamond's pleas, the Guardians did not reverse their decision; and despite his prediction, no disaster occurred that night.

But on Wednesday, 5 October there was to be a further march to the workhouse where a large number of single unemployed were going to demand admission as paupers. The logic of this tactic was that the strikers' demand was for 15/3d. per man per week, whereas it cost about 16/- to keep one person in the workhouse for a week. Large numbers of police were stationed at the march's starting point, and another large force blocked the entrance to the workhouse. Despite the massive police presence, between 150 and 500 single unemployed (depending on which version of the events one is to believe) did manage to sign themselves into the workhouse that night. Once in, they caused a disturbance. The police were called and arrested a few people later referred to in court as "leaders" of the disturbance; they were charged with "insubordination". The remaining protesters demanded eggs for breakfast the next morning and were summarily ejected from the workhouse. (Approximately twenty young single unemployed men used the same tactic one week later in Derry. They signed themselves into the workhouse to emphasise their total poverty but, on finding conditions in there so bad, they scaled the walls in the middle of the night and slept in an adjoining field).

Meanwhile, outside the Belfast workhouse on that Wednesday evening the police began to attempt to disperse the crowd. They pushed it down the Lisburn Road and into Bradbury Place and Sandy Row. Frustrated and in militant mood, the crowd responded by breaking windows and looting shops; or, as Barney Boswell, laughing, redefined it: "It wasn't a matter of looting; it was confiscation". The police response was to make repeated baton charges. Geordie Loughrey has clear memories of the evening's events:

> "Well, things got a wee bit hot and the next thing we knew was the people were driven down the Lisburn Road. The action of the police in forcing the people back, that started the riot. When we got into Sandy Row, two or three times the police would come swooping on, trying to chase the people away. But along Sandy Row the doors would open up and everyone – it didn't matter who you were, what you were – you were just brought into the house. Doors closed again while the police were about. As soon as the police would go away again, the people all got out onto the road again, kicking up, shouting slogans. The police didn't come into the houses. That was what really surprised me, to tell you the truth. They did it on parts of the Falls.
>
> We came along the Sandy Row that day until we were past what used to be the old Sandro picture house. We had to get into a house after the police came along. As soon as the police had gone again, the next thing I knew the people were out onto the streets. There was a lovely big shop there selling mostly bed clothes – blankets, sheets, pillows, curtains, all this sort of stuff. The next

thing I knew was they started to hammer the windows. They smashed the windows in and inside of no time that shop was completely cleared out. By this time my friend and I were beginning to get a bit worried when we saw the looting. We hadn't expected anything like that, so we made our way towards Hope Street. We had to go into the houses a couple of times; every few minutes the police would come flying by in the tenders. So we got into Hope Street and just as we got halfway down it, a police van came up, unloading a lot of police. I was able to run as hard as I could towards Great Victoria Street. My friend unfortunately went into St Andrew's Square, which happened to be a dead end and he got caught and got a few thumps with a baton while I got out of the road."

Police baton charges were not confined to the Sandy Row area that evening. Some distance away, in Saint Mary's Hall, an audience of strikers had gathered to listen to Geehan report on a meeting he had had earlier that day with the mayor and the Ministry of Labour. Some slight concessions had been mooted at the meeting, but the strikers rejected them. To cries of "Up Birkenhead" and "Up Russia", they voted to hold out for their full demands. As they left the hall, they were baton charged by police in Castle Street.

Thursday, 6 October was relatively quiet as regards street fighting, but there was a bustle of activity all the same. Bates met with the Board of Guardians and put some pressure on it to increase the number of days of work for each person on task schemes by 50%, thus giving them some more money. In the evening there was talk of a general strike at the Trades Council. Also that evening there were a number of strike meetings held in various parts of Belfast. At one on the Shankill, Harry Finlay and Betty Sinclair of the RWG urged the strikers to avoid any riots such as those of the previous evening.

On Friday, October 7, the strikers met again in Saint Mary's Hall and rejected the Board of Guardians' offer of 50% more work per person on task schemes. Geehan announced that their complete demands still stood and that if they were not met, they had five or six other tricks up their sleeve. The government, he said, would be "sorry by the end of next week". One of these tricks was to be a march on the workhouse on the following Tuesday when 80,000 were expected.

By Monday, 10 October, the strike was a week old. The relief committee had opened food depots to distribute a large amount of food that had been gathered from shops and sympathetic firms; the Belfast Co-operative Society provided 500 gallons of milk. Tommy Fitzpatrick, a striker, was involved in the collection and distribution of food in the Docks area:

"I rapped on a door and I asked the people – they might give you bread, milk, sugar, different things. That was people who were working; they could afford it. The dockers were very good to us.

They had a collection amongst themselves. So we were able to give out half a crown."

On the Shankill, Charlie Hull was involved in collecting for strike relief also, and recalls that "the side street shops gave more than the larger shops on the Shankill gave". Sean Mac Con Uladh recalls that in the Oldpark area he and others were able to collect meal from the flour mills and left-over bread from local bakeries.

Not all of these local committees operated smoothly, however. Tommy Boyd recounts one unsavoury incident:

> "We put a fellow from North Queen Street in charge of it. We had to go to work, you see, but Billy McMullan gave us the docket to store it in the dockers' hall in Corporation Street; and this fellow – if he didn't get the hand down – he flogged the stuff when we were at work. A dirt bird! He had to go to England. We'd have got him if he'd come back, although there was no shooting much at that time."

In the evening of 10 October there was a brief riot when the police broke up a meeting in Cromac Street. Although it was five days since the last street fighting, the Cromac Street violence was a foretaste of what was to happen the next day, for, with all the plans ready for a huge march to the workhouse, Bates banned the march under the Special Powers Act. Despite the ban and the drafting in of 500 extra police (meaning there would be 4000 police on duty in Belfast), Geehan assured a meeting of women workers and wives of strikers that tomorrow's demonstration was still on:

> "The mass of workers, organised and unorganised, employed and unemployed, are determined that we will no longer live under rotten conditions of poverty."

Liam Mulholland is certain that "there was no ODR man who wanted any violence" at the march. But violence on a large scale was to be the order of the next day. Things started off peacefully enough. The marchers began to gather at five points in the late morning of Tuesday, 11 October – Canning Street (North Belfast), Templemore Avenue (East), Tennent Street (Protestant West), Clonard Street (Catholic West) and Glengall Street (Protestant South). The intention was to converge in a massive show of strength on the workhouse where the Board of Guardians was to meet. The police, however, displayed their strength first, moving in to enforce Bates' ban, beginning in East Belfast. Alec Salmon was not one of the marchers, but he witnessed the ferocity of the police's actions:

> "There was a brave lot of sore heads. I was fairly young and I was in Templemore Street. That's a good bit away from Templemore Avenue. And I looked out of the door and there were six peelers and they'd chased three fellahs from Templemore Avenue. It's a long street, and they chased them from there and left them lying with the blood running out of them with their batons."

The violence in East Belfast was not without its own brand of black humour. Laughing, Tommy Boyd recalls:

"There was one fellow over where I lived that was on the outdoor relief. I had to coax him to go just to the one over by Templemore Avenue. We wanted them all there to swell the ranks. I said: 'It's up to you; you're on this, I'm not. I'm a docker'. And I got him to go. He was the first man to get his ribs cracked!"

With East Belfast's contribution effectively nipped in the bud, the police turned their attention to West Belfast, and especially the Falls Road. Police gunfire around the Albert Street area on the Falls left Samuel Baxter, a twenty-year-old Protestant flower seller from Regent Street, dead. Fourteen other civilians received gunshot wounds. One of the most seriously wounded was John Geegan, a forty-year-old Catholic from Smithfield. The fighting on the Falls was the fiercest. Trenches were dug, paving stones thrown at police, barricades built and watchman's huts at ODR schemes burned. The Falls was also the scene of most, if not all, of the shooting. Hence John Campbell, Guardian, and secretary of the Labour Party, found it "noteworthy that although the recent trouble was spread all over the city, only in a Roman Catholic area did the police use their guns."[14]

Shooting apart, the violence on the Shankill was widespread, as James Kelly, sent by his newspaper the *Irish Press* to cover the Tennent Street march, can testify:

"I remember a woman with a shawl come running to the people I was talking to. She shouted: 'They're kicking the shite out of the peelers up the Falls. Are you going to let them down?' And that seemed to be the flashpoint for the riot. These people started to burn a watchman's hut that had been used in an ODR scheme. The crowd dispersed in a panic when armed police came up in a cage car. Harking (another reporter) and I took refuge in a shirt factory in Agnes Street and we saw some of the Protestant workers actually shooting at the police. We heard later that they were B Specials, but I don't know. After the police left, rioting and looting broke out. Reporters often talked about what they should do in a baton charge – proffer their press card. I know one reporter who did that and nearly got his back broke with a baton. The only thing to do is to run like hell. The police made no exception. They went about it in a workman-like fashion and there was no quarter given. That was a terrible afternoon on the Shankill. You could hear fire engines, shouts and roars, men crying, batons landing on skulls. It was a hell of a scene. We didn't realise that much the same thing was going on up the Falls."

In essence this is the same story Kelly told in the *Capuchin Annual* of 1944 (excepting his reference to the B Specials, NI's auxiliary police). Whether, as he claims, the fighting on the Shankill can be traced to one single incident and person is highly debatable. But what does seem beyond doubt is his description of the ferocity of police behaviour. Their most committed ruthlessness seems to have been saved for the Falls, however. Whether or not one accepts Peter Carleton's remark that "they never bothered to use guns in the loyalist areas", the number of casualties suffered on the Falls is evidence of their willingness to use them in nationalist areas.

As a result of police actions, the ODR marchers were thus confined to their own areas, rioting until quiet was restored as a result of an 11 P.M. to 5 A.M. curfew, the first curfew in Belfast since the "troubles" of 1922. And, spared of the aggravation of tens of thousands of unemployed outside their gates, the Board of Guardians had been able to meet in relative quiet. Despite the events on the streets, they refused to concede, instead announcing that they were going to stop all relief payments to all ODR workers who did not report back to work immediately.

Rioting recommenced the next day, 12 October. There were more trenches dug, more barricades, more arrests made and more people injured, although no one was killed. However, John Geegan, seriously injured in the previous day's violence, died. As on the previous day, it was in the Falls area that the heaviest rioting and the most violent police action was experienced. The police stopped delivery of food in the lower Falls "in an effort to smash the resistance of the workers in this district".[15] In addition, James Collins, a Nationalist member of the Board of Guardians, was one of many people – including four blind people – taken from their beds by police to dismantle barricades in pouring rain. Although unionist papers tended to play down this incident, the feeling that perhaps the police were over stepping the mark was not confined only to the pro-ODR *Irish News*. The Nationalist Party could hardly fail to support the strikers after such treatment to one of their leading members. Yet it is obvious that the party was uneasy about the extent to which things had got beyond control. Speaking at a meeting of still-determined strikers in Saint Mary's Hall on 12 October, Joe Devlin, leader of the Nationalists, referred to the government:

> "They may find it necessary to yield to angry popular outbursts what they contemptuously denied to the parliamentary representatives of the toiling masses."

For their part, the government seemed to be playing a double game, determined to end the strike by foul means and fair. The Board of Guardians was the most intransigent factor in the matter. In the interests of defusing the whole situation the Unionist government was putting pressure on the Guardians to make some more concessions to the strikers. However, the government did not find it contradictory simultaneously to condone police heavy-handedness against those same strikers. Moreover, the police began to play the sectarian card, beating Catholic strikers more viciously than Protestant ones, and seeing republican subversion where it most definitely did not exist. Speaking to a Unionist Party meeting on that same

Wednesday, Prime Minister Craigavon said that "if the mischief makers who had come into Belfast had any designs by the trouble they had created towards obtaining a republic, they were doomed to disappointment. I am not a man to be intimidated". It was at that same meeting that he used one other ploy, that of attempting to buy off skilled workers. Magically he pulled from his hat the announcement of an order of ships to be built by Workman Clark's, the first order in many, many months.

Things were fairly quiet still on Thursday, 13 October. It was reported in the press that Geehan and others of the relief workers' committee were lying low, expecting arrest. Dawson Bates meanwhile held a meeting with the Board of Guardians and more or less ordered them to concede to some of the strikers' demands. So, on Friday, 14 October the Guardians made a new offer to the strikers. A number of the original five demands were conceded, a major omission being the extending of relief to the single unemployed.

The new rates on offer for ODR were:

Man and wife	20 shillings per week
with 1 or 2 children	24
with 3 or 4 children	28
with 5 or more children	32

It was up to the strikers now to consider the offer.

Meanwhile, Craigavon's red and republican scare tactics received an extra boost when veteran socialist Tom Mann arrived in Belfast for the funeral of Samuel Baxter on 14 October. The *Belfast News-Letter* screamed that communists had been called in to organise the strike. The fact that, in James Kelly's words, "Mann was a benevolent old boy with a white moustache, the very antithesis of what is expected of a communist", was irrelevant to Craigavon, the *Belfast News-Letter*, and the police. Mann was openly tailed by detectives from the moment he stepped off the Liverpool boat. As he reached the gates of Milltown cemetery in the funeral procession, he was arrested by these detectives and taken to nearby Andersonstown barracks. From there he was transferred to police headquarters where he was met by a chief superintendent:

> "He asked, 'Was it your intention to hold public meetings?' I said, 'It certainly was', and that I was intending to hold a meeting at the Customs House steps on Sunday night. He then said that would be impossible, as they could not allow such a gathering."[16]

At that point he was served with an exclusion order. Under the Special Powers Act the NI government had no power to deport anyone from NI, so communists were confined to Clogher in Tyrone, and republicans to Limavady in Derry. When we asked Paddy Scott why those two places, he replied by asking if we could think of anywhere more inhospitable for a communist or republican! Mann was given an order excluding him from every part of NI except Clogher. In effect, it was an order to leave on the next Liverpool boat. He did so that evening.

On Saturday, 15 October, the ODR strikers met and agreed to accept the Guardians' offer. Geehan addressed the meeting, stating rather over-enthusiastically that "poverty and destitution have been swept away". The hyperbole can perhaps be forgiven. Something major, even if limited, had been achieved as a result of the solidarity of Belfast workers around this single issue. The strikers had every reason to feel flushed by their success.

All except the single unemployed, that is. On Tuesday, 18 October, 300 of them met and expressed their disappointment. They stated that if they had no satisfaction by the end of a fortnight, they would recommence the strike. But, despite the support of others, such as Court branch of the Labour Party, which condemned Geehan for calling off the strike before satisfaction was gained for the single unemployed, this threat of a new strike fizzled out.

There was no victory march through Belfast to celebrate the end of the strike. Although one was mooted, it would almost certainly have been banned. Perhaps this fact was enough to dissuade the organisers.

The ODR strikers returned to work on Monday, 17 October, two weeks after the strike began, and the curfew was lifted the next day. There were some complaints in the following days that the authorities were reneging on the agreement and continuing to pay some ODR men in kind, not in cash. But there was no victimisation of strikers, a number of local offices to consider claims for ODR were opened, and the number of people receiving ODR expanded rapidly.[17]

As a grim postcript to the events: ten days after the strikers recommenced work, the inquest was held into the deaths of Samuel Baxter and John Geegan. The coroner stated that "the police handled the situation in a courageous and tactful way".

Assessing October 1932

Prior to the ODR strike, the *Irish Workers' Voice*, paper of the RWG, stated in an editorial that Northern workers should realise:

> "that British imperialism, which has partitioned Ireland, carving off the industrial North from the agrarian South, which has rendered derelict the mighty technical forces of the Lagan, which has brought hunger into thousands of Belfast homes – this imperialism has nothing to offer them". (27.8.32.)

It was, in one sense, a short step from this admonition to the conclusion that if Belfast workers marched and rioted together, then they had in fact realised the significance of what the RWG had said. For the RWG, then, the events of the ODR strike were a prophecy come true. "A victory for the relief workers is a victory over imperialism, a blow at the whole hunger system of capitalism," proclaimed the *Irish Workers' Voice* on 15 October. And one week later, after the strike had ended:

> "With the artificial barriers swept away, Catholic and Protestant workers fought side by side against the police of their common enemy."

The problem in this interpretation, however, is that it is tautological: if workers march together, then sectarianism is dead; the workers marched together, therefore sectarianism is dead. This interpretation was echoed in the Communist Party of Great Britain's *Daily Worker,* which saw "Catholics and Orangemen united against the common imperialist enemy" (8.10.32.) in a struggle for "bread and independence". (10.10.32.)

But, to listen to reminiscences of eye witnesses of, and participants in, these events is to find major flaws in this interpretation. For a start, despite all the violence, the events did not have the magnitude that one would expect of a pre-revolutionary situation. As a prologue to what the *Irish Workers' Voice* (8.10.32.) referred as "the dictatorship of the proletariat", it passed many people by, as Jack McGougan, a trade union leader recalls:

> "There is a tendency to overestimate the extent and impact of the ODR strike. It was possible to live in Belfast without knowing much about it. There were huge marches for a short time."

Moreover, it is apparent that the consciousness of some of the marchers was neither anti-capitalist nor anti-imperialist. Alice Quinn was in the riot on 11 October, and remembers exactly why she ended up at it:

> "Me and Billy Knox from King Street, we went to see the march and were all rammed into a bar because there was shooting going on. It wasn't for the outdoor relief, like; we'd no money to go and see the pictures, so we just went to see the march."

Jackie Quinn (no relation) had similar motives:

> "I marched with all the young fellows as a bit of excitement, but really I don't think I was marching with the conviction that people were getting treated the way they were treating them on Outdoor Relief. I don't think at my age then it meant much to me. I just marched along with the crowd."

It would be easy to dismiss both Jackie Quinn and Alice Quinn as atypical of the marchers and rioters – on the one hand a young man looking for excitement, and on the other a young woman mill worker merely there to watch. In fact, all that is unusual about them is their frankness concerning their apolitical motives for being there. Many others claim a more heightened political consciousness than they, but the vast majority of them are also sceptical of the "pre-revolutionary, anti-imperialist" interpretation. Take Tommy Patton, then unemployed, but later (1982/3) Lord Mayor of Belfast:

> "The people were shoulder to shoulder for one thing and I think they realised it was only for one thing. Unity was very limited. A

> united Ireland was the last thing they thought of. The strike was not organised for a political purpose."

Where, then, does that leave the RWG interpretation? It reveals it as a romantic myth begun in the midst of the very events themselves. The RWG (later CPI), as a result of their central involvement in the events, understandably sought to preserve the history of the period. But, given that most other forces in NI society quickly proceeded to forget the events, the CP interpretation became isolated and unchallenged. In short, it was the romantic myth that was preserved, not history. This is not to deny the level of poverty in 1932, nor the magnitude of the agitation and the police repression; nor is it to negate the importance of the RWG's involvement. It is, however, to point out that many elements of the myth are untenable. The strike was not pre-revolutionary and anti-imperialist, neither in the minds of most of the strikers and marchers, nor its possible effects. Geordie Loughrey, whose experiences in Sandy Row on the night of 3 October we have recounted earlier, is adamant: "I just wanted an improvement in the system; I never thought of changing the system". The struggle was about reforms *within* British capitalism, and was consciously and unconsciously part of a wider struggle that led, in stages, to the emergence of the United Kingdom's own particular form of social democracy, the welfare state. Barney Boswell may have joined the IRA as a result of his political awakening in 1932 ("the ODR riots made me a rebel"), but that was a path not trodden by very many. In addition, the republican movement's official involvement in the strike was non-existent. But, most importantly, the ODR struggle was, as we said, a struggle for reform within *British* capitalism. Even organisationally, despite the all-Ireland nature of the RWG and its Irish National Unemployed movement, the eyes of the strikers and marchers looked more often to the east, to Birkenhead and Jarrow, than to the south.

The unity of 1932 was on a single issue, and was thus extremely superficial. One did not need to know the religion or politics of the person marching beside one. The most enticing, but perhaps most misleading component of the romantic myth is therefore the assumption that Belfast's traditional sectarianism was struck a near-mortal blow by the ODR agitation. Listen to James Kelly,[18] not himself an RWG member, but very sympathetic to them:

> "Hunger stalked the pavements in Belfast. But something very queer was happening besides. There was a strange stirring up those long narrow side streets where the Orangemen lived. The big drums were silent and the paint was peeling from the gable where King William was wont to appear with his white horse. Empty stomachs and starving children brought an awakening in those little kitchen dwellings where the sash hung over the fireplace. Catholics and Protestants suffered alike and suffering

brought a new sense of unity."

Reality was much less mystical than that. In the real world the greatest blow to the RWG vision was, paradoxically, the success of the strike. The "unity" of the ODR strike was as short-lived as the length of time that the issue of ODR remained an issue.

Afterwards, the RWG's problem was to respond to the sort of challenge raised by Jackie Quinn:

"If they were so sincere working together, how the hell were they broke up? Nobody ever answered that."

On the contrary, the RWG/CPI did provide a plausible answer which has been the main one in the intervening years. It is the final element in the romantic myth. Simply put, the argument is as follows: the unity of Protestant and Catholic working class in the ODR struggle was perhaps the key element in making the situation pre-revolutionary. To defuse the risk of revolution, the state needed to break up the unity of the working class. It did so by beating the Orange drum very loudly, and many Protestants, workers included, heeded this siren call. As Betty Sinclair sums it up:

"The government here and the government in London were very worried about the unity of the working class. Class – that's the greatest thing they fear."

But, if the unity was not as great as the CPI argues, then perhaps that lack of unity is itself enough to explain the apparently subsequent disunity. Perhaps the government's action in whipping up sectarianism was only one element, and maybe not the major one, in the "decline" of "working-class unity". Perhaps, finally, it was not the government that was the villain of the piece as such; sectarian relations were so "normal" in Belfast that they broke through to the surface, especially when that surface was as fragile and temporary as the unity of 1932.

There is no denying that the Unionist government was eager to intervene to end the strike. Their intervention was at a number of levels: increased repression on the streets (including the first curfew since 1922 and the deaths of two demonstrators), pressure on the Board of Guardians to concede to some of the strikers' demands, and the making of impressive promises, such as Craigavon's announcement of "new orders" for Workman Clark's during the strike, and attempts at whipping up a witch-hunt directed against both republicans and communists, with the latter viewed as the more important target. For example, in the middle of the ODR strike, on 12 October, Craigavon denounced the agitators who had "come into Belfast" to cause trouble in the hope of achieving a republic.

But it was the press which took up this theme most hysterically. On 13 October the *Belfast News-Letter* announced that "most of the agitators are from England and Scotland", and there was one from Dublin. The *Daily Mail* of the same day went even further afield in search of its aliens, reporting that a "husky Russian" was among the rioters! For its part, the

Belfast Telegraph seemed the most committed to tarring the strikers with the communist brush, highlighting the communist influence in the riots in editorials on 12, 14 and 15 of October.

The irony is that in their virulent anti-communism the Unionist government and press had an unusual bedfellow, the Catholic Church. Peter Carleton recalls that in Saint Peter's Church, shortly after the strike, a priest attacked the communists and their "foreign influence". As a direct result, he claims, a meeting in Leeson Street a few days later, held to protest at the Special Powers Act, was attacked by a local crowd because of the presence of some RWG speakers. Harry Diamond, aware of the Catholic Church's antagonism, was in a quandry; he was politically active on unemployment alongside communists, yet did not want to be branded as a fellow traveller. Bishop Mageean solved his dilemma for him:

> "Collins and I went to see the Bishop and we explained that the predicament we were in was that, if we took part in this with prominent communists, we could be labelled. Betty Sinclair tried to address a meeting at the corner of Dover Street and was chased off the road during the thirties. That's the sort of thing you were up against. So we explained to the Bishop that, in our judgement, the rights of the poor were legitimate, and he recognised that too, and he said: 'Well, I'll take steps to ensure that there'll be no comeback'. He assured us that, if we came into any difficulty, he would see that, as far as it lay within his power, there would be no repercussions of the kind that we feared."

It was not only from the Catholic Church that opposition came. On 17 October the *Belfast Telegraph* carried a long article about one Shankill minister's attack on local Protestants for forgetting the Bible and lowering the prestige of Ulster by allowing themselves to be waylaid by Bolshevism. And Milotte notes that Protestant Belfast experienced a well-organised youth anti-communist evangelistic campaign which lasted three weeks and employed the skills of twenty preachers in the aftermath of the ODR strike. As Peter Carleton put it, "There wasn't a pulpit all over Belfast – Catholic, Protestant – that wasn't denouncing communism".

The establishment's wish to drum up a red scare was made extremely easy by the centrality of the RWG in the strike. The RWG would have strongly disagreed that their involvement was the cause of the unrest, but they certainly pulled no punches in declaring their own reasons for being involved. Milotte[19] thus concludes that:

> "no member of the RWG – or, more accurately of its leadership – would have denied the allegations levelled against them by the Unionist establishment that they were communist agitators out to smash the state and unite Ireland in a Bolshevik-type Republic. They made no bones about that fact."

Certainly, Geehan, as the most public RWG person involved, was at no pains to hide his communism. On 20 October he declared:

> "I came into this fight as a communist and I am going out of it as a communist. Those who do not like that in a good proletarian way can lump it."

Without such obvious communist presence, politicians and churchmen could have attempted to conjure up a red menace anyhow. With their presence, however, a witch-hunt was inevitable. It united even the trade union movement with the establishment on this point, those same trade unionists whom the RWG was constantly denouncing as "social fascists". For example, Bob Morrow, secretary of the Belfast Trades Council, wrote to A.A. Purcell of the British TUC, praising the RWG for taking up the cause of the unemployed, but condemning their "would-be revolutionary leaders [who] went into hiding on Monday and let the fighting be done by the poor fellows that don't hardly know what the Labour Movement stands for".[20]

More practically, in the aftermath of the strike the Trades Council agreed on 10 November 1932 to begin organising the unemployed themselves. An Unemployed Workers' Association under Trades Council control was formed, claiming by February 1933 to have 1500 members. But, by June 1933, R. Rooney of the Association told the Trades Council that the organisation was in a bad way, with few members. He suggested winding it up "as the unemployed, in his opinion, were satisfied with their position".[21] In July 1933 the Unemployed Workers' Association was disbanded.

At one point the Trades Council had written to the Minister of Home Affairs asking the government to recognise officially the Unemployment Workers' Association as the only legitimate voice of the unemployed.[22] Similar constitutionalism had been shown by them during the ODR strike, leading Craigavon, never noted for his support for the trade union movement, to be glowing in his praise of them. On the day when the Trades Council met with him to try to end the ODR strike, he said:

> "I publicly thank them for coming to meet the Ministry, because I am a great believer in the trade unions if they are properly led, and if the leaders will meet the government, it is infinitely preferable because we shall then have some responsible persons with whom to negotiate rather than having a rabble running round the town." (*Belfast News-Letter* 13.10.32)

Against such odds, the surprising fact is not that it should have taken riots to gain concessions, but that it only took a few days of rioting for the state to concede the strikers' demands.

It was not mere paranoia that led the establishment to see RWG comrades at every turn. However, in the case of an anti-republican element in the witch-hunt, the establishment was on much shakier ground. The involvement of republicans in organising the strike was minimal, and the official involvement of the republican movement was nil. Reinterpreting trouble in republican terms was a phenomenon well known in Belfast. But it was a phenomenon which held remarkably little sway in the middle of the events of the first fortnight in October.

The Ulster Protestant League and popular sectarianism

Milotte[23] notes one telling statement by a Shankill Road man arrested for rioting during the ODR strike: "It is very unfair, I am a loyalist". It would be dangerous to make too much out of this statement. However, it is an interesting portrayal of the complexity of consciousness. The myth of 1932 would have us believe that sectarian consciousness gave way to socialist consciousness. Yet here was at least one working-class Protestant ODR supporter for whom some seeds of sectarianism and socialism could peacefully coexist in the one consciousness.

This point needs to be stressed because to first appearances sectarianism "died" in the autumn of 1932. But a closer view shows that at most it was quiescent. A valuable way to illustrate this point is to look at the Ulster Protestant League (UPL). On the day the ODR strikers won, the UPL issued a statement neatly conjuring up both the traditional scapegoats of unionism. They deplored the fact that poverty and hunger:

> "were used as a cloak by the communist *Sinn Féin* element to start a revolution in our province. We also greatly deplore that some few of our loyal Protestant unemployed were misled to such an extent that they associated themselves with the enemies of their faith and principles." (*Belfast News-Letter* 15.10.32)

In issuing this statement, the UPL was acting true to form. Founded in 1931 ostensibly to "safeguard the employment of Protestants" as the recession took hold, it turned much of its attention in subsequent years actively to opposing communism in Belfast, either through the press (including its own paper, the *Ulster Protestant*), or, when it felt confident enough, on the streets. It was especially active against the RWG as the communists succeeded in organising the unemployed from late 1931 on. A favourite ploy was to disrupt communist or socialist meetings using the ultimate symbol of loyalist dominance, the Lambeg drum.

It was obvious that the UPL had friends in higher places. James Kelly thought it "significant that they were always given the use of the Unionist Party headquarters in Glengall Street" for their meetings and socials; and, as it openly advertised these events in the *Ulster Protestant*, it was lost on no one that the UPL was acceptable to the Unionist establishment. More than that, after the ODR riots the UPL was wooed by the Unionist Party. Its potential in providing anti-communist "shock troops" was not one to be ignored by the government. However, it is a long way from acknowledging their usefulness to the sectarian state to arguing that it was a creation and mere puppet of that state. The UPL represented the extreme of popular sectarianism, a phenomenon which pre-dated that organisation, and has survived long after its demise. At various points in NI's history the state has employed that popular sectarianism to its own ends. After 1932 the government, aware of the threat that the politics of unemployment raised, was eager to welcome any sectarian forces on its side. But it cannot be said that all sectarianism derived from the state, to be switched on and off at will.

Popular sectarianism was a relatively independent force, sometimes meshing well with government wishes, sometimes clashing with them, and sometimes a harbinger of the government's own subsequent sectarian actions. And it was a force that was always there. It had its ebb and flow, but it never disappeared.

Thus, even in the midst of that "socialist summer" of 1932 which culminated in the ODR strike, sectarianism was alive and well. As Farrell[24] notes, in March 1932 an AOH parade in South Derry was fired on and two Hibernians wounded. In June pilgrims going to and from the Eucharistic Congress in Dublin were attacked in numerous separate incidents in Larne, Lisburn, Loughbrickland, Lurgan, Portadown, Banbridge and Kilkeel. And on 27 August, after an Orange rally, a crowd wrecked a number of Catholic pubs in Dungannon. If popular sectarianism retreated in October 1932, it was perhaps only in order to regroup.

Class and sectarianism after 1932

No sooner had the dust of ODR settled than perhaps the most violent official strike in NI's history to date took place – the railway strike of 1933. In 1920 railway workers had earned 64/6d. per week; but a series of five wage cuts had reduced their weekly wage to 38/9d. by 1932. In November 1932 the railway companies approached the Railway Wages Board seeking a further 15% wage reduction. The board conceded that they could make a 10% cut. The NUR opposed the cut, and received backing from other unions who were certain that this was the prelude to a whole round of severe cuts affecting many other industries. The strike began on 31 January 1933, and the railway companies quickly hired blacklegs, many of them students from Queen's University, to drive the trains and buses. In the following months these blacklegs became the main targets for the strikers' disdain. Two blacklegs were killed when the Dublin to Belfast train was derailed on the first day of the strike. Many other incidents of stone throwing, bombing and derailment took place. Tommy Boyd recalls that the blacklegs "wore berets on them, and they thought they were great". He recounts that he and some friends stood on a bridge as some of these scabs were driving an engine through. They threw stones down on them and "cut the skulls off them", but had to scatter when a policeman called Larmour "came flying up the other side of the bridge with a rifle".

The strike was an official one, but also had the support of the RWG and the IRA. On 28 February an IRA unit fired at a group of blacklegs at the GNR station and was pursued by an RUC patrol into the Lower Falls. There one policeman was shot dead and the IRA unit escaped. Charlie Hull can remember that night well:

> "I remember standing listening to the shots on a still March (*sic*) night with the frost in the air. I was standing on the corner of Conway Street with a security man out of Stormont. I said to him, 'There were shots', and we were very clever, those of us who lived in the west side of the town; we could have told nearly the street a shot came from. We could tell that the shot came from down near the railway. And the police wanted to know where I was, and I was able to say I was with him, thank God!"

Amazingly, despite establishment paroxysms over the IRA's involvement, the strikers, most of whom were Protestant, did not seem perturbed. Charlie Hull, himself a Protestant, perhaps indicates why when he says:

> "The IRA weren't the cause of the strike; the conditions were the cause of the strike, and the silly people who brought in the blacklegs to run the trains were the cause of the policeman getting shot."

On the other hand, the establishment, as previously during the ODR strike, was very concerned at the communist and republican involvement. Many bishops used the occasion of their Lenten pastoral letters during the strike itself to condemn communism outright. And Lord Brookeborough, then Minister of Agriculture (and later Prime Minister) followed in Craigavon's footsteps by redefining the events in anti-republican and increasingly sectarian terms. On 12 July 1933 he urged employers not to employ Catholics, pointing out, "I have not one about my place". One year later he returned to the theme, stressing that "99% of the Roman Catholics in Northern Ireland were disloyal".

The railway strike dragged on until April 1933, when the NUR agreed to a package involving a 7½% cut in wages and the retention of any blacklegs who wanted to remain. Their militancy thus produced little by way of results. But the extent of the militancy was enough to convince the RWG that there was support for radical politics in Belfast. So, in June 1933 the RWG reformed as the Communist Party of Ireland. However, a strange fact of Belfast radical politics at the time was that the street militancy did not translate into constitutional support for radical political candidates. Thus, in the January 1933 elections for Belfast Corporation, the tens of thousands who marched for ODR did not unite to back radicals. The NILP lost its only seat in Dock ward. And Geehan, standing in Court ward, lost miserably. Similarly, in the Board of Guardians elections at the same time three unemployed candidates (in Clifton, Shankill and Court wards) all lost, leaving the Board's make-up 29 Unionists, four Nationalists and one NILP member. In like manner, in the wake of the railway strike the CPI's optimism was dealt a blow when there were no major shifts in the make-up of the Board of Guardians after an election in May, nor in the Stormont parliament after the election of December 1933.

Despite this, there was still militant activity, as ever, on the old question of ODR and the Board of Guardians. In June 1933 Harry Diamond, himself a Guardian and exasperated at the failure of his fellow Guardians to discuss adequately the issues of unemployment and poverty, resorted to rather unconstitutional methods. Unlike Jack Beattie in parliament the year before, Diamond had no mace to throw; but there were other objects that could be thrown. Diamond had put down a motion on unemployment which, as he recalls:

> " . . . had appeared two weeks running on the agenda, and when it came to the day it was to be debated, the chairman said: 'That motion's out of order'. I thumped the table and said: 'Well, if that's not discussed, there'll be nothing else discussed here today'. The Chairman, Adam McKegney, told me to sit down and take the next business. I could think of nothing else. I just saw this floor mat at my feet. Well, Lord, I lifted it and heaved it at him and it just fell on the desk in front of him. He was such a doper that he says: 'Who threw that?' There was about seven lady members and they were screaming at the pitch of their lungs. They immediately passed a motion and described my conduct as blackguardly. I was suspended, to be expelled from the Board until a full apology was made. The Master of the Workhouse was told to escort me out. Says I: 'If you put a finger on me, I'll sue you', so he ran away and told the Chairman he couldn't do this. So, they had a bit of a collogue among themselves and the next thing one of them went out of the Boardroom and about four of these big workhouse attendants came in and so I was put out. I turned up the next week and they spent an hour haggling. At the end of it one young fellow got up and he said: 'Look, Mr Chairman, we're businessmen. We're wasting our time'. They went on to next business. I didn't apologise."

Later that same year, exactly one year after the ODR strike, the question of ODR again became a political issue, not just behind closed doors, but on the streets. In October 1933 the government decided to revert to relief rates that existed prior to October 1932, that is, the low rates that were at the centre of the ODR struggle. The CPI attempted, not very successfully, to mobilise opposition. They organised two marches to converge on Belfast in time for a commemoration of the ODR strike on 11 October. One group of 30 marchers left Derry, but was turned back by police at Glengormley on the outskirts of Belfast. A group of 70 left from

Dublin, but most of them failed to get beyond the border where the police were waiting for them. And to cap it all, a few days before the commemoration the IRA shot dead a policeman in Belfast. The government immediately banned the ODR commemoration, as if it was related to the IRA's action. Tommy Geehan reluctantly agreed to the ban, but another CPI member, Arthur Griffin, was arrested for breaking it and sentenced to three months. Four days after the aborted commemoration, on 15 October, Harry Pollitt, general secretary of the CPGB, and Sean Murray, first secretary of the CPI, were served with exclusion orders; Pollitt was sent back to England, and Murray "back" to Dublin even though he was a native of County Antrim. At the end of October Murray appeared in Belfast again and was jailed for one month for disobeying the exclusion order.

Yet, within a few weeks of all this militancy the smouldering fire of sectarianism emitted a bright spark. In November a Catholic publican, Dan O'Boyle, was shot dead in York Street. It was the first sectarian killing since 1922. But it was a sign of what was to come in the spring and summer of 1934. The UPL had been relatively quiet for a while, and although it may have been involved in the York Street killing, its public profile was low. However, in May 1934 a proposal by the Catholic Church to hold a missionary exhibition in the Ulster Hall proved the occasion for them to go into action. James Kelly regards the Catholic Church's decision as "silly" and itself a sectarian one, given the significance of the Ulster Hall "as a kind of Unionist Valhalla going back to the Edward Carson and Randolph Churchill meetings of 'Ulster will fight and Ulster will be right' ". The thought of "fenians" using its hall was too much for the UPL whose pledge was "neither to talk with nor to walk with, neither to buy or sell, borrow or lend, take or give or have any proceedings with them [Catholics] at all." (*Irish News* 16.10.32.) The UPL itself held a meeting in the Ulster Hall to begin a campaign of opposition to the exhibition. What was notable about this meeting and subsequent campaign was the extent to which UPL people were willing to be public about their involvement and intentions. Major J.H. McCormick, a Unionist Party MP, was prominent at the meeting. And Mrs Dorothy Harnett urged those present to "get training in firing"[25]. There was some violence afterwards when a crowd returning from the meeting attacked Catholic homes in the York Street area. In being so public, the UPL dignatories had the example of Cabinet ministers to follow. It was still fresh in everyone's mind that only two months previously (19 March 1934) Lord Brookeborough had reiterated his call to Protestant employers not to employ Catholics, and, when there was some public outcry over his statement, he received backing from the Prime Minister himself: "I am an Orangeman first and a Member of Parliament afterwards", boasted Craigavon. In such an atmosphere McCormick, Harnett, and the others could afford to feel relatively invulnerable. Though convicted later of incitement to disorder, Mrs Harnett was merely bound over to keep the peace.

This was happening at a point when the attempt to organise Ireland's working class into a unified anti-imperialist, anti-capitalist organisation was well under way in the form of the Republican Congress. The Congress had less effect in Belfast than elsewhere, and much less than one of its organisers, Peadar O'Donnell, would have hoped for from the most industrialised part of Ireland. But the Congress did succeed in sponsoring an Unemployed Workers' Movement conference in Belfast in May 1934, which was followed by a meeting of 3000 at the Custom House, the largest working-class gathering in Belfast since October 1932. Furthermore, O'Donnell is personally credited with forming the James Connolly Workers' Republican Clubs in traditionally working-class areas such as the Shankill and East Belfast. These clubs provided the core of the Protestant contingent from Belfast which went to Bodenstown on 18 June 1934 for the annual Wolfe Tone commemoration, only to get into a scuffle with more traditional elements in the IRA. The Belfast contingent held its own separate commemoration in the nearby town of Sallins, and the next day marched through Dublin to Connolly's grave in Arbour Hill where an oration was read by a Shankill Road republican, Robert McVicker.

Meanwhile the sectarian wave was building up towards a crest. In July 1934 shots were fired into Catholic North Thomas Street (in the Docks area), but no one was injured. On 16 September a Protestant crowd invaded New Dock Street and Marine Street. Forty Catholic homes were wrecked and a crippled young man was injured; he died later in hospital. Barney Boswell recalls the incident:

> "There was a woman there, McCombe, and she had a crippled son, a hunchback, and he lay at the window for years and years. And the kerbs were up – it was ready for concreting – and there were stones about. And one of these jokers lifted one of the slabs and threw it through the window and killed that boy. He was forty years of age – Andy McCombe, they called him."

Thus, 1935 started out with the twin forces of class and sectarianism operating side by side. Class militancy at the beginning of 1935 centred on two seemingly unrelated issues, both of which had their origins in 1934. The first of these was that in July 1934 the government had rescinded a 10% cut in unemployment benefit that had originally been imposed in 1931. At the same time, it was announced that the administration of unemployment benefit was to become the responsibility of the new Unemployment Assistance Board (UAB) as from January 1935. In one sense this was good news, in that the administration of transitional benefit, conferred on the Board of Guardians in 1931, was to be taken from them and given to the new UAB. But the CPI, the Trades Council, and others feared that the UAB would try in its own way to keep down the financial costs of unemployment to the state. Sure enough, the UAB defined its brief initially in the narrowest of terms, taking in for the most part only skilled workers. As Devlin[26] points out, the Ministry of Labour promised that a further 100,000 workers would be included in the scheme within two months. But it was two years before the scheme was extended to other workers, and then only to 5000 of them. And it was 1939 before the UAB became fully operational with the disbanding of the Board of Guardians. In that interim many insured and paid up workers, and those workers who did not have enough stamps (200 over ten years, or 30 over two years) were still subjected to the vagaries of the Board of Guardians.

The second issue arose out of the CPI's by now annual attempt at an ODR commemoration in October 1934. The commemoration was banned, but this time Geehan broke the ban and was arrested. The case became a *cause célèbre,* and the fine of £10 imposed on Geehan was opposed not just by him, but by his party, the Trades Council, the NILP, and the NCCL.

In January Geehan's appeal was heard and the fine reduced to £5; still he refused to pay. At the same time unemployment benefit was cut, and a campaign of opposition swung into action. Its high point was a protest meeting at which 3000 were present, and where the demands were for a restoration of previous unemployment benefit levels and the lifting of the fine on Geehan. The government in London had backed down in February after a similar campaign against cuts in unemployment benefit by the British working class. But the Unionist Party diehards held out until 11 April when they finally gave in and restored the unemployment benefit levels. Geehan, however, was arrested for non-payment of the fine.

April 1935 also saw the successful conclusion of a rent strike organised by the CPI-backed Tenants' Defence League. A campaign against cuts won, a successful rent strike, joint action by the organised labour movement – to the CPI, at least, it looked as if the revolutionary wave of 1932 was again on the rise.

1935: The sectarian riots

At exactly the same time as socialism appeared to be on the rise in Belfast, that other standard element of Belfast life, sectarianism, was daily growing in strength. Throughout April there were numerous shooting incidents, mostly in the York Street area of North Belfast, and mostly involving Catholics as victims. But, if April was bad, May was worse. In two of the worst incidents, on 13 and 23 May respectively, James Madden and Harry McKeown, both Catholic, were injured by gunshots. In May the Silver Jubilee of George V occurred, and as part of the celebrations the Duke of Gloucester was scheduled to visit Northern Ireland. From the first few days in the month the UPL went into top gear, mainly against the CPI. They attacked and broke up CPI meetings in Custom House Square on 5, 12 and

19 May, and another party meeting in Library Street on 27 May. In addition, they issued an ultimatum to the government that, if the government would not deal with the communist threat, they, the UPL, would. Belfast was once again experiencing its street battles, but very different ones from those of 1932.

These attacks must have come as a shock to the CPI, rejoicing as it had in the faint flickers of a new socialist dawn. What quickly became apparent was that the UPL activity was no mere bump on the road to socialism, but was a harbinger of what the rest of that summer was to be like. The realisation of the strength of sectarianism struck the organised labour movement too, but, cautious as ever, the Trades Council and NILP cancelled the May Day march in the interests of "peace". Whether or not this gesture was supposed to influence the UPL is debatable: although it may have kept trade unionists off the streets, it did nothing to curb the UPL's street activity.

On 8 May there were disturbances in the York Street area in which three people were injured. On the following day Catholic millworkers were attacked by the crowd in the same area and in the course of the evening a number of serious incidents occurred. Two bombs were thrown in the Catholic end of Vere Street. And Patrick Mallon of Steam Mill Lane was shot in the stomach and seriously injured while walking in Nelson Street. By 10 May the police decided that things were bad enough to warrant a curfew. In addition, the Duke of Gloucester was to arrive the following day, and a curfew was one possible way of casting a calm veneer over the city to please the Royal gaze. The *Belfast News-Letter* pointed out that:

> ". . . the last time that a curfew was enforced in Belfast was in October 1932 when there was a riot consequent on the demand by the unemployed for an increase in the outdoor relief allowances."

The curfew had the desired effect. The Duke's visit passed without incident and the curfew was lifted on 14 May.

Inspired by a nationalist boycott of the Jubilee celebrations, the UPL and other loyalists increased their campaign of terror against the CPI and Catholics throughout June. On 12 June the UPL wrecked both the Socialist Party and CPI headquarters. On the same evening shots were fired from Protestant Duncairn Gardens into Catholic Lepper Street, and some Catholic shops were wrecked in North Street. Two days later, apparently for the first time, Catholics responded in kind. When shots were fired into the Catholic end of Ship Street, fire was returned and two Protestants were injured. On 15 June, Mrs Brown, a Catholic from Dock Street, escaped injury when shots were fired into her house. Fifteen year old Annie Quinn was not so lucky on 16 June; she was shot and injured while going to Mass.

It was on that day, 16 June, that the CPI publicly announced that it was going to form a workers' defence league to combat sectarian attacks. The league never materialised, so the thorny question of whether it could have operated in the midst of sectarian warfare, or whether it would itself have fallen foul of sectarian division was never put to the test. But, partly in response to the CPI's announcement, Dawson Bates banned all public meetings and demonstrations. In point of fact, the only such gatherings at that time were loyalist ones. So, Bates' attempt to nip the CPI challenge in the bud ended up only antagonising loyalists. Thus, on 19 June, the Orange Order became the first group to break the ban. And on 24 June the head of the Orange Order, Sir Joseph Davison, said that the Twelfth marches were to go ahead. Three days later Bates capitulated to Orange pressure and rescinded the ban. In the atmosphere existing in Belfast in that summer of 1935, it was inevitable that the July marches would be the catalyst for even more serious trouble. As a foretaste of what was yet to come, Protestant crowds wrecked Catholic homes in Brown Street on July 2nd and in Spamount and Lepper streets on 11 July. The stage was set for the Twelfth.

Ironically, on the last day of parliament before the Twelfth (on 10 July) MPs had a heated discussion of the riots of the previous May. T.J. Campbell, Nationalist, blamed the disturbances on the "weakness and vacillation of government". Furthermore, when trouble had occurred the Minister of Home Affairs himself had gone to York Street and "hob-nobbed and fraternised" with the very element in the community causing the trouble. In reply, William Grant, Unionist, said that the trouble was due to the sullen and anti-royalist attitudes of Catholics during the Jubilee celebrations. In conclusion, J.W. Nixon, Independent Unionist, stated ominously that:

> "Protestant processions should and would take place in Belfast, and if anything went wrong, there were ways of dealing with the trouble."

The events of two days later were to prove the validity of his prediction.

It has been said that the first casualty of war is truth. The accounts of what happened on 12 July 1935 differ totally depending on whether the source is a Catholic one or a Protestant one. It would be tempting to aim for some point in the middle and call that "truth". But the fact is that some of the accounts are too contrived to be true. Listen, for example, to the Orange Order's official account of what happened on that day:

> "The Orangemen were returning home by the route approved of by the Commissioner of Police, peaceably and quietly – their minds still occupied with thoughts of their message of loyalty and devotion to his Majesty and his gracious reply thereto – when they were fired upon almost simultaneously by gunmen at five different well-known danger points. These gunmen, from the screens formed by openly hostile crowds, which for some reason yet to be explained were allowed to collect at these danger points, directed their fire against unarmed men, women and children. It is to the credit of the Orangemen that not one of them left their ranks."

Apart from the fact that the piety of this account is too transparent to be real, there is any amount of evidence from witnesses of the events that major riots did take place and that countless Orangemen broke ranks to join in the fighting. They may well, as Henry Kennedy recalls[27], have stuffed their sashes in their pockets before doing so, but it would have taken more than that to disguise their participation from journalists, and police, not to mention the Catholics with whom they were fighting hand to hand.

The first incident of the day occurred at 6.30 in the evening as the Orange procession returned from the Field at Belmont in East Belfast. The procession was passing Stewart Street in the Markets when a drunk woman shouted something at the marchers. She was pushed by one of them and fell. Two Catholic youths attempted to help her and were pursued down Stewart Street. This riot was over very quickly, but it left three Catholics injured by gunshot wounds; there were no Protestant casualties. The procession continued and by 7 P.M. had reached the York Street area. The most serious riot occurred at this point. Protestant accounts have it that the march was attacked by Catholics; the Catholic account is that the Orangemen invaded their street and they fought back. What is beyond doubt is that the incident which sparked the riot occurred beside a bar, Sheridan's, at the corner of Lancaster Street. The Catholic residents of the street had agreed to stay indoors in the interests of safety, but had appointed some men as pickets to stand at the entrance to the street with the armed police who were on duty. As the procession passed, two of them, James Leddy and George Allsop, were standing with a Sergeant Brennan when some of the people following, but not in, the procession rushed up and hit them. No one seems to know precisely why this happened. The pickets ran into Sheridan's and out the back door, over the wall and into Lancaster Street with a number of Protestants in pursuit. While few marchers may have seen the initial incident, all witnessed the chase, and within seconds Lancaster Street was filled with hundreds of Orangemen. It took no time for stones to give way to pistols. The street cleared and there was a brief lull. Kennedy[28] remembers that lull:

> "The space opposite Lancaster Street was quiet and almost empty except for a youth sitting on the pavement with his back against the wall of the public house, and with the innocent air of someone enjoying the evening sun. Another man was bending over him. I did not know it at the time but the youth, a follower of the Orange procession, was dying with a bullet through his chest."

His name was Edward Withers, and he was eighteen. When the ambulance had removed him, the rioting recommenced, and at one point the battle was a three-way one, with Catholics, Protestants and police all firing, the last of them bringing an armoured car on the scene to pump rapid bursts of machine gun fire down both Lancaster Street and Little Patrick Street. Eventually the riot died down. In addition to Withers' death, there were many people injured. One of these, John McKay, a Catholic, was to die within the next few days.

The Lancaster Street riot was only a few minutes in progress when another Catholic was killed half a mile away. Mary and Samuel Broderick walked out of their house in Marine Street. Mary was carrying their one year old baby. As they came towards the Protestant end of the street, a group of men opened fire on them. Mary was hit and died instantly. As she fell, her husband Samuel had just time to catch the child.

About half an hour later a Catholic man, Joseph McDonald, was chased by a crowd at the corner of North Street and Royal Avenue. It was claimed that he had opened fire on the last of the Shankill lodges returning home. He was "rescued" by police, but, although no gun was found on him, no spent cartridges were discovered and he later claimed that a written statement of guilt signed by him had been made under duress, he was found guilty of firing on the marchers.

As 12 July drew to a close, a riot occurred in Isabella Street, on the border between the Catholic North Queen Street area and Protestant York Street. Thomas McDowell, a Protestant, was one of those seriously injured in the riot; he died some days later.

On Saturday, 13th July there were no major riots during daylight hours. The *Belfast News-Letter* misleadingly described the day as quiet "save for isolated incidents". In fact there were at least four Catholics injured in separate shooting incidents during the day, one a young boy and a seventy-four year old woman. A curfew had been imposed, to begin at 10 P.M. Half an hour before it did, a procession of Protestants, led by a band, the Billy Boys from Glasgow, marched with a wreath to the home of Edward Withers. The *Belfast News-Letter* recounts that the crowd stood to attention while the Billy Boys played "the King" and that as soon as it was finished shots rang out and Thomas Jordan and William Little, both Protestants, were killed. In London *The Times* was more cautious; pointing out that "it is alleged that several shots were fired" at the band, it went on to say that the two Protestants were killed in the "orgy of destruction" against Catholic homes in the area. For its part, a *Glasgow Herald* editorial asked:

> "Why do the authorities permit a party of people to march behind a band carrying a wreath to the home of a man who had been shot the night before? Of course, the wreath was a sincere tribute to the dead, but the manner of its delivery cannot be called anything but an ostentatious piece of provocation for the living."

In the rioting of that evening 48 Catholic homes were burned, and troops were called out for the first time to patrol the area.

On the 14 July, Sabbath or not, trouble spread to Sandy Row, Donegall Place, and the Lower Ormeau Road. There were incendiary attacks on Catholic houses, small riots and a number of shooting incidents, but no deaths. Despite these occurrences, the bulk of the trouble throughout July was confined to the York Street area. For this reason, on 15 July the police began to erect barricades at the entrance to a number of Catholic streets in the area. Though they may have been publicly presented as a way to keep people *out* of the area, the barricades had the effect of making Catholic residents feel even more confined and under seige. Jackie Quinn claims that nobody in the area really welcomed the barricades.

There was a small riot in the Brown's Square/Millfield area on the evening of Monday, 15 July. During it, James Andrews, a seventeen year old Protestant, was shot and seriously injured. About the same time, the Billy Boys were marching along Donegall Place heading for the boat back to Glasgow. Five Catholic men were chased by a large crowd accompanying the band. The *Belfast News-Letter*, echoing the claims of the crowd, says that they had produced revolvers. Four got away, but the fifth was chased by about 200 people into a billiard hall in Fountain Lane. There he had the dubious honour of being rescued by police only to be charged in connection with the riot.

Tuesday, 16 July, was quiet until the funeral of William Little, killed on the thirteenth, took place in the late afternoon. As the funeral arrived at the corner of Donegall Street and York Street, part of the funeral crowd rushed the International Bar. The bar was popular with Catholics, reason enough in the volatile atmosphere of the times for it to warrant attack. A free-for-all took place in the bar until the police arrived and arrested ten Catholics who had been playing billiards. They were led away to the cheers of the crowd who then turned their attention to nearby Academy Street, where they set three Catholic homes on fire. Later that night William Osborne, a Protestant, was shot and seriously injured in a riot in Nixon Street. Meanwhile, the police had begun erecting the barricades in New Andrew Street, New Dock Street, Marine Street, Ship Street, Fleet Street and Nelson Street.

Up to this point the CPI and the trade union movement had been remarkably quiet. But the CPI, recovering from the initial blow to its hopes of a socialist awakening, began agitating against the sectarian riots. By 1935, however, the CPI, in line with Comintern policy, was into a new phase of working through the labour movement, rather than condemning it as class-collaborationist. So, the CPI's efforts were directed in the main to persuading the Trades Council to issue a manifesto, which it did on this same day, 16 July. The single practical suggestion in the manifesto was:

> "[a] request that the Lord Mayor, as Chief Magistrate of the City, should immediately convene a conference of all religious and political organisations to consider what further effective steps can be taken to restore peace." (*Irish Workers' Voice* 20.7.35.)

The chances of success of such a conference were doubtful. To take just one political organisation: did the Trades Council seriously believe that the Orange Order, the first group to "disturb the peace" by breaking the ban on parades, would attend such a conference? And, even if some agreement had been reached at the conference, how would this have influenced working-class rioters? Even the CPI realised the flimsiness of this action and independently called for a "monster demonstration" and a one day general strike. Neither took place. Nor did the peace conference.

William Osborne, shot on the sixteenth, died on Wednesday, 17 July. But the city was quiet that day up until the funeral of another Protestant, Thomas McDowell, who had been shot at Lancaster Street on the Twelfth and died a few days later. Such was the anticipation of trouble among the "mourners" that they rushed an empty house in Peter's Hill where a man was seen at a window. He turned out to be a detective! Not to be so easily frustrated, the crowd attacked a Catholic in North Street. The police got him offside, but about 2,000 of the "mourners" swept along Royal Avenue beating up civilians and police and looting shops. There was trouble again as the funeral procession returned home, ending in the police being engaged in gun battles with Catholics at both Peter's Hill and Hartley Street (in the Old Lodge Road area). There were fifteen incendiary attacks on Catholic homes and pubs later that night, and, for the first time, 150 B Specials were called up for night duty to relieve the RUC who were said to be exhausted from peace keeping.

There was another death on Thursday, July 18, James Andrews, a Protestant who had been shot on the fifteenth. The day was remarkably quiet, however, with only eight incendiary attacks reported that evening, as well as a number of evictions. Friday the nineteenth was even quieter, with some evictions and three incendiary attacks. The surprising absence of violence on both dates was undoubtedly related to the fact that there were no funerals. But the lull came to an end on Saturday the twentieth with the funeral of James Andrews. At Berry Street a section of the funeral procession broke away and attacked a Catholic man whom, they claimed, had made an insulting remark. In the middle of the furore a shot was fired from the crowd at the police. The funeral procession meanwhile had moved on and part of it attacked another Catholic on the Newtownards Road; he was badly beaten. They also tried to storm Foundry Street, but did not succeed because of a large and unusually forceful police presence. Later that evening there was rioting in Ardoyne and shooting in York Street and Agnes Street, and this ended the first day of the second week of rioting.

Sunday, 21 July, saw two more deaths, one being that of a Protestant, Edward Scarlett, in Hibernia Street, East Belfast. The *Belfast News-Letter*, probably quoting police sources, concluded that his death was "a real mystery". But Catholic sources were quick to point out that he was "a Protestant with strong Catholic associations".[29] He was shot in a Protestant main thoroughfare and his assassin ran off into the heart of the Protestant district. The other person to die that day was John McKay, a Catholic injured on the Twelfth.

Monday, 22 July, was to be the first day back to work after the holiday. Things did not augur well, as already threatening slogans had appeared. One near Harland and Wolff's read: "Catholics who cannot swim, learn to before Monday". So:

> " . . . on the day that work was resumed mobs were allowed to collect round the gates of some of the largest mills and factories in Belfast, brandishing sticks and iron bars and shouting in violent and vile language what they intended to do with the Catholic workers when they came out. When the Catholic workers emerged, old and young alike were attacked, some of them being pointed out to the crowd by their Protestant fellow-workers. Some of these girls were slashed with razor blades, others were struck, others knocked down."[30]

There was less trouble than might have been expected, however, probably because many Catholics stayed away from work.

The intimidation of workers was one source of inspiration for a short-lived rent strike which began in Ardoyne on the same day. Tenants vowed to withold rents "until all workers are properly protected in their homes and in their work, and until such time as peace is restored in the city". The intimidation of Catholic workers also led to a number of ugly retaliatory incidents in the South. Already on the seventeenth all Protestant businesses in Ballina had been smeared with red paint, and slogans such as "Remember Belfast" and "Boycott the Orangemen" appeared. Four days later, there were reports of "orgies of destruction" directed against Protestant businesses in Clones and Limerick. But, on the twenty-third, some in the South directed their attention to the Protestant working class there. A serious but unsuccessful effort was made to call a general strike in Galway unless all Protestant workers were dismissed. Meanwhile, on the same day a Protestant church was burned in Kilmallock, and Limerick dockers refused to unload Belfast ships.

For their part the Orange Order in the North attempted to organise a boycott of Catholic businesses, especially public houses, and indeed any businesses which employed Catholics. But this was less a response to the embryonic boycotts in the South than to the moves being made by the Nationalist Party to raise the question of the Unionist Party's collusion in the riots. The Orange Order released its lengthy statement blaming the trouble on "that portion of the populace which ever arrays itself on the side of sedition and disloyalty" on the same day, 24 July, that two Nationalist MPs, Cahir Healy and J.F. Stewart, arrived in London to publicise their dossier of complaints against Unionist politicians. The Orange Order, the Unionist Party and the Unionist press was furious at such effrontery, but such fury did not reach the streets. The war was fast becoming one of words, not of stones and bullets. On the twenty-fourth troops were returned to barracks and work at some mills was reported to be completely back to normal. There was still some trouble, however. York Street Flax Company had to close on Thursday the twenty-fifth until the following Monday after Protestant women refused to work alongside Catholic women whom, they said, had been guilty of "provocative conduct". One suspects that in the atmosphere of the times for a Catholic even to turn up for work might be taken as a provocative act.

On Sunday, 28 July, the Republican Congress held a protest meeting in Trafalgar Square in London where the Nationalist MPs were among those protesting at official sponsorship of sectarianism in NI. Despite Unionist disgust at this "vilification" this meeting marked the last activity on the streets of that Twelfth fortnight. The troops were in barracks, the funerals were over, the curfew was about to end and the barricades would soon come down. By the end of July, as far as the press was concerned, Belfast was back to "normal". But, there were still a few reminders of what had happened. In all 430 Catholic homes had been burned, 514 Catholic families (2241 people), had been intimidated out of Protestant areas. The *Belfast News-Letter* fudged the issue of intimidation by stating that:

> " . . . residents who were not of the same religious persuasion as the majority in a district received warnings to leave at once, and in many cases the warnings were heeded." (19.7.35.)

In fact the intimidation was overwhelmingly one-sided. The relief committee formed by the Catholic bishop, Dr Mageean, to care for the Catholic homeless, found only one case of a Protestant family being intimidated out – in the Whiterock Road, close to MacRory park, where the refugee Catholic families were living in tents. It can be conceded that this committee had an axe to grind; but even the fiercely loyalist *Belfast News-Letter* and *Northern Whig* could produce no evidence of a mass eviction of Protestants similar to that experienced by Catholics.

Rehousing these Catholics was a problem, even with the 2,000 guineas collected by the *Universe* from English Catholics. One of the immediate consequences of the evictions was that many Catholics squatted in partially built houses in Glenard estate, Ardoyne. Ironically, as James Kelly points out, this was to have been "a Protestant estate which, when built, would have turned the Oldpark constituency into a safe Unionist seat". Betty Sinclair was one of those involved in helping people to settle in the new estate, a dubious exercise in the eyes of some given that she was Protestant and the squatters were Catholic:

> "A woman came to see me and told me we had to stop helping these Catholics otherwise she was told to come as a deputation to tell me that our house would be burned down. I knew her very well, she was one of those people who belonged to a Mission Hall, very Christian. I said: 'Well, you can go ahead and burn the house down. It doesn't belong to us and we don't have much in the way of furniture or that. But, I don't think that Ewart's mill

directors would be very pleased with its workers burning down its property and it might be worse for you than for us in the end.' Nobody ever came back again but for two years none of the Protestant people in Hooker Street spoke to me."

There were other reminders still around of the intensity of the troubles, many of them perhaps less visible than charred houses. Court cases, both civil and criminal, arising out of the riots went on for months afterwards. (Approximately 95% of the £21,669 paid out in compensation was to Catholics, according to Bardon.[31]) Some of the injured were still hospitalised. One of these was Edward Brady, whose girlfriend recounts in heart-rendering detail the incident in which he was injured. Returning from the city centre at about 9.30 P.M. on 13 July, they passed a group of about fifty men at the corner of Boundary Street and Shankill Road:

"One of these men caught the lapel of Edward's coat and asked: 'What are you?' Edward replied: 'I am a Catholic'. Immediately this man struck Edward in the mouth. The rest of them started to strike him and kick him. We ran up Boundary Street and two women standing at the door pulled us in and shut the outside door. A crowd gathered outside and began to shout and yell. The woman of the house said: 'God, if you don't get out of this they'll wreck the house'. The other woman said: 'There's an empty house next door. If you get in there you'll be all right till the crowd goes away'. Edward ran out into the yard and he got up on to the shed, and the woman helped me up after him. We got down into the yard of the empty house. There was a short step-ladder in the yard. We put it against the wall and climbed into a room through an open window. We were in the room for ten or fifteen minutes. A few minutes later I heard the front door of the empty house being burst in. I heard the crowd shouting: 'Trail the Fenians out'. Edward climbed out of the window and down the ladder. I felt very weak and cried out for him to go on himself. But he wouldn't go. He waited for me. I climbed down too and we put the ladder against the shed. Eddie climbed up on to the shed and I was just getting on to the shed when three men rushed out into the yard. One of them lifted a sheet of tin and shouted: 'You ——— ———' and threw it up at Eddie. He jumped from the shed on to the wall of another yard and slid down into the yard and I saw him go in by the back door of the house. That was the last I saw of him that night. The three men got up on the shed. They went down into the same yard that Eddie went into. About twelve more men came into the yard and one climbed up on the shed. He said: 'Where's your mate?' I said: 'I don't know where he is'. He struck me on the face with his fist and said: 'Tell me where your f——— mate is'. I said: 'I don't know', and he struck me again. They went away and

I heard some of them shouting: 'He's in the last house in the row'. I pulled myself together, jumped on to the other wall, and down into the yard of the last house in the row where Eddie had gone. I went into the house but Eddie was no longer there. I looked out to see if I could see where they had him when a woman gripped me by the hair and pulled me out into the street. A crowd of men and women got round me and began to maul me. A man dazed me with a blow on the back of the head with his fist. Two or three of them said: 'Let the women at her'. They kept on beating me with their fists on the head and face and driving me on in front of them. I staggered down Boundary Street. I turned a corner and collapsed beside a blank wall. While I was on the ground I heard two shots from the direction of the Shankill Road but very close at hand.

A man then picked me up and carried me down Boundary Street into a Catholic house. He said he was a Protestant but he didn't go in for that carry-on. He said also that he needn't go up the Shankill for he would get a hiding for saving me.

I saw Eddie several times in the hospital during the next three weeks before he died. He died on August the eighth."[32]

Aftermath

The events of the second half of July 1935 did not come out of the blue. They were the culmination of a build-up of sectarianism in the spring and summer of that year. As an editorial in the *Irish Workers' Voice* of 27 July stated:

> "The pogrom was not caused by a revolver shot on the 12th, any more than the Great War was caused by the revolver shot at Sarajevo."

Interestingly, from the very first day of the riots it was referred to by some as a pogrom. The word conjured up the awful days of 1920-22, when over 500 people had been killed in Belfast, many of them Catholic. It captured the fear of Catholics, especially those in borderline areas such as York Street, that they would be massacred by hordes of marauding Protestants.

But it was a word that did not fall easily on loyalist ears. The loyalist assessment had a number of variations to it. The first was that of the Prime Minister on 20 July, that the trouble "has never been so serious as has been made out". The Unionist Party agreed:

> "Regrettable as the disturbances have been, their bulk must not be exaggerated. The population of Belfast is about 450,000, and the population of the area affected about 4,500. Therefore not more than 1% of the population has been affected."[33]

But even the most recalcitrant unionist had to admit that *something* happened, even if it was only the Lancaster Street riot on 12 July. That was easily explained. As far as unionists were concerned, Catholics started the riot by attacking law-abiding Orange marchers. Furthermore, the unionists refused to see even what they defined as a Protestant "response" as a pogrom. As the Dean of Belfast[34] put it:

> "To describe the shooting and evictions as a one-sided pogrom is absurdly unjust. It is a queer pogrom in which twice as many of the supposed assailants were killed as the inoffensive victims."

The Dean went further, and in the face of all evidence to the contrary, stated that "there were no murders or evictions until the unprovoked attack on the orderly Orange procession of 12th July". This was easily refuted by nationalist propagandists. Less easily dismissed was the proportion of casualties: seven Protestants dead to two Catholics. The nationalist reply was that one of the Protestants (Scarlett) was killed for being a "Fenian lover", and that the others were killed in street fighting (where they could as easily have been hit by police or army bullets as Catholic ones), unlike one of the Catholic victims (Broderick) killed half a mile from any riot. They could have added that a third Catholic (Brady) died three weeks after the Twelfth. Such retorts, however, fell on deaf ears as far as the establishment was concerned, leading the nationalists to publicise their argument in London. Dr Mageean also called on British Prime Minister Baldwin to initiate an inquiry into the government's involvement in the causes of the riots[35] but to no avail. For unionists such actions were tantamount to disloyalty. The establishment assessment remained relatively unruffled by these nationalist and episcopal moves.

Not surprisingly, this dominant assessment was shared by the unionist media and the police. As regards the media, Kennedy,[36] a journalist and an eyewitness of the Lancaster Street riot, was appalled to find that the *Belfast News-Letter* and the *Northern Whig* of 13 July had "accounts of the riot radically different from my own", in which the people of Lancaster Street were portrayed "as a community of murderous ruffians". Naïvely, he arranged to see the chief reporter on one of these papers to point out the error of his paper's report, only to be informed that the report was based on his, the chief reporter's, own first-hand experience of the riot!

For their part, the police adhered to the "Catholic mobs attack peaceful Protestants" reading of events. The *Belfast News-Letter* presumably quoting police sources carried a story purporting to show the police as beleaguered keepers of the peace. Rather, it revealed their reluctance to act against Protestant rioters:

> "The police were very seriously handicapped in dealing with a situation of the utmost gravity by reason of the attitude assumed by a number of small bands and other minor processions which, despite the strongest possible persuasion, persisted in exercising what they protested was their right to march down York Street

> after the trouble had begun. In one instance, policemen were thrust forcibly to one side and were threatened with deacon poles. The police were powerless to enforce their requests that the marchers should desist and proceed along another route."

Yet, these same police showed no hesitation in firing a machine gun into Catholic streets. It is no coincidence, then, that when police prosecutions were brought against those arrested in the Lancaster Street riot, it turned out that all were against Catholics. This fact was taken by the loyalist community not as the evidence of bias that it was, but as proof that the loyalist reading of events was correct. And so the stage was set for even more trouble.

The Nationalists rightly made much of police "forbearance", as they sarcastically termed it. Even the mildest of Catholics were amazed at the RUC's frequent low profile. Kennedy is such a Catholic. He recalls[37] that on 12 July he stood and watched a Protestant man:

> " . . . firing a revolver repeatedly in the direction of Lancaster Street. It looked so harmless in action, the reports of the shots so faint, the small puffs of smoke so innocent that it was incredible that this was an instrument of death. Even more fantastic was the fact that nobody except myself seemed to be paying any particular attention to him – not even the two policemen standing within two yards of him or the dozen other policemen within fifty yards."

Less mild Nationalists than Kennedy came up with some firm conclusions. The first was that the chief cause of the riots was the action of Unionist politicians in whipping up sectarianism. In a public statement on 22 July, the Nationalist members of Stormont declared their:

> " . . . belief that members of the government, by their bitter sectarian speeches advocating the boycott of Catholics, are, in the main, responsible for provoking the tumult and orgies of destruction let loose upon the city in the last two weeks."[38]

This was the central plank in the Nationalist Party case presented at Westminster that same month, in which, like Dr Mageean, they called for a public inquiry into the riots. In their argument the Nationalist Party had support from an unusual source, T.E. Alexander, the Belfast city coroner, who had stated during an inquest into one of the riot's victims on 22 July:

> "Poor people who commit these riots are easily led. They are influenced almost entirely by public speeches by men in high and responsible positions. There would be less bigotry if there were less public speech-making of a kind by so-called leaders of public opinion."[39]

Needless to say, the CPI agreed with this assessment. Geehan did his part to conjure up the romantic myth of 1932 in an interview he gave to *Irish Workers' Voice* on 20 July:

> "With all my conviction I want to tell my fellow workers that this

> trouble is the work of our capitalist enemies; it has been diabolically organised. I urge every unemployed man especially to remember the lessons of 1932 and to work might and main to end this strife and restore our unity for the real struggle – the struggle for food and clothes, for our wives and children."

That politicians' sectarianism influenced public opinion is undeniable. However, that it alone was the cause of the riots is too far-fetched a conclusion. The strength of popular, everyday sectarianism cannot be underestimated. Geehan's call to a "real" struggle ignored the fact that that other struggle, the sectarian one, was equally real in people's lives. In fact, it could almost be argued that the sectarian struggle was so normal that all talk of "restoring" working-class unity was wishful thinking rather than realism. Sectarian speeches by Unionists such as Brookeborough and Craigavon could contribute to a flare-up of sectarianism, but there were times when the politicians were found leading their people from behind, as it were, or, alternatively, contributing to trouble by default rather than by action, as when they failed to stand up to the Orange Order over the ban on processions. Sectarianism as a part of Belfast's everyday life had a vitality of its own.

Of course, the Nationalist Party's conclusion fitted its overall assessment of the Northern state, that it was inherently sectarian and irreformable (just as its publication of that assessment was taken by Unionists as proof of the Nationalists' well-known disloyalty). In this belief in irreformability (or at least in the inability of the unionist state to reform itself from within), the Nationalists again had somewhat unlikely backing, this time from the editorial writer of the *Manchester Guardian* on 13 July:

> "Craigavon's government is now in a difficult position. Its prestige is gone. All see it for what it is – a government which has chosen to seek support for a new state from the strength of ignorance, sectarian prejudice and the passions of faction . . . Evidently this is no matter of merely local importance in which the British government need take no interest."

Yet, this is precisely what the British government was going to do. When Dr Mageean wrote to Baldwin on 16 August demanding that Baldwin exercise his right and duty under the 1920 Government of Ireland Act to investigate the Northern Ireland government's use of powers devolved to it, he received a single sentence reply from V.M. Watson of the Prime Minister's office:

> "The Prime Minister is at present absent from London, and I am therefore writing, in his absence, to acknowledge the receipt of your letter to him of the 11 August."

The imperial cabinet was not about to call on the provincial government to account for its stewardship. Partition and devolution were not questioned for a second. In short, Craigavon's position was not made any less tenable as a result of the riots, despite the Nationalists' wishes to the contrary.

To nationalists the expensive and palatial parliament building at Stormont, opened shortly after the ODR riots on 6 November 1932,[40] was the surest symbol that sectarianism had been well and truly institutionalised and was here to stay. Together with partition in 1921 and the British government's full-blooded recognition of the border in the Ireland Bill of 1949, the opening of Stormont was one of the trinity of events that confirmed the minority's worst fears about discrimination under a Unionist majority.

And if institutionalised sectarianism was alive and well, so also was popular sectarianism. The troubles did not end with the lifting of the curfew at the end of July 1935. On 20 September a riot occurred in Greencastle, north of Belfast, and a twenty-seven year old Protestant, George Clyde, was shot dead. A Catholic, John McKiernan, also twenty-seven years old, was shot dead the following night, probably in retaliation. Similarly, a Catholic woman was shot and injured in her own home in the Docks area. Throughout September and November there were a number of shooting and bombing incidents in the York Street/Docks area. The wave of sectarianism may have crested, but it was still there.

The wave of class militancy was in relative ebb also after 1935 despite a continuing high level of unemployment; in fact, 1938 marked the highest level of unemployment ever in the state, 28.3% of the insured population. There were industrial rumblings from time to time, but there were no major strikes in the late 1930s to match the railway workers' strike of 1933, nor any major unemployment agitation such as that around the ODR issue in 1932. The CPI, in line with its "popular front" strategy, continued unsuccessfully to put forward candidates in parliamentary and Board of Guardians elections, and to forge a union with the NILP and W.J. Steward's Progressive Unionists, formed in 1937 as a protest against rising unemployment.

By the end of the thirties the Belfast scene had changed, or was about to change, dramatically, at least for a short time. The IRA had gone on the offensive, carrying its military campaign to Britain itself. The approach of World War II turned back industrial decline temporarily and proved a god-send to Harland and Wolff's and Short's. Unemployment started to decrease till it reached 3.8% of the insured population in 1944, the lowest it had ever been since the state was founded. Geehan, one of the most active and well known CPI members, had resigned and the membership of the party had declined severely. And the prospect of a larger war than the intermittent one on the streets of Belfast seemed to soften the edge of sectarianism, at least in its popular form. World War II was not a "major breach" in the walls between the working-class communities that had been strengthened in 1935, as Kennedy[41] hoped; but for a while it appeared to be. The waves of class militancy and sectarianism were at a low ebb, but they would be in flow again in the years after the war.

FOOTNOTES

1. Budge, I; O'Leary, C. 1973: 151
2. Isles, K. S., Cuthbert, N. 1957: 31
3. Belfast Trades Council Minutes, 3 December, 1931
4. Ibid: 3 March, 1932
5. Cited in Johnstone, T. M. 1930: 6
6. Ibid: 8
7. Figures given in Bardon, J. 1982: 217
8. On the rise of the RWG and CPI, see Milotte, M. 1977
9. Public Record Office of NI, Cabinet Minutes, CAB 4/304/21; quoted in Milotte, M. 1977: 283
10. Belfast Trades Council Minutes, 6 October, 1932
11. Figures from Milotte, M. 1977: 282
12. Farrell, M. 1978: 87
13. Devlin, P. 1981: 79
14. Quoted in Devlin, 1981: 130
15. Hannington, W. 1940: 63
16. Mann's press release; quoted in Hannington, W. 1940: 64
17. Devlin, P. 1981: 133-5
18. Kelly, J. 1944: 307
19. Milotte, M. 1977: 298
20. Quoted in Milotte, 1977: 295
21. Belfast Trades Council Minutes, 22 June, 1933
22. Ibid: 6 April, 1933
23. Milotte, M. 1977: 300
24. Farrell, M. 1980: 136
25. Ibid: 137
26. Devlin, P. 1981: 176
27. Kennedy, H. 1972: 102
28. Ibid: 101
29. Confidential Document, n.d: 16
30. Ibid: 14
31. Bardon, J. 1982: 230
32. Quoted in Confidential Document, n.d: 37-8
33. Ibid: 28
34. Dean of Belfast. 1944: 387
35. Catholic Bulletin. 1935: 689
36. Kennedy, H. 1972: 101
37. Ibid.
38. Catholic Bulletin. 1935: 685
39. Confidential Document. n.d.: 23
40. "XQ". 1933
41. Kennedy, D. 1966: 149

2. The Working Class Experience: Unemployment and Poverty in the Thirties

Introduction

It is unfortunate that a statement which begins as an accurate description can, through usage, end up as a cliche. There is no denying that the 1930s in Belfast were indeed hungry, yet the extent of such hunger can be lost on us half a century later. For many people in the depression, their life chances consisted of only two options: the world of low-paid, often casual work; and the terror of unemployment. Of course, there were rich in Belfast, as elsewhere, whose decadence was a marked contrast to the poverty of the working class. But, though the affluence of the rich was tied inexorably to the hunger of the poor, both being sides of the inequality of inter-war capitalism, it is on the poor, both the unemployed and those at the bottom end of the jobs hierarchy, that we will focus here.

Unemployment in the thirties

We have examined in the previous chapter the drastic growth in unemployment in the 1930s. For those laid off the immediate shock of unemployment was bad enough; at least they *might* be lucky enough to have unemployment benefit. But as the length of unemployment for most people increased in the thirties, there emerged the second and more serious problem, that of trying to survive when the unemployment benefit ended. Harold Binks, an ex-trade union official, put it like this:

> "The 1930s was a very difficult time for working-class people. In my view, it was more difficult than the present time because there were less jobs. For example, if a man was unemployed, he was able to draw 17/- per week. If he was married, he drew 15/- for his wife and he could draw 2/- per week for any child up to sixteen years of age. He could draw those rates for a period of up to six months and after that he was able to draw another six months called 'transitional benefit', but at the end of his transitional

benefit, as far as the state was concerned, he could live on grass or whatever he liked."

Alice Quinn told us of the specific experience of her family in this respect:

"I wonder how my own mother managed, because my father, he died in the States – he went to sea. There was no widow's pension, no family allowance. I was married before the family allowance came out. There was no widow's pension, and when it did come it was only ten shillings. All she got was one pound and one shilling to keep four of us and her."

Nor was Alice Quinn's experience unusual. Studies of poverty at the time were few but they do exist. Dr James Deeny, a general practitioner from Lurgan, investigated the health and financial circumstances of 205 women in his area in 1938. He found that the sources of income varied markedly in the five income groups he identified (see Table 1). There were insufficient people in Group 1 to make it worth recording.

TABLE 1: Sources of income, Lurgan, 1938[1]

Source of Income	Group					All groups
	2 (poorest)	3	4	5	6 (least poor)	
Earnings	41%	66%	73%	81%	86%	70%
Unemployment Benefit	48%	27%	14%	9%	7%	20%
Other Income	11%	7%	13%	10%	7%	10%

In presenting these figures to the Statistical and Social Inquiry Society of Ireland, Deeny drew the obvious conclusion (yet one that seemed astoundingly novel to the other Society members) that the:

"table shows plainly the relationship between poverty and unemployment. A much greater proportion of the income of the lower income groups is derived from unemployment benefits."[2]

He also pointed out that "the people of the sample were not the poorest in Lurgan by any means; in fact, they could be regarded as industrial aristocrats".[3] Yet, even they did not have enough income to cover the necessities of life.

Around the same time, in the winter of 1937/8, two poverty surveys were carried out in Belfast, one by the Presbyterian Church's Social Service Committee, the other by the Methodists' Temperance and Social Welfare Committee. Both revealed incredible levels of poverty. The Presbyterian survey covered 436 households in one working-class housing estate. The researcher, Beacham from Queen's University's Department of Economics, derived a poverty line based on the British Medical Association's 1933 assessment of minimum food requirements and the work of Rowntree. On this basis, Beacham considered that an income of 20/6d. was a minimum requirement for a family of husband, wife and one child, but hastened to add:

> "Any household with a net income below the appropriate minimum needs standard is in extreme poverty. Any household with a net income from 0% to 50% above the appropriate minimum needs standard is faced with a continuous struggle to make both ends meet and has an insufficient margin to meet probable contingencies or to provide such simple luxuries as would make life worth living."[4]

Using his harsh measure of poverty, Beacham found that on this one housing estate:

> "at least 33% of the families . . . are in considerable economic distress, whilst a further 29% are living under conditions which may be termed as 'barely sufficient' and probably intolerable for any length of time."[5]

In addition, 24% of the households were found to be wholly dependent on state benefits, with 31% partly dependent on such benefits and 45% wholly supported by wages. Of the first category, those wholly dependent on state aid, 70% were in extreme poverty.

In the Methodist study[6], 705 households on one housing estate were surveyed. Of them, 76% were found to be below Rowntree's 1936 poverty line. Of the households dependent only on wages, 58% were below the poverty line. Of households maintained by a combination of wages and state aid 13% were below the poverty line. And 40% of the households were totally dependent on state benefits; of these, 89% fell below Rowntree's poverty line. In short, like the Presbyterians, the Methodists discovered that those on state benefits had not enough to survive. But, in addition the Methodists provided evidence that even those in employment on this working-class estate were more likely than not to be in extreme poverty.

In short, low pay and unemployment were the twin prospects for most working-class people. As regards the latter prospect, the long-term nature of unemployment in the thirties was something that was shocking and, relatively speaking, new to the workers of Northern Ireland, as Winifred Campbell recalls:

> "Short time unemployment was common enough. It simply meant a tightening of the belt for a while. If essential payments fell behind they could always be cleared off at so much weekly, once work was resumed; but this was something different. As months stretched into years, people began to despair. Every possible economy became the way of life."[7]

Housing and rent

> "First priority was the rent. That must be paid, otherwise a family could be evicted and their belongings seized in lieu of rent. Next came food, a necessity of life. A long way behind came fuel, clothes, utensils, bedding."[8]

The rents that working-class people had to pay for housing in the thirties varied greatly. One person, Florrie Addley, recalls:

> "There was no such thing as a basic wage; you could have come out in one week with four shillings, and the next week had way over a pound; there was no such a thing of having a basic of, say, a pound, unless they were fixed-pay workers, as we called them. A pound a week then was a terrific wage. When I started, I had six shillings, and my husband and I, when we married in 1939 – he was a salesman, you know – and he had two pounds a week, and the rent was ten and sixpence a week. That's a sixth of your wages and they talk now about the big rents – and they'd no help whatsoever."[9]

Similarly, the Methodists in their survey found that people were paying on average 9/7d. a week for rent in 1938, and that on an average income of 45/6d. for a family of four. Of course, the quality of housing varied as much as the rents did. Dr Carnwath, in his report on the health of Belfast in 1941, reported on the worst of working-class housing he had seen:

> "Damp, mouldering walls, many of them bulging, rickety stairs, broken floors, crumbling ceilings were common defects. Some of the 'houses' were mere hovels, with the people living in indescribable filth and squalour. Considering the accommodation, the rents seemed high. In a group of three of the worst houses, each sublet to three tenants, and rents were 1/9d. a week for a small attic which it was an adventure to approach."[10]

At the other end of the range of working-class housing was the parlour house. Florrie Addley recalled the status that having such a house bestowed, even if such status was arguably more affected than real:

> "Anyone who had a parlour had a decent suite in it, and sometimes they used to joke and say they'd nothing in it except a big aspidistra to cover the window so that nobody would see in! We had a decent suite, and you weren't allowed in it unless on special occasions, or, as in most parlour houses, if there was a death, they were laid out in the parlour."

Overall, the quality of housing for working-class people in Belfast had improved in a generation. Dr Carnwath noted that "in respect of over crowding", the position was "considerably better" in 1937 compared with 1926; however, he added, it "cannot be regarded as satisfactory". If there was one major factor in the continuing poor quality of working-class housing, it was the state's failure to see the provision and maintenance of such housing as a duty. Since the end of World War I the authorities in Ireland had had statutory obligations to aid house building. However, the Acts encouraging such provision had fallen into disuse, and an added element in the inertia on the issue was the conservatism of the Unionist Party which took over the reins of government of the new state of NI after partition. As a result, very few new houses were provided out of state funds between the wars, as Table 2 shows. Although in some years, especially in the 1920s, the total number of houses provided with at least partial state aid looks respectable, the state's direct involvement was minor; in no case did urban or rural authorities directly provide more than a minority of state-aided housing; in fact, in 1936/7, they directly provided *no* houses at all. For the most part state help went to bolstering the private sector. This disproportionately affected the chances of the working class, throwing them into the market where their incomes enabled them often to acquire housing only at the lower end of that market.

TABLE 2: Houses built with state aid in Northern Ireland, 1921/37[11]

Year	Urban authorities	Private builders	Rural authorities	Total
1921/3	478	237	–	715
1923/4	24	102	–	126
1924/5	73	675	59	807
1925/6	882	1,382	91	2,355
1926/7	123	1,504	379	2,006
1927/8	91	2,142	388	2,621
1928/9	198	3,620	704	4,522
1929/30	300	4,540	155	4,995
1930/31	144	5,036	33	5,213
1931/2	37	2,565	173	2,775
1932/3	15	554	56	625
1933/4	20	446	11	477
1934/5	50	1,151	–	1,201
1935/6	20	3,717	–	3,737
1936/7	213	4,712	–	4,925

Binks refers to one ingenious working-class response to the problem of bad housing and high rents, what he calls "the rent repayment business".

"People organised themselves in cells, as they were called then. They used to come around and knock at the door, find out if people had paid their rent and how much. The rent book would be looked at and the woman be paid back because they had stopped the rent collector at the end of the street and relieved him of all the rent he had collected. The rent agent couldn't reclaim the money because it was marked paid in the rent book. I don't know who the hold-up men were, but I suspect that if they were not in the Communist Party, they were sympathisers."

Feeding the poor

One of the consequences of being poor in the thirties was not having enough good food. Frances Maguire recalls how forcefully that conclusion impressed itself on her as a child:

"I remember my mother reading that it costs five shillings to keep a dog in a dog's home and they give us two shillings to keep a child. I always remembered that, and it always influenced me all the days of my life after that, that human life was so cheap, even in relation to animals."

To make ends meet was a constant struggle that required the utmost ingenuity and careful planning. The remarkable fact is that the poor were able to make a little go a long way. One means of doing this was to buy the minimum amount of food required at any one time. Florrie Addley's father owned a corner shop in the Docks area, open seven days a week:

"We sold the jam loose out of a big jar. It intrigued us as kids, because even as kids, we had to help in the shop. I loved anyone coming in for jam, because you had to weigh their cup first and whatever jam, quarter pound, you put the other weight on. And there was no such a thing as packet butter or anything. The butter was bought in a butter-box and set on a slab, and you had to use the things to cut it up."

Another tactic was to buy as cheaply as possible, either by queueing up at a shop which had a reputation for being cheaper, or by buying the cheapest possible cut. Barney Boswell remembers buying a pound of broken biscuits for a penny, or a penny worth of broken cheese. Frances Maguire remembers the queues for stale bread in West Belfast:

"You would have seen people going with a white bolster-slip or a pillow-case and they would have got a shilling's worth of bread. Now that would mean most people wanted loaves and it was great if you got it all in loaves. But then you could have got what you called small bread. That was scones and baps and barmbracks and such bread like that, a veda loaf or a small wheaten loaf. Some people would have went for that. You might have got a couple of gravy-rings threw in, all this sort of thing, but mostly the majority of people would have preferred just getting a shilling's worth of bread. I remember that you could have seen people going up to the bakery after three o'clock. Mr Kennedy was very good in relation to that, more so than most, like Hughes. You might have got maybe some fresh bread with him and you maybe got something extra, or something like that, where Hughes didn't give you that."

Anne Boyle remembers similar queues in North Belfast:

"A loaf was only tuppence ha'penny. People queued up at six o'clock in the morning at the City bakery up the Oldpark Road. I have seen kids all the way from Ardoyne, standing in their bare feet. Everybody was there with their pillow-cases to get stale bread. You got sixpence worth of stale bread, and you could have got threepence worth of stale buns. It would be up to the good will of the one who was serving you what kind of bread you got."

Certain shops got the reputation of selling specific commodities cheaper. So, they were obviously places the poor preferred to shop, queues or distance notwithstanding. Frances Maguire again:

"I remember McNeill's at the top of Cupar Street where you could have bought potatoes. People came from all over and walked to the top of Cupar Street and down with a stone of potatoes in one hand and a stone of potatoes in the other hand. And there used to be, off the Springfield Road, a shop where you could have got a quart of milk for thruppence ha'penny. It was tuppence a pint, so most people walked there to buy at that price. The cheaper you got it, the better it was."

Leo Boyle has similar memories to those of his wife, Anne:

"Eggs were bought from Gracey's of York Street, sixpence for a bowl of cracked eggs. You didn't ask for a dozen or a half-dozen. You might have got fourteen or fifteen if they liked you."

Working-class people tended to try to get by on cheap, filling foods – bread, potatoes – with other things being relative luxuries. Soup and stew were popular staple foods. But fresh milk was rare. Anne McKenna recounts that:

"It wasn't every family that had sweet milk. Buttermilk, yes, and condensed milk, tinned milk. Now, I was ten, eleven years of age when I saw that on the table in the house opposite me – it was calf's milk."

Harold Binks cited one source of fresh milk. In the morning boys and girls would wait, barefooted, at the cattle pens at the Albert Bridge to get the milk from cattle which were being shipped to England, milk that would otherwise have been thrown away. Hygiene surrounding the collection of that milk must have left much to be desired, but for the poor it was worth it to have sweet milk.

Buttermilk was the more likely drink in working-class homes. But, there was more than one way to drink it, as Charlie Hull remembers. You could:

" . . . take a bucket of stout with a bucket of butter milk, or alternatively, if you couldn't afford the stout, you got a bucket of buttermilk – a penny in the gas and the gas tube in the buttermilk really made a nice intoxicating drink."

Meat was an even greater luxury than sweet milk. Florrie Addley:

"There would have been soup, maybe for two or three days in one of those big pots. I remember all you ever seemed to get was soup. You would never have got – well, I remember getting maybe sausages, but I never remember getting fried steak or anything."

And the Addleys were not among the very poorest families in Belfast.

As well as sausages, there was cheap pork, as Anne Boyle recounts:

"You could buy pork cheap and bring it home and burn all the hairs off it with a red-hot poker and then we'd put it in the oven and eat the crackling and skin and all."

Leo Boyle told us of one other type of meat the poor could just afford:

"The sides of meat were hung up in butchers' shops and the blood would be drained off them, congealing at the bottom. This is what people got when they bought stewing meat. It was dirty looking, but it was richer than other cuts. But the few people that had money never touched it; they selected their cut, but the ordinary average family was glad to get it."

Finally there was rabbit hunting. This occurred either in the mountains to the west of Belfast, or on the Dufferin estate in Crawfordsburn (where one ran the risk of getting caught by gamekeepers) – both could provide free meat. Charlie McGlade never went rabbit hunting himself, but he knew of those that did:

"Fellahs would set off about twelve o'clock at night to go away over the mountains and try and catch rabbits. These lads would go over the mountains so as to be there early in the morning when you would get the rabbits and the hares quicker. You always said that you couldn't eat a hare, but it made a beautiful soup. But rabbits are different; they're edible. I was only a young lad and I was working, and I should have been glad to be working; but I was jealous of these lads setting off at that time of night to go away over the mountain."

So, rabbit hunting was not only a source of meat, but also doubled as recreation for young men. In addition, it could help augment a person's income, as John Nicholl explains:

"You could sell the surplus to Ewing's fish shop on the Shankill Road. They would have given you 2d. for a rabbit, maybe 3d. for a large one, and they would have sold them for 6d. at that time. They also sold the pelts and they got additional money for them."

That luxuries were rare was evident also on festive seasons. Leo Boyle used to see:

"... people going down to Sawer's on Christmas Eve and waiting on the remnants of the turkeys, buying gizzards and turkeys' necks. They couldn't afford a turkey or a chicken for Christmas, and made soup out of that."

Recalling the diet of the poor in the thirties, and with her tongue slightly in her cheek, Anne Boyle concluded:

"I'll tell you this: we were nice and slim then! We had nice figures because we didn't need to diet!"

More accurately, as the quotation from Frances Maguire at the start of this section pointed out, the poor were under-fed and badly fed.

In Sickness and in health

Paddy Scott came from a middle-class family. As such, he had certain advantages over the mass of people to whom the thirties meant hunger and poverty. Yet, what he saw from his relative social vantage point was enough to move him:

"I remember going over to Queen's as a student, walking over the Antrim Road, and one of the incidents that struck me then, which left an indelible mark in my memory, was seeing young children with deformed legs, gaunt looking; I subsequently discovered it was rickets due to malnutrition. I also noticed the women were gaunt, lifeless, and particularly the young men were gaunt, drawn, thin, and their eyes were lifeless, expressionless, which gave me the impression that they were people who had lost all hope. The experience of seeing in 1932 the great hardships you could read in the eyes of the unemployed and the sense of helplessness, if you were sensitive at all, you couldn't help but have a reaction. It had a tremendous effect on me and made me a socialist."

Scott's subjective impressions can be verified from some statistics of the time. Influenza, diarrhoea and other ailments were widespread in Belfast, and claimed the lives of many, especially working-class people. But of all the ailments, pneumonia and tuberculosis were the harshest killers. Dr Carnwath's figures make this clear and also reveal Belfast's position relative to elsewhere (see Table 3).

Although pneumonia was the greatest problem, it was tuberculosis that held the greatest fear in popular consciousness. Tuberculosis, or consumption, was to the thirties what cancer is to the present day, a disease the very name of which strikes fear. So much so that numerous euphemisms arose; one was to say that people had gone "into decline". Anne Boyle recalls:

"There were twenty-eight in my class at school and when I was about twenty-five, I would say that more than half of those girls were dead, mostly from tuberculosis. There were whole families wiped out with tuberculosis. I remember the sexton of Sacred Heart chapel, Paddy McKernan; all he had was four daughters, and those four daughters died within a couple of years. They were teenage girls. That was in a lot of families, but people didn't know how infectious tuberculosis was. They thought it came out of the air, and they used to close the windows to keep you warm and sweating, which kept the germ active."

TABLE 3: Death rate from various diseases, per 100,000 population, Belfast 1936/40, and County Boroughs of England 1938[12]

	Belfast Annual Average 1936/40	County Boroughs of England 1938
Scarlet Fever	2	1
Syphilis	4	4
Diptheria	8	9
Whooping Cough	11	4
Measles	19	5
Other Tuberculosis	21	12
Influenza	24	11
Epidemic Influenza	46	13
Pulmonary Tuberculosis	88	66
Pneumonia	97	75

TABLE 4: Death rate from pulmonary tuberculosis for various age groups, per 100,000 population, Belfast average 1936/40, and County Boroughs of England 1938[13]

	Age Groups (in years)							
	0-5	5-15	15-25	25-35	35-45	45-55	55-65	65+
Belfast	12	10	117	144	121	121	110	71
England	8	6	81	89	80	94	95	46

There had been some improvement as regards tuberculosis in the two decades before the thirties, especially as far as the younger members of the population were concerned. For example, for every 1000 people in NI in 1911, one child under 5 died of tuberculosis; but by 1936, the average was one child under 5 for every 10,000 of the population. Yet Belfast had little reason to rest on its laurels, as is shown by comparing its rates for each age group with the rates elsewhere (see Table 4).

One main reason for Belfast's poor record was the quality of the corporation and state-provided medical services. Carnwath in particular singled this reason out for special attention in his detailed report:

> "In its personal medical services, however, Belfast falls far short of what might reasonably be expected in a city of its size and importance and I believe the reason is that the Council is not quite certain what it is doing, whether it is worth doing, or whether they are the people to do it."[14]

This accusation of bureaucratic confusion was echoed within a few years of Carnwath's report by Belfast's Socialist Medical Association:

> "The worst feature (of medical provision) is the multiplicity of bodies responsible for health questions. In NI the Ministries of Labour, Home Affairs and Education and the local authorities all play some part in medical care. In addition, hospitals may be voluntary, controlled by the local authority, or by the Poor Law. There are eight schemes for tuberculosis. Co-ordination of all these services is obviously the first requirement."[15]

But, above and beyond the obvious problem of administrative replication, it must be added that the health of the poorest was not often a priority for the medical services. Dr Carnwath gives one humourous, but telling example:

> "The cleansing of verminous children is carried out at the clinics by three helpers of the charwoman type, but not quite as well paid, who also act as dental assistants. This might suggest to the cynical observer that the Council attached more importance to the cleaning of the steps of the City Hall than to the cleansing of heads of children."[16]

In addition, there was no national health service, which meant that the expense of medical treatment or hospitalisation was proportionately greater for the poor than the rich. William Patterson recalls what it was like when his wife Ida was in hospital in the thirties:

> "When Ida was in the City Hospital – that's the hospital now, but it was the Union at one time – if you had got an egg, you had to take it up to her. You had to get your own food brought up, you know. And you had to pay so much, whatever you could afford to pay. And anybody going into the Union, if they went in overnight, they had to do a day's work the next day before they got out."

It should not be surprising then that the quality of ante-natal and post-natal care was not great, and that consequently the infant mortality rate was high. Throughout the twenties and thirties in NI the number of children under one year who died per 1000 live births never fell far below 70 (see Table 5). The main causes were officially given as, firstly, "developmental and wasting diseases", and secondly, bronchitis and pneumonia. Dr Carnwath adds that "dirt, unclean milk and maternal ignorance" were contributory factors. But the contribution of poor medical facilities to such high rates must also be included.

TABLE 5: Infant mortality rate per 1000 live births in NI, 1922/38[17]

1922	77.2	1931	67.9
1923	76.5	1932	73.4
1924	84.6	1933	83.0
1925	86.4	1934	79.7
1926	84.9	1935	69.7
1927	77.7	1936	86.3
1928	77.9	1937	76.9
1929	85.6	1938	77.4
1930	67.9		

Once again, in this regard Belfast's record is poor in comparison with that of other cities as Table 6 shows.

TABLE 6: Infant mortality rates per 1000 live births, 1901 and 1938[18]

	1901	1938
Belfast	154	96
Salford	209	75
Liverpool	189	74
Preston	219	71
Manchester	204	69
Leeds	189	64
Sheffield	202	59

Yet what is astonishing is that although the city with the highest infant mortality rate in 1938, Belfast had the *lowest* rate only 37 years previously. In short, other cities had improved their care of mothers and young children at a much faster rate than Belfast in the first third of the century.

The reality behind these grim figures is caught in the recollection of Anne Boyle:

"There was so much infant mortality that it seemed as if every

> week blue baby-coffins were coming out of every street. I had three brothers and a sister dead before they were two years old, out of eleven of us."

Nor was it only upon the infants that the hazardous business had such terminal effects. The number of maternal deaths in childbirth was high, leading Professor R.J. Johnstone, MP, to conclude:

> "Maternity is a more dangerous occupation in NI than in the Free State or in England."[19]

But the biological hazard facing women was made worse not only by the poor quality of medical services, but also by the supremacy of men. Saidie Patterson recalls:

> "Men were the head of the household. The men had their meal by themselves and they got it first. The children got what was left then, and if there was anything left, the mother got it."

Frances Maguire agrees, and draws a direct link between this custom and the hazards of bearing children:

> "It was a habit that the wife usually tried to give him as much of the food that she should have got, which then had a reflection on the children when they were born, because her body was half-starved."

So, it was little wonder that for many working-class women, whether employed or unemployed, bad health was the order of the day. Women had to face the problems of raising children, making ends meet, housework, and often paid employment, with less nourishment and fewer vitamins than their husbands and sons. Dr Deeny in his study found that all women, regardless of being employed or unemployed, were less tall than they ought to have been, heavier than was healthy for them, were anaemic, had bad posture and poor skin colour, among other defects. In fact, he concluded:

> "The women can therefore be divided into two classes. Those who do not overcome poverty and so suffer from malnutrition; and those who do at the expense of their health."[20]

It would seem, then, that in health, as in many other aspects of life in the thirties, there was a sexual inequality.

Domestic relations

The experience of unemployment and low-paid employment was not confined solely to men in the thirties. But the problem of making the everyday decisions about paying the rent, buying food and clothes, etc., when there was not enough money to cover expenses, was an experience disproportionately reserved for women. In the home, men were served, while women did the serving, as Frances Maguire recalls:

> "The women did everything. She baked. She knitted. She washed.

She cooked. She pressed. Now, the man: he did nothing. I remember my mother saying, you know: 'He bears the heat and burden of the day'! But even that was carried over into the thirties, where the woman went out to work. The women that I worked with went home and did everything. The man did nothing. He sat like lord and master. She made the lunch, and then she came home and made the tea and then she washed, cleaned and ironed. She did everything. The majority of the men wouldn't do that, because it was woman's work. Even a woman would have felt strange if a man would have been washing and cleaning. If he did that, he was an old jinny."

Of course, men did some things around the house, such as mending shoes. But most of the domestic chores were left to women. Thus, when Anne Boyle talks of the many ways in which "people" had to economise, it is clear that she is not talking about *all* people:

"People went down to the tip head at Duncrue Road with buckets and went through the garbage for cinders and anything else that would burn. What was very common was men with patches on their clothes and boots. People patched their coats, trousers, boots. These had to be sewn on; there were no stick-on patches. The women had to sew them on. The women made pillow-cases and sheets from flour bags. They could have bought flour bags in Rank's or Andrews' flour mills for sixpence each. You washed and bleached the flour bags, sewed four of them together and binded them. That only cost two shillings or half a crown for a beautiful sheet that would last for ages. I remember once some of them made underwear for a girl getting married. It was made out of flour bags and covered with little pieces of lace."

The domestic division between the sexes was equally evident when it came to childcare. Frances Maguire again:

"A man wouldn't have pushed a baby in a pram. He wasn't an Englishman! Where the Englishman would have taken a baby out in a pram, under no circumstances would an Irishman do that. All he had to do was hand over his wages, and that was the sum total of his responsibility."

Alice Quinn makes the same point in words so similar that it is clear that the sexual division was ingrained to the point where, for a man to even give a slight hint of taking on a woman's role, was a source of grave embarrassment to him:

"You can see them pushing prams now, so the men must be coming round a wee bit. They wouldn't have done that fifty years ago. Not here, not in the North. I don't know about England. I think they might always have done it there, but not here. If the child had've cried in the middle of the night, he nearly would have

> blamed you. And if anyone had've come in when he was nursing a child, he would've hurried up to get it back on your knee. It was almost a disgrace for anyone to see him nursing a wee child. He'd be called a wee jinny."

Being left holding the baby at home was problem enough. Having to keep down paid employment while being the only person deemed able to look after the children was even worse. Florrie Addley tells of one mother's solution, and of her own mother's understanding of that mother's predicament:

> "Well, I remember, he's a very prominent citizen in Belfast now, and I'd shudder to give his name, and his mother worked in the mill. Now they were decent people, and the father, I think, was a bit of a gambler, and where he went, I do not know. But this child used to be left on the step of our shop, and I think he was only about two. And I remember my mother bringing him in and not knowing whether she had done right or wrong because he had the measles and she was worried about us all taking the measles. But she wouldn't see the child left there. The woman wasn't cruel; she had no option."

Nor was the arrangement of male supremacy and female inferiority confined to the home. It took in many other aspects of working-class life as well: at work, in terms of unequal wages and the male bias of the trade unions, in politics and in leisure. When asked if women had voted in the same way as their husbands, Alice Quinn replied:

> "I never heard of that. In fact, to tell you the truth, I don't think that half of them did vote. I don't remember my mother going out to vote. If she did, she never said."

And Lucy McErlane recalled that:

> "Men and women, husbands and wives, would have gone out together, but women wouldn't have gone into a pub."

Outside of housework, the most obvious sign of the arrangement was that it was women who had the much greater amount of worry in trying to make ends meet, attempting to help the family and, by extension, the community, to survive, even in the most basic, material sense of the word.

Making ends meet

We have already pointed out that part of the everyday task of making ends meet was buying the cheapest food and avoiding luxuries. But even that was not enough. Clothes, shoes and fuel were expensive items, so that running a house and raising a family required economising at every moment. When clothes could be made rather than bought, they were. When boots could be mended again, they were. When a coat was only needed one day a week, it was pawned for the other six days. Winifred Campbell provides an account of some of the things that were done in the house in order to make ends meet:

"Small pieces of soap were rendered down into a sort of cleaning jelly. Teeth were cleaned with salt and water and men gave each other a haircut. Only powdered ash from the fire was thrown away; every cinder was carefully picked out to back the fire. The floors had to be scrubbed with water only in order to save precious soap. Little boots went from child to child until they were past wearing. Even then, they were filled with dampened coal dust and used for fuel. Men and women had only the clothes they stood up in – all the others had long since gone to the pawn shop or been made over for the children."[21]

The pawnshop was an important link in the chain of survival. It is easy in retrospect to condemn pawnshops and their owners as exploiters of the poor. But what must be remembered is that they were the only places to which the poor in the thirties could turn for badly needed cash. The banks would not have let the poor in the door, never mind give them a loan. And, although the interest rates charged by pawnbrokers were high, they were not nearly as high as those charged by the only alternative source of money then – moneylenders. Hence Anne Boyle's conclusion:

"The pawns were a good thing. It made you independent of moneylenders and neighbours because it was your own property that you were bringing to the pawn. People preferred pawning to borrowing. If they did get into the moneylenders, they were sunk completely because the moneylenders were a menace to society."

Belle O'Hara agrees:

"Sometimes you were better going to the pawn as making yourself mean to people for the loan of it, for you were classed like a beggar. So, I never bothered. I just pawned. You were just as well paying the interest to the pawn as you were paying the interest to the moneylender."

None of this is to imply that being dependent on the pawn was a bed of roses. The interest rates were high, and the paradox was that you went to a pawnshop because you were in debt, but going trapped you further in debt. In time, there might be nothing left to pawn, except those things which were most valuable, financially and emotionally. Anne McKenna recounts:

"The number of women who pawned rings, wedding rings, and who never got them back! There was an awful lot of that. When they had given everything, the last thing was the ring because it was gold and you got a better price for it."

Moreover, given women's centrality in facing the problems of running the home, going to the pawn could become a source of domestic friction, as Belle O'Hara recalls:

"See him, he pawned his waistcoat, and he used to get four bob on it up the Shankill. Know what he done one Saturday night? He couldn't get money nowhere. And I got him a grand pair of boots. They were cheap them days, and he came in that night and I says: 'Jasus, where's the boots?' Says he: 'They're in the pawn'. Come home in his stocking soles and he'd no boots to go out on Sunday. Pawned them for drink, pawned them for drink."

This was one of the incidents which convinced Belle O'Hara that she was going to cut her ties with the pawnbroker:

"I said: 'By God, I'm not going to pawn no more clothes. I'll try and work on the way I am, till I'm going to work and try to make myself in the right position. When I got out of it, I kept out of it. I was always sensible, wise like that."

But making the break was not just as easy as she seems to say. As a result, for many working-class women, the pawnbroker just became one more element in the daily juggling to keep going. Making ends meet required them to keep a number of balls in the air, hoping that not too many would land at any one time, that not too many creditors would call at the door simultaneously. This meant in turn a great deal of ingenuity, with women becoming adept at pulling the wool over a number of people's eyes, including, on occasions, those of their own husbands. Alice Quinn, with obvious glee, recalls:

"God help our poor husbands. When we got them out to work, a neighbour would come knocking to borrow his suit. It was pawned for a few shillings. One suit could have been passed to a dozen people and the oul' fella never caught on!"

Of course, such ingenuity in making ends meet was not confined to women. Where men showed their skill was in finding odd jobs to bring in some money in an economy where regular jobs were becoming fewer and fewer. In Chapter 3 we look at some of the tasks men performed in this grey world of casual labour. But it was not only men who were involved in the endless hustle for odd jobs. Women and children played their part too. In fact, in the pursuit of every extra penny possible, children could be as ingenious as the next person when it came to giving the "customers" exactly what they wanted. Alice Quinn remembers:

"Ah, we were crafty then! When a boat came in we would sing to the sailors 'When Irish Eyes are Smiling', and everyone loved the Irish, and we would have got a couple of coppers."

In short, when times were rough, people helped themselves, individually and collectively as best they could, but, what level of support was there for the poor from government and voluntary bodies?

Helping the poor: the official response

The relatively laissez-faire state of the 1930s had little motivation to help the poor. We have examined elsewhere the state's main provisions for the unemployed poor, through unemployment benefit and outdoor relief. Beyond that, about the only intervention of the state was to "encourage" voluntary bodies to help the poor in some way. One example of this was the NI Council of Social Service (NICSS), set up under the auspices of J.M. Andrews, then Minister of Labour, in 1938. There was no breach in the walls of laissez-faire involved, however, as the annual grant from the government to the organisation amounted only to £3,000. Moreover, charitable and voluntary work were quite compatible with the concept of laissez-faire, the state leaving matters to others. This was a division of labour with which NICSS members were content; theirs was a task which, in their judgement, only they could do:

> "There is another side, however, [to poverty], often overlooked, no less fundamental than that which can be solved by money. It could hardly be met by the state, for it demands intimate personal contact and imaginative initiative. It arises from the fact that the unemployed man (sic) often feels 'unwanted' by society and experiences the deadening results of too much spare time."[22]

The emphasis, therefore, was on the psychological well-being of the poor. Although the Council involved itself in practical activities – obtaining plots of land to rent to unemployed men so they could grow food, running physical fitness classes and a male voice choir, starting "women's groups" where unemployed girls could learn domestic service or where "women of all ages come together to spend an hour knitting for the troops"[23], helping the YMCA run workcamps for unemployed men – the thrust of all these activities was to occupy the unemployed in mind and in body, keep them off the streets and thus have "healthy" unemployed people in a "healthy" society. In short, the schemes did nothing to combat poverty or its causes.

The workcamps are a good example of the overall approach of the NICSS, and indeed of other such voluntary bodies of the time. The YMCA had been running them since 1931, and NICSS joined in, in 1938. The NICSS report explains that the essential features of the camps:

> " . . . have been that the men have been taken for ten days to canvas camps in the country or at the shore. Mornings have been spent in work for the good of the community; afternoons and evening in games and holiday pursuits. The camps have been led and staffed by young men – students, teachers, civil servants – who have voluntarily given up a part of their holidays. They have gone to the camps to live intimately with the men; not only to act as leaders in work and play, but to cultivate that spirit of personal friendship and understanding which is at the bottom of much

social work . . . It will be noted that the camps combine three features of importance in dealing with the psychological problems of unemployment; an opportunity to do useful work; contact with men from different social levels and from other parts of the Province; life in the open air with good food and regular exercise."[24]

Norman MacNeilly was in charge of one of these camps. He not only confirms the psychological/social work nature of their philosophy, but also shows that certain sections of "the community" benefited a lot from the "useful work" that was done:

"The summer camps were the idea of Adam Scott, whose brother was the head of the NI civil service at the time. The men stayed at the camps generally for a fortnight, sometimes three weeks. These camps were arranged in a way perhaps as belonging to an age of patronage. They were run on the estates of Lord Dufferin (at Helen's Bay), Lord Londonderry (at Clandeboye) and the estate up at County Londonderry: I forget whose it was. In the first year there was only one camp. The basis of the financing was simple. The lads worked for Lord Dufferin for four hours in the morning, from 9 o'clock to one. The first year was the cleaning of timber, trees, plantations, if you like. There were no mechanical saws in those days. There were crosscut saws and the ten pound axe. The four hours work were fairly tough. The camps were organised by the National Council of YMCAs. We never had any government grants or anything like that."

The reluctance of statutory and voluntary bodies to become involved in helping the poor in a material way seems to have been widespread. Thus, the Mission Halls which helped many in Protestant areas through soup kitchens, mother and child clubs, etc., often seemed embarrassed to admit that their activities were so this-worldly, and ended up making ridiculous assertions, such as, that the poor came for the gospel and not the food. In March 1936 J.G. Crawford, president of the City Mission, stated:

"The Mission made no attempt to carry away the people on a wave of excitement; there were no rewards of a worldly kind beyond affording relief in cases of absolute want. They did not rely on enticing words of wisdom in order to get people in. It was the Gospel, nothing but the Gospel, that drew the people to the Mission Halls, and induced them to send for the Missionaries when they were in distress."[25]

One wonders, though, if Crawford's euphoria derived less from a realistic reading of the situation than from a very real fear of churchmen that (in the words of David Irwin, secretary of the City Mission in 1932) there was, because of poverty:

"a spirit of restlessness abroad which had an unsettling effect on

> the people and many have cut themselves off from and are hostile to all organised religion."[26]

Thus, it was probably a combination of self-respect, the proselytizing that one would have to endure, and the realisation that the missions were reluctant to get their hands dirty with the financial aspects of the problem of poverty, which led many to avoid approaching the missions at all. Winifred Campbell writes:

> "Food and clothes could be applied for at one of the Mission halls – but that was the very last straw and the people of our street somehow held out without that."[27]

There is evidence of a similar wariness on the Catholic side, and for a similar combination of reasons. When asked if he had ever approached the St Vincent de Paul Society (SVDP) for help in the thirties, Barney Boswell replied:

> "Not a chance! Who would go to them? I'd crawl on my knees before I'd go to them."

Leo Boyle reaches similar conclusions:

> "The SVDP Society did more harm to the people by showing themselves at people's doors. People were humiliated when they came. Everybody knew they were SVDP."

And his wife Anne adds:

> "People were trying to hide their poverty and they were exposing it. They always came after twelve o'clock mass and the world and their wives saw them. All they gave was a half-crown chit for food which they brought to a grocer's. That's about all you got. At First Holy Communion or Confirmation they supplied a dress and they just had the one person who made the dresses and all the dresses were exactly the same. People didn't want to take them because you were identified as a SVDP's child. So, the Church charities didn't work so well."

All of this seems to run contrary to Devlin's treatment of the SVDP Society. He produces figures [28] to show that throughout most of the twenties and thirties the Society spent much more on the alleviation of poverty than did the statutory authorities. Moreover, like the other Catholic charities, the Society "extended no relief to the Catholic destitute except in cases where relief was refused by the statutory authorities".[29] It is possible to dismiss the reminiscences of the Boyles and Boswell, seeing them merely as expressing their own idiosyncratic pride and unwillingness to accept any "handout" from any charity, including a Catholic Church one. On the other hand, Devlin may have exaggerated the role of the Church in the alleviation of poverty, and in doing so glossed over the ideology involved in official Catholic charity. Take Kennedy's account of the Church's activities in Belfast to care for the Catholic poor:

> "One Belfast parish began to help the unemployed in the years of

depression. Classes were organised, lectures and talks given, outings arranged to places of interest in the neighbourhood. A dramatic society presented plays in the Parochial Hall. Money was raised to send a number on a pilgrimage to Rome in the Holy Year, 1933. On a wider scale, a Catholic Social Conference in Belfast in 1937 pinpointed some of the evils of the time and suggested practical steps to remedy them. Two proved particularly effective. One was the establishment of a Social Service Bureau to deal with moneylenders and hire-purchase sharks preying on the poor, and to give legal aid to those in difficulties with landlords or Government bureaux. The other was the setting up of a Workers' College to give trade unionists a training in philosophy, economics and public administration."[30]

Although Kennedy offers this as proof of the beneficence of the Church authorities in the face of widespread poverty, it is difficult to see how these interventions could have been of much practical help to the poor. The Catholic Church, not unlike the Protestant Churches, seems to have explained poverty either in terms of the laziness of the poor or as a trial sent by God. In this light, practical relief for the poor was not the chief priority. This is borne out by Anne Boyle's recollection of one priest, a Father McAuley:

"I remember him during the thirties when he got up and said to us to get up off your backsides and go out and do something yourselves. He said you can't expect God to come round the corner with a bag of flour on his back. Then the people didn't know where to turn. He had no sympathy whatsoever for the poor people, absolutely none."

Given such attitudes, it should not be surprising that many of the clergy would have been opposed to any political agitation on the part of the poor. Anne Boyle again:

"I remember the day the ODR riots started. It was my last year in school and we were coming out of school and I was the very first out. Fr MacNamara (Diocesan Religious Examiner) run out because of all the shouting and screaming. The police were baton charging in Glenpark Street. I was crying and I remember this. The priest said to me: 'Why are you crying?' I said: 'Oh, everybody's fighting'. He said to me: 'Is your daddy in it?' I said: 'No, he's in England working'. He said: 'Well, you've nothing to worry about. They're only a bunch of hooligans, a lot of hooligans'. I've always remembered him saying that. The men he was calling a lot of hooligans were getting eight shillings a week and they had to work half a week on the roads. They got food chits; they got no money."

Frequently abandoned by church and state, the poor were often thrown back on their own resources. Self-help was the mainstay of the working class in the thirties. But voluntary bodies were quite happy to "hijack" self-help schemes because they required little commitment from the bodies themselves other than administration. One example is the case of the Belfast Council of Social Welfare:

> "In 1938 a worker in Messrs. Harland and Wolff Limited developed tuberculosis and was ordered into a sanitorium for several months but his National Health Insurance benefit was quite inadequate to maintain his wife and young family during his absence from work. The case came to the notice of the Council and they made a weekly allowance to the family till the breadwinner could be restored to health. Unaware of this, the man's workmates raised some money among themselves to help the family. When they brought this money to his wife, she told them that they were already being provided for by the Council. The workers got in touch with the Council and asked from what source they got the funds which enabled them to shoulder so heavy a burden. When they discovered that this came from the charitable purse, they made a collection among themselves for the Council's work. The interest thus aroused soon spread to other departments and later to other firms – especially Messrs. Short Brothers and Harland. At this time the employees of these firms contributed sixpence a week each – apprentices threepence – from wages to their respective Central Charities Funds which were administered by employees committees. . . . . At the peak period the Council received about £1,000 a year from the workers' contributions."[31]

This continued until 1948 and the establishment of the National Health Service. Although a scheme operated by a voluntary organisation, this scheme existed only because of the self-help abilities of workers. In fact, self-help was the oil in the machine of the day-to-day life of the working-class community.

The working-class community

The church, state, and voluntary bodies were right about one thing, that the experience of unemployment and poverty was demoralising. Where they were wrong was in gearing their policies towards a minimal alleviation of the symptoms of economic crisis, rather than towards the cause of those symptoms. As we saw earlier, Paddy Scott witnessed this demoralisation on his way to Queen's University each day. Florrie Addley saw it too from her parents' shop:

> "Men all stood at corners. You would have been identified as

what corner you stood at. They would have said: 'Oh, sure you know him, he stands at the corner of Henry Street'. Of course, they were all pubs too. They'd nothing else to do, nowhere else to go."

The long-term effects of this demoralisation worried many in the church and the state. We already noted the fear of David Irwin, secretary of the City Mission, that the Protestant poor were abandoning organised religion. On the Catholic side the clergy would seem to have had less reason to worry, at least in terms of attendance at Mass. The emphasis on obligation was accepted by most, so much so that the few who did not attend were marked people in the community. Anne Boyle recalls:

"You knew the people who didn't go to Mass or confession. If they took any sickness, even with the blitz, everyone said that the bombs only fell on those people that didn't go to Mass. If they took any sickness it was because they didn't go to Mass. That was pure superstition."

For their part, the state authorities were also worried, especially about the possible links between poverty and crime. In 1938 a Stormont working party reported their findings on the causes of juvenile delinquency in a lengthy Command Paper. Unusually for the time, they went far beyond a narrow or merely punitive approach to the question. But, although they recommended the abolition of whipping of juveniles (a punishment still meted out by the courts at the time), and saw the relationship between bad housing, unemployment and crime, there is no denying that the elements of fear and the desire to control juvenile delinquency were paramount in the working party's minds:

"In many instances the parents are personally to blame, either through ignorance or negligence, if their children become delinquent. In others, however, the conditions in the home are such that it is almost impossible for the father and mother to look after their children properly. This is especially so when a large family is crowded into one or two rooms, and the children are inevitably forced on to the streets where they are very liable to get into trouble. . . . Unemployment has, we think, an important bearing on juvenile delinquency. If the father is unemployed there is probably financial instability in the home and the lack of a feeling of security may have a detrimental effect on the character of a boy or girl. If, on the other hand, the juvenile himself has left school and is unable to find employment or can only obtain casual or blind-alley jobs, there is the possibility that he may drift into the streets and eventually become delinquent." [32]

But demoralisation was not the only feature of working-class life in the thirties. Another important element was the sense of community:

"United by a common poverty, we lived a sort of communal life. Help, such as it was, was given and received with simple dignity". [33]

> One sign of this communality was, as Florrie Addley remembers, that: "Doors were left open; there was nothing in their houses you could have stolen. The house that I was born in was a parlour house, and you were a kind of a wee bit snotty if you were born in a parlour house. But I remember in our house our sitting room was locked and probably any valuables were in it, but the big door, as you would have called it, anybody could have walked in. I never remember big doors being closed, only at night."

And Frances Maguire would agree with Winifred Campbell that even the poorest were willing to help each other in any way they could:

> "People at that time were so kindly that if anybody wanted something, they would have lent a pot or a pan or something like that. Pots wore out and you didn't have a pot, so if the woman next door wasn't using it, she would lend hers to you."

Florrie Addley recalls that even those who had trouble making ends meet themselves didn't hesitate offering food to a neighbour:

> "You know, maybe a neighbour would have come and said: 'I was passing and you'd a good smell' and everybody got a share. What you had, you shared, especially food-wise, with people which you knew hadn't."

This daily communality ensured that people, especially women, could help each other, spreading the tasks such as food preparation and child minding around a little bit, so that the burden was not over-heavy on any one pair of shoulders.

Beyond the day-to-day sense of community, working-class life was punctuated by the frequent ritual of wakes, which were as much a time to celebrate the solidarity of the living as they were to pay respects to the dead. Leo Boyle remembers that neighbours rushed to support bereaved neighbours:

> "When a person died, the first thing the neighbours did was to ask if there was any insurance. If there was no insurance, the people buried them. They went round and collected money. They dressed the dead, brought in their own sheets, fixed the house up, loaned furniture."

When all the preparations were finished, the wake itself could begin. Florrie Addley recounts:

> "They would have kept the dead for about three days, and it didn't matter where they got the money, like, with Irish hospitality it had to be. There was drink and cheese and tinned beef, and you were supposed to make door-step sandwiches; and there was a great big crepe bow put on the door and all the family wore a great big black armband which must have been about five or six inches wide."

Charlie MacGlade recalls that for the slightly more pragmatic and irreverent young men in his area, wakes were the source of a free meal:

"During the hungry thirties fellows would look up the *Irish News* for deaths in Catholic districts and they'd see such a person dead. They would make it a point to go along to the wake. There were wakes then and they were more like parties than anything else. There'd be fellahs there telling stories and there'd be a bottle of Guinness going, and there'd always be a cup of tea. Fellahs who were unemployed would go along to those wakes and say: 'Ah, missus, sure I knew your husband well,' 'I knew your son well', or whoever, 'and he was a decent man' and all this, just to get into the wake, and in lots and lots of cases they probably didn't know the man at all, but they were getting a bottle of Guinness, a bottle of stout and a bit of a feed."

So, the wakes were many things to different people in the community – a free meal, a religious event, a local party. As the last of these, they were an example of the community entertaining itself. There were other examples. Frances Maguire remembers house parties:

"where, to make a bit of money, somebody in the street would give a party and then people would have come and paid money to get to the party. It would have been more the young element would go."

Anne Boyle has memories of other forms of self-made communal entertainment:

"There was always football matches and they were free. They were in the brickyard and they were all round the town and everywhere. Do you know where Glenard is built now? Well, that was called the rushie fields. There were games up there and they came from every part of Belfast to them games, big lorries and trucks and all. There was tug-of-war, there was bowling, everything you could think of."

In addition to community self-entertainment, there was the growing phenomenon of mass entertainment. Of course, there were some older forms of mass entertainment, such as dances, but the thirties saw the development of other experiences for the working class, cinema and radio, for example. Leo Boyle remembers the dances of his youth:

"The boys used to go out to the dances when I was very, very young, and I remember the girls used to go with the shawls on them, and bare legs with maybe black shoes. It was the old figure dancing then, and it would be 2d. or 3d. to get in."

Like Leo Boyle, Frances Maguire can easily remember prices, this time for the cinema:

"The Clonard for the front stalls was four pence; back stalls was sixpence and the balcony was a shilling. And in the Diamond it was fourpence and sixpence."

In the Diamond also children could get in with jam jars, which were returnable for money then. There was some opposition to the cinema, perhaps on the grounds of corruption of the morals of the young; but it was not an opposition which Florrie Addley's mother shared:

> "I remember some woman saying what a sin it was to go to the pictures, and my mother said they're the best god-send ever there has been, for at least for threepence the men can sit for a couple of hours off the street."

Libraries could fulfill the same function, as Anne Boyle remembers:

> "Whenever the weather was cold the library in Oldpark there had warm reading rooms. You got the books that you weren't allowed to bring out, and you would have booked that for the next day to finish it, and you would have gone down and spent an hour sitting there reading in a nice, warm library."

Of course, there were still some forms of mass entertainment that were beyond the means of the working class. One which Frances Maguire remembers was radio:

> "Very few people had a radio, and if you had a radio, by heaven, you were up a step above buttermilk!"

Another such luxury was a holiday. Frances Maguire again:

> "You were very rich if you went on holidays. I remember a lassie that lived next door to us and her aunt was taking her to Lourdes. The whole street was up to see them going away to Lourdes; the whole area came to watch the spectacle. Somebody able to go to Lourdes! And I remember they were queued up, all right round, because this was a great thing. Nobody could have afforded that."

Luxuries were few, and poverty never far away for the working class of Belfast in the 1930s. True, the shared experience of poverty was at the base of the great sense of community which existed in working-class areas, but it would be wrong to romanticise the experience of poverty, as it is all to easy to do in retrospect. For a start, the quality of community relationships could perhaps blunt the edge of poverty, but it could not substantially counter the problems of ill-health, bad housing, and so on. Moreover, the community was a double-edged sword in a way, a source of support, and yet also a cause of restriction and isolation. Florrie Addley, from North Belfast, knew nothing of East Belfast across the river:

> "Well, the Shankill now, you had a wee bit of leaning towards, and the Falls and Grosvenor Road, but once you crossed the bridge, you went in fear and trembling. I didn't know anyone that lived over there, and anyone that went over there, we thought it was like going to America; you would never see them again."

Remarkably, East Belfast was a predominantly Protestant area and Addley herself was a Protestant. So, there is no sectarian element in her social distance from East Belfast. When such a sectarian factor was added, the isolation could be even greater. And in the Belfast of the 1930s that factor was never far away, whether in the workplace or the community. In short, confined in what later generations would refer to as ghettoes as a result of class and sectarian divisions in society, the working class endured severe hardship. They were able to alleviate that hardship by pulling together. And they were even able to momentarily transcend their situation on a few occasions, through industrial or political action directed towards the cause of the hardship – the unequal distribution of resources whereby the poor were poor *because* the rich were rich.

The rich

The focus of this chapter has been on the poor of Belfast. But it is worth recalling, however briefly, that if hardship and demoralisation were all too often the daily experience of the working class, this was not true for some people in NI. Although they were never known for their ostentatious display of wealth, the rich in Belfast and elsewhere in the industrialised North knew how to enjoy their money. While tens of thousands suffered from malnutrition or had no clothes except those they stood up in, there were others who could afford to take up the advertisements in local papers for world cruises and who continued to socialise on the scale to which they had previously been accustomed, the depression notwithstanding. Paddy Shea looks back on the pastimes of the rich then in the town of Enniskillen. He quotes from a weekly column by Millicent Trimble in the Fermanagh paper, the *Impartial Reporter*:

> "Were it not for the stir of the social world, life and business would be very dull in Enniskillen in January and February. We have had a succession of dances. Each had its own special character. The glory of the Fermanagh County Hospital Ball, the rollicking gaiety of the Fancy Dress Dance, the hunting Pink and 'horsey' atmosphere of the Hunt Ball, the Legion Ball with its many ribbons and medals on the breast – and now, the Constabulary."[34]

Shea goes on to note that on one occasion everyone at a local sports meeting was fed from exactly the same menu as the chief guest at that event, the Earl of Belmore; he quips that perhaps this was "the beginning of the egalitarian society in Enniskillen". But, while some may rejoice in the past frolicking of "a pleasure-loving people", one is left wondering about the other citizens of Enniskillen and vicinity. No fancy dress balls for them, unless they were to come wearing their rarely seen suits and dresses retrieved from the pawn for the event.

At a time when a fully-insured, recently paid-off male worker was able to draw 17/- a week unemployment benefit, there were others who were drawing much more than this from public funds. XQ[35] itemises the salaries of some of the top public figures in NI in 1932:

Prime Minister: £2,720 plus £1,488 allowances
Minister: £1,700
Permanent Secretary: c. £1,700
Inspector General of the RUC: £1,750
Attorney General: £2,125

It would have taken the unemployed man sixty-one years to make the Prime Minister's annual salary (not including allowances) at the rate of 17/- a week. But even this is a ridiculous comparison, as 17/- was the maximum he could get; it lasted only for the first six months of unemployment. After that came transitional benefit, and then, possibly, outdoor relief.

In the same year that the ODR workers had to riot before getting any more money from public funds, the same politicians had no hesitation spending £30,000 of public money on building Stormont. The original plans were for an even more grandiose building than now exists, a building resembling a US state capitol, replete with copula. The British Treasury refused to contribute any more than £1,700,000 to the building of this structure, so the Unionist Party revised their plans to come up with Stormont as we know it. However, they still went over the treasury budget by £30,000 and had to "find" that additional money somewhere in NI's normal expenditure. [36]

Finally, the inequality which permeated NI society then is perhaps best shown by an example given by Florrie Addley about one of the directors of Gallaher's tobacco firm (whose name she could not remember), who had pneumonia:

> "We lived very near Gallaher's, which was just the one building at the time. I don't know whether it was a Gallaher or not, but whoever it was lived above the offices in York Street, Virginia House they called it. They had taken pneumonia, whoever it was. And there were trams all along York Street then, and they made a heck of a racket going along the lines, you know; they were square sets. And whoever it was that lived in Gallaher's, I remember sitting while they laid turf because he was coming up to the crisis. It seems that with pneumonia then there was no such a thing as penicillin, and there was a crisis in the pneumonia seemingly after nine or ten days. We used to notice they tied up the knockers in case there would be a noise, and we would have noticed this and be told as children: 'Oh, be very quiet and keep away; there's a crisis coming'. Well, this had happened to him, and they laid turf, carts and carts of turf, laid from Earl Street to Brougham Street to deaden the noise of the trams; so they must have been – to us they were very, very wealthy."

A disease may not recognise the wealth of a victim before striking, but such was the power of even sick rich people that they could make sure that everyone else recognised it.

FOOTNOTES

1. Source: Deeny, J. 1940: 77
2. Ibid.
3. Ibid: 89
4. Beacham, A. 1939: 12
5. Ibid.
6. Methodist Church. 1938
7. Campbell, W. 1976: 14
8. Ibid: 15
9. In fact closer to one quarter than one sixth
10. Carnwath, T. 1941: 5
11. Source: *Ulster Year Book*, 1938
12. Figures derived from Carnwath, T. 1941: 12
13. Figures derived from Carnwath, T. 1941: 20
14. Ibid: 48
15. Socialist Medical Association, n.d: 13
16. Carnwath, T. 1941: 44
17. Source: *Ulster Year Book*s
18. Source: Carnwath, T. 1941: 31
19. Quoted in Midgley, H. 1933: 17
20. Deeny, J. 1940: 84
21. Campbell, W. 1976: 14
22. NI Council of Social Service. 1940: 6
23. Ibid: 25
24. Ibid: 23
25. Murray, S. 1970: 50
26. Ibid.
27. Campbell, W. 1976: 15
28. Devlin, P. 1981: 84
29. Ibid: 81
30. Kennedy, D. 1966: 148
31. MacBeath, A. 1956
32. Lynn Committee. 1936: 11, 13
33. Campbell,W. 1976: 15
34. Quoted in Shea, P. 1981: 129
35. "XQ". 1932
36. "XQ". 1933

PART TWO

Part Two examines in depth the experiences, activities and beliefs of many of our respondents. Chapter 3 looks at the experience of paid employment, obviously concentrating chiefly on the shipyards and linen mills. We let our respondents tell us in their own words about finding work, working conditions, wages, trade union organisation, etc. And throughout the chapter there is a stress on the continuous interplay between class and sectarian issues. Chapter 4 encapsulates the reminiscences of those socialists and communists to whom we spoke. It looks at their activities and attitudes, focussing, among other things, on their assessment of the Outdoor Relief strike and the Spanish Civil War. Throughout the chapter we emphasise the divisions among socialists and communists on the national question. Chapter 5 focuses on those people for whom the national question was paramount, the republicans. We examine their activities and beliefs also, concentrating, among other things, on their assessment of the Outdoor Relief strike, the Republican Congress and the sectarian riots of 1935. Throughout the chapter we look at the divisions among republicans on social issues and politics beyond the national question.

To each of the chapters in this section is appended a profile which tells the life story of one of our respondents in greater detail. We have chosen each of these life stories as being in some way typical or representative of the work experience in Belfast in the thirties, the experience of being a socialist activist, and the experience of being a republican activist. (On the problems of ascertaining how each of these life stories can be said to be "typical", see our "Afterword on Ideology".)

3. The World of Work

For those lucky enough to have a job in the thirties wages and conditions were hardly luxurious. Messenger argues that her research into labour conditions in the linen industry "seems to cast a shadow over the validity of some of the more pessimistic statements that have been made regarding the overall quality of life for many workers".[1] She accepts that right into the 1970s linen workers suffered from long hours, low wages, bad conditions, authoritarian foremen and so on but does not see this as exploitation. The argument is that these workers were better off than their predecessors or rural labourers and that they were "imbued with an ethic which exalted work well done".[2] It is true that exploitation – like poverty – is relative, that is to say it must be seen in context and not measured against the present day. However, any objective assessment of the world of work in Belfast in the 1930s must stress the intensity and degradation of work in those days. It is no use saying that workers made the best of it – Messenger constantly stresses the singing and "larking about" of the mill workers. That only goes to show that working people have an inexhaustible reserve of energy and hope for a better life. It cannot be used to "prettify" the exploitation of Belfast workers in the 1930s which we will examine mainly through examples from the shipyards and the linen industry.

The engineering industry of Northern Ireland was heavily concentrated in Belfast – in 1935 ninety per cent of the labour force was employed in the city. This was because Belfast was the major centre for Irish industry and because the port allowed free entry and exit of raw materials and exports. During the First World War the shipyards were kept busy but as the slump in world trade set in after 1929 business declined. Throughout the 1920s the shipyards produced over 100,000 tons per year, with a peak of 168,000 tons in 1930. Then, output was halved in 1931, and in 1932 and 1933 Harland and Wolff launched no ships at all, while the output of the "wee yard", Workman Clark, was only 6,000 tons in 1932 and 14,000 tons in 1933.[3] In 1934 Workman Clark's yards closed down but Harland and Wolff was kept going through the slump by government financial assistance. By the mid 1930s shipbuilding had begun to pick up in Belfast as Britain began its rearmament programme. From September 1939 to August 1945 over 150 warships from landing craft to aircraft carriers were built in Belfast and Harland and Wolff also produced some 10% of Britain's merchant ships.[4] Before 1939 the company employed 26,000 workers across its subsidiaries but this figure rose soon afterwards to 51,000 workers of whom half were employed at the Queen's Island in Belfast.

The linen industry expanded rapidly in the second half of the nineteenth century, stabilising at 844,000 spindles for the whole of Ireland by 1900. Unlike the shipbuilding industry, the First World War disrupted production in the linen industry because it was difficult to import flax. During the 1920s and 1930s production and employment rates in the industry fluctuated but there was a steady downward trend as cheaper materials came on the market. The Second World War likewise did not lead to a boost to the industry as raw material sources were cut off and users switched definitively to newer products. The last weaving factory was built shortly before the First World War and the maximum number of powerlooms – 37,789, of which 22,000 were in Belfast – was reached in 1920.[5] There were approximately seventeen spinning companies in Belfast during this period, with an average of 750 employees per mill. About three quarters of the workers in the linen industry were women with men taking the more "skilled" (i.e., better paid) jobs and supervisory positions. It is important to note as Betty Messenger points out that by 1935 technological and social changes had considerably modified the industrial climate in the linen mills and factories. The 1930s are thus a period of fluctuation and transition for the linen industry and its workers. The industry was particularly affected by severe cyclical fluctuations in employment with 1930-31 and 1937-38 marking the worst recessions.[6]

Finding work

The first step for anyone unemployed is to find a job. During the 1930s hiring practices gave the job-seeker practically no rights at all. People would be hired and fired at will by the employer or more usually the foreman. It seems that this exercise in degradation had the purpose of instilling "loyalty and discipline" in the prospective worker. A number of people described to us their experience in finding a job.

Alice Quinn, a linen mill-worker, recalls:

"We had to wait until we were fifteen to get into York St but still and all we needed the money. It was hard enough to get in; you couldn't just walk in, except you had somebody to speak for you, or taking a chance going down standing in the lobby, as it was known. In the morning you would have seen a whole crowd of wee girls all standing in the lobby for the overseer to look and see if he needed any."

Florrie Addley got her job as a damask weaver also when she was fifteen but in a roundabout way:

> "No jobs were available then and there was a man used to come into our shop and he was a gambler, he would have borrowed the shirt off your back as they say. . . . He was in trouble, and I think he borrowed a lot of money off my mother; now a lot of money then would have been ten shillings, and whether my mother had asked him for it or not I don't know, but he had came over, maybe for money, and my mother asked him if there was any prospect of me getting a job, so he must have got a good loan, for I got started and that's how I got the job."

Jobs weren't advertised as now, rather it was through word of mouth that you heard of vacancies. Florrie Addley recalls:

> "The first job ever I got was in Milewater mill. It's still vivid in my memory, there might have been fifty or sixty women standing there although they wouldn't all have been my age, there might have been older women it seems. I learnt afterwards that they were opening a new room which had been closed through lack of work, and I was fairly big for my age, fairly tall and sprouted up, and maybe this is why they picked me. One of my pals and me got started cleaning this . . . and it was filthy, the dust was about a foot high on all this machinery and we were brushing. I only stuck it two days for it nearly killed me . . . I just remember a man saying, 'you, and you'. That's the way they picked dockers too – it wasn't what you knew, it was who you knew. Things were very bad then."

John Nicholl confirms this:

> "I did search for work. I went to the shipyard every morning in the week with a lad called Davey McGrath who had served some time in the army, three years in the army, and nine years reserve. He and I went down, and there were hundreds of men looking for work. You had no chance unless someone knew you. Both he and I had never worked in the shipyard, so it was absolutely impossible to be acquainted with anyone."

In the shipyards it was membership of the Orange Order which was the surest way of getting a job. John Nicholl remembers:

> "I'd become fairly aware of it [i.e. sectarianism] in the sense that, all around me, there was people getting work. I remember one particular instance of a chap who came away from County Tyrone somewhere and he married the daughter of a neighbour of mine in Berlin Street, and in three or four weeks he became a tram driver. And if you can understand my frustrations at that one. I'm living in the locality, couldn't get a job, not that I'd anything personal against the lad, but it taught me that something was wrong with

> the system when this can happen and it made me really start to think seriously about things then. If you didn't have no political influence or no influence in the sense that you were connected by some secret organisation, then you had very little opportunity of getting work and that's the way it worked for me."

What secret organisation did he mean?

> "Well, I would say the Orange Order. A fellow who was connected with the Orange Order would have had a ten times better chance of getting a job than I had. Now, I don't know whether it would be from the Order's point of view or whether because he knew more people who were in work than I did . . . The other things that revealed these things to me was an uncle of mine who was a plumber – I had two uncles plumbers. One of them was a plumber in the shipyard, the other was what was known as an uptown plumber. The fellow in the shipyard was subsequently paid off after a number of years and he walked straight onto a job as a navvy, notwithstanding that there was thousands of navvies at that time unemployed, men who had spent years and years at the game and knew something about it, but he was able to walk from one thing to the other. That galled me not because he got a job, but because it was so easy for him to get a job . . . because he had particular connections."

Apart from the patronage system exercised by the Orange Order there was a well-established practice of family employment in the shipyards. John Hyde recalls:

> "The shipyard men were family men. In the old shipbuilding and engineering unions, the booklet that they had laid down very clear that a man who worked in the shipyard and wanted his son in had preference against those who did not work in the shipyard. This suited the employers to a large extent because, well, if a boy wasn't conducting himself, or was wanting to move somewhere after getting considerable training, the father when he was home at night would probably lay down the law to his son a little. So, the shipyard considered that, with the two working all out of the same family, if something came up, a word or two from the foreman to the father and it was all settled."

The shipping magnates thus gained a certain stability amongst their workforce by encouraging the practice of family patronage.

Probably the worst aspect of all in the hiring practices of the 1930s was the playing off of worker against worker. Bobby Hurndall remembers:

> "We had endless people down outside the shipyard when it did restart in 1934. When they did get a few orders you had crowds of men outside the gates, waiting for the foreman to give them the O.K. to start. They were clutching their caps, saying 'Good

morning' to the foreman in the expectation of getting a job. Most of them were disappointed – it was a long time before there was anything like full employment in the shipyard again."

John Hyde also told us that in the 1930s:

"I have seen two to three hundred joiners standing outside the back gate of Harland and Wolff's joiners' shop waiting on a job, and only twenty men were required. And yet those men, when the end of the day came, when they were leaving and going back to their homes some just stayed around the shipyard hoping to see someone who they knew could possibly say the word for them and getting them or at least give them some hope of a job . . . ."

The foreman would exploit his authority over hiring and "play games" with those waiting for work in rainy weather. As William Patterson recalls:

"You went down in the morning at ten past eight and you waited till nine and it would still be pouring and the gaffer would come around and say, 'What the hell are you still doing here since you know its going to be a wet day', and you went home. The next day you'd go in and it was raining and you'd stay to nine o'clock and you'd go home and you were maybe on your way home when the rain would stop and you got ate the next day for going home. It didn't matter what you'd done you were always wrong."

Tommy Cochrane remembers particularly the viciousness of the foremen towards those who were out of work:

"With the same four people that I'd been travelling about with, my mates, I went down every morning to Workman Clark's north yard to try and get a job. . . . We hadn't a bloody chance. Of course, there was hundreds looking jobs. Anyhow, the boss was that damned ignorant with us . . . they treated you as if you were bloody dirt, some of them. When you went down to look for work, you felt you were crawling. That's the way they set to make you feel. It was the system, the system was rotten."

In this way unemployment was brought to bear on the world of work to create fear of joblessness and respect for the foreman. According to some accounts it was not so difficult to get a job in the mills. Belle O'Hara, an ex-mill worker, told us:

"There was nothing like the mills for you never wanted a job. You got the sack one day or in one room and you could have went down below the next day and got in. You never wanted a job. The work was hard in the mills. You got two sides, maybe all your one ends fell down and you were getting into a bog one day, and jumping up and down the next. Oh aye, it was hard work in the mill but I loved the mill, really loved the mill."

This was probably true though wages were low and conditions were bad. Lucy McErlane remembers how she left Jennymount mill to work in

Gallaher's where she learnt to strip tobacco. Her mother didn't like her working in the mill and considered Gallaher's "a step up". Work was heavy and dangerous and there were no prospects for promotion but Lucy McErlane thought it was very difficult for a Catholic to get work in Gallaher's so she was very lucky to get in.

When people had jobs the nature of employment patterns was such that they would regularly lose them. It was effectively a system of casual labour which predominated in Belfast in the 1930s. As Charlie Hull recalls:

> "Even the nature of work in the shipyard then was of a casual nature. When I came out of my time as an apprentice I was working for a few months, then paid off . . . When I went to work in Barrow-in-Furness in 1937, came back after the July holidays, got started at Harland's again, got working for six weeks and two days, where they were putting down the wooden decks of a big Union Castle liner, at the end of six weeks and two days paid off again. Then off a couple of months, brought in again. That was the pattern for most of the workers. There were a certain few who were always there, who were well known to the foreman and well established. For the vast majority of workers it was only with the advent of the war, and the aftermath of the war, that we got full employment and continuity of the employment."

Bobby Hurndall explains how the 1930s slump affected the shipyard:

> "In 1931 the recession following the Wall Street crash in 1929 began to hit Harland and Wolff's. As ships were launched the slipways were left idle. Towards the end of the year the shipyard was denuded completely of ships. I started to serve my time as an apprentice shipwright 21 July 1931. My father had been killed on 29 of June on the White Star liner, *Georgic,* and I was allowed to start my apprenticeship as soon as the July holidays were over. I was the last apprentice shipwright for over two years. There was no work. Corn was growing at the old waterway gantry in the Queen's yard. That state of affairs continued until around 1933. There were sixty apprentice shipwrights scattered about the yard, tidying up, gathering chains, oiling wire mooring ropes, and various other maintenance work. As the older apprentices finished their five year apprenticeship they were immediately paid off."

Shipyard workers, unlike the women in the linen industry, did however have a certain degree of geographical mobility. When the going got bad in Belfast they would move to the Clyde or Tyneside yards over in Britain. Jim Salmon says:

> "I done it myself and I knew other people who did. My own brother, he was a foreman and he went to Barrow-in-Furness, he went to Cammell-Laird's too on different periods when there was slackness in Belfast. When there was slackness in Belfast you had

nowhere else to go except across the water. As soon as Workman Clark's was closing they went over to Cammell-Laird's – the head man there was a Workman Clark's man originally. So Cammell-Laird to me became Workman Clark's on the Mersey. When you went there, I knew the managers and they knew me, and I was able to talk to them. If you were going to another job yourself some colleagues might follow your job up and somebody else behind to do it, that sort of thing."

John Hyde tells a similar story:

"It was as near a man feeling at home in Birkenhead or Cammell-Laird's as he would in Workman Clark's. If the work went out there, with a bit of a fall out with the gaffer, or if the work went a bit slack, and a man was working in Harland and Wolff, he would lift his cards and the next thing you would hear of him he was in Cammell-Laird's or he was in John Brown's or he was on the Tyne – he could have been anywhere. He just went over; he felt that maybe there was more overtime, or perhaps there was a job where there was a bit more money. It was nothing for any of the shipyard men to be found working in any of the shipyards in Scotland or England. It seemed to work out all right. Even when they discussed work on the dole, this was a way that word got round, but especially in their trade union rooms, or the bars they frequented. Some day a mate might say 'I'm off, they're building a big one over in some other yard. I don't like the gaffer up here, I'm getting fed up with him'. The man he'd be talking with would say, 'Do you think . . . ?', and the two of them would go, and that would be all there was about it."

Outside of the skilled engineering trades and the linen industry, work in Belfast was even more sporadic and casual. These were part-time jobs through which people simply tried to make ends meet. William Patterson and his wife, Ida, recall one such case:

"I think his mother sold pillow-cases up there, she's a widow . . . and she'd have got sixpence a dozen . . . and she'd have been sitting there until two o'clock in the morning and you never heard a machine going as fast in your life. And after they had been sold they had to be turned out and folded. She'd do six dozen every day. I'd put them on a push-car and carry them over to Somerset's, carry them up the stairs, get another six dozen and back home again . . . you never heard a machine going as hard in your life . . . some days she might only have got two or three dozen."

Anne Boyle tells of the people in Sandy Row:

"They were very poor, but enterprising and hard working. They made the mill girls tea at lunch-time for a penny, or a penny bowl of soup or a penny bowl of rice. When I worked in the Linfield mill, all I had with me was two pennies for my tram fare, so, if I bought the tea, I had to walk to or from work. People were selling things from their homes: apple pies, soda bread, hot peas, pigs' feet, candy apples, candy. There was no relief at all and people were helping themselves. It was a great thing for fellows in their teens if their mother could buy them a pony and cart to go round with fish or vegetables. I think the saddest thing was the teenage fellows; they had nothing, no hope. They were young and they wanted things."

Leo Boyle, likewise remembers how:

"Every street had its shoe mender. They charged a shilling, one and six, for soling. Everybody that I can think of was doing something to help their homes. I remember people going out during the snow with yard brushes on their shoulders and going to the big houses up the Antrim Road and Cliftonville Road and cleaning their snow away for a shilling. There was great jealousy among the men over this, how many houses they got in a day."

Here we see how the 'world of work' merges with the world of the jobless – it is a grey area of part work, part unemployment.

Working conditions

Having examined how people got jobs, and lost them, we now turn to the conditions at work. As regards the labour process the 1930s was a period of "rationalisation" and productivity drives. This was done partly through new capital investment and the adoption of new production techniques. One study mentions an increase of 30,000 horsepower in the linen mills during this period, and the introduction of new "labour-saving" machines in the shipyard.[7] A contemporary account claims that "with the introduction of the deck caulking machine one shipwright can do the work of twelve". The economic crisis could not, however, allow for systematic introduction of new technology and the main element in "rationalisation" was a demand for a quicker and more intense work effort. Davis describes how "working conditions deteriorated everywhere as shrunken workforces struggled to keep pace with relentlessly increased rhythms of production. Textile operatives were forced to supervise more machines; boiler makers and engineers raced against one another; and outside the doors of every plant the unemployed waited to take the jobs of those who couldn't take the pace".[8]

We shall now see how the workers of Belfast experienced this process.

As Anne McKenna recalls:

"In the clothing industry you worked extremely hard; the old method of making the garment right through was disappearing

. . . You would have got a dozen cut-out trousers with all the accessories and then you made the entire garment right through . . . . What we got then was the introduction of the conveyor belt from the States . . . Most factories always had a five minute break . . . every hour on the conveyor belt system; they said you needed that. But in the factory I was in, it didn't happen, you only got a five minute break every two hours. . . . You were that tired, you see, your head was down all the time because nothing stopped the belt. That work came down. You had to work to the belt. On that bench, forty pairs of trousers were made every hour."

Anne Boyle had a similar experience:

"I was working about 1934-35. I used to walk it from the Oldpark Road to Linfield mill in Sandy Row. I worked as a winder. I worked from 8 in the morning to 7 at night for seven and six a week. Joe Devlin got the hours changed, to stop at 6 o'clock and then half five. There was nothing like a tea break or coffee break. You got an hour for your lunch and that was it. We had a three minute break, I think it was, every 2½ hours or 3 hours, to run to the toilet. Outside of these breaks, you had to get permission to go to the toilet because there would be nobody to take over your job. You had to call the boss to get permission. There was no union for us."

Saidie Patterson specifically mentions:

"In 1931 or '32 we were offered more machinery, say to have you look after two looms. One loom could be as wide as a room. Well, to offer women more looms to look after, or more frames in the spinning industry . . . !"

Was there any change in her wages as a result of this extra responsibility?

"Yes, you got less. It was less money for more work. You were putting the money in the coffers of the boss."

What about the shipyard workers, the "aristocrats of labour" in Belfast according to some? Tommy Patton is adamant that:

"Shipyard men were very highly respected, hardworking men, who in my opinion, were imposed on in every way you could think, I have seen them working in the rain, snow and everything. I have seen them sent home two and three days a week because of the bad weather and done without pay. The riveter's job was a very hard job because he never got paid for anything only putting in rivets and if he wasn't putting in rivets, he wasn't getting paid. The riveter maybe had to run after a plater, a caulker, a line man to get the job right. That could maybe take a day and a half of his time and he hadn't earned a ha'penny. When he did start, he had to work like a beaver. They had to kill themselves to get in as many rivets as they possibly could to get a fair week's pay."

Alec Salmon describes another aspect of the shipyard:

"The conditions look bad looking back but in them days that was part of the school; that was the way you worked. You went down and the place was freezing, the sheds were old galvanised sheds and they would've skinned you and you couldn't light a fire. Some of the boys, when it came to getting their coats on would have lit a fire and if the gaffer came round he would tell them to get it out. You went down to them big sheds and there was no heat in them, and you went down and worked in them. That was part of the work though and you never thought much about it. At Christmas one time I went out to the water to make tea and the water was all ice so you broke the water all up and got it into your bucket, but you weren't worried about the cold you just went up onto that boat with snow and whatever was going in January, February, March; you never thought about it."

John Hyde confirms that the labour process in the shipyard was "rationalised" after the 1930s in a similar way to the mills:

"The war provided a certain amount of employment but the good days were ending then in shipbuilding generally. Things were changing, the same amount of men were not required to build a ship – new methods, new materials had interfered with the old particular type of what was known as 'ships built by shipyard men'."

One small way in which technological change affected the shipyard workers was the move from riveting to electric welding. John Hyde again:

"To a large extent new methods and new materials were used in all trades. New fittings were used, and new methods for using the fittings, but all faster. The result was that a terrible lot of requirements, craft requirements, that used to be needed in the old pre-war days, were no longer required."

This was effectively a process of de-skilling – taking away the craftsman's skill and knowledge and vesting it instead in management 'specialists'. It had the added advantage of reducing the number of workers. For John Hyde:

"When I left Harland and Wolff, although my particular section was pretty well catered for, there wasn't one eighth of the people of my trade employed when I left compared to when I went in – far, far from it."

Accidents were a common feature of work in those days. Industrial injuries were seen by employers as something which workers just had to accept as part of their lot. Protective clothing for example had to be provided by the workers themselves. Scotty Best describes one such industrial accident and official reaction towards it:

"There's a big chain there, with 3 inch links, five-eighths in diameter – so we connected that up and started screwing away. All of a sudden my hand was on the beam lee and it smashed up against that and my finger dropped into the middle of my hand. When that happened I fell down twenty or thirty feet among all the scrap iron and the cuttings that was on the tank top. Sammy Young catched me by the throat and held me there against the bulkhead until Mingham and the other big mate got me over the big bulkheads and lowered me down onto the ground. The foreman met me and said 'Ah, you've just broke your finger'. I was off for nine weeks, and during that time I refused to take my compensation until such times as I saw a doctor, because I wasn't satisfied with the treatment I was getting. They couldn't do anything with it, the smashed bone was acting as a brake, and he said the rest of the hand was no use. If the smashed bone had come out at the back of the knuckles it would have penetrated the skin. I couldn't close the hand and the doctor said the decision was up to me. I asked what he meant, and he said to have it amputated. When I came back in again at the end of twenty-five weeks I met the two foremen and they said to me, 'There's your mate up yonder', and they sent me up a seventy foot ladder."

William Patterson tells of another incident:

"If you were working in below the bottom of a boat with maybe seven or eight riveters and the sparks flying off and no glasses the only chance you had of getting a pair of glasses was going over and buying a pair or else if there's somebody working in Cammell Laird's or Birkenhead they brought you a pair home. . . . The only thing they supplied was a glove and if you went down with a docket for a glove he'd get the book out and say, 'Oh, you got one three weeks ago, it's too early', and it didn't matter if it was hanging off you. If you'd have went back to the foreman and said that they'd no gloves in the store he'd have said, 'Well you know what to do'. In fact, I saw me going into the town into that place in High Street and buying a glove for myself before you'd go to the foreman for a docket for one."

William Patterson had burn marks about his neck from the sparks flying off during riveting and he told us how doctors at the hospital had photographed them because they found them "interesting".

Some trade unionists like John Hyde were acutely sensitive to the importance of working conditions:

"Down in the tanks of big tankers and bulk carriers there was noise, dirt, filth – everything's there. There's some things that you can't clear up but you can do the best you can to provide for the safety of the men as far as is humanly possible and their health. To offer men a few extra shillings a week is no answer to a man's health, and we've always tried to put forward, that when conditions got really bad and away from normality that we tried to get something replaced that lessened the danger rather than agree to a small increase. We always tried to get the conditions changed, not a few coppers or a few shillings at the end of the week."

In the linen mills and factories conditions had not changed drastically since the turn of the century. Armstrong described the situation in the Belfast linen industry then as follows:

"The risks inherent in work in the spinning and weaving section of the linen industry can easily be gauged from the character of the processes. The most dangerous aspects were the omnipresence of dust in the preliminary processes and the great heat and moisture associated with spinning . . ."[9]

Alice Quinn worked in the wet spinning end during the 1930s and says simply "You couldn't describe it", her friend Mrs McBride adding "You were murdered". Concerning accidents, Armstrong describes the great reluctance of the linen bosses to introduce fencing of machinery, adding that the long hours were a contributory factor in the frightful injuries caused by this work. Alice Quinn tells of one common cause of injuries:

"And then if a drag had've fell on your toe, that was you. You can just picture yourself, although its years since I'm out of it: there was a whole frame you see, and all the bobbins were there; at the back there was a big piece of cord, and to make the bobbins tighter there was a big drag, and you had to drag it. If the string broke then the drag would've fell on your toe – some of them were 26 ounces, some 10 ounces – you'd be running around with a broken toe. Your head had to be nearly off before you could go out to first aid."

Workers just had to put up with bronchitis (from moving out of the heat and damp into the cold outside), lung diseases (from the spray from the spindles) and phthisis or "the pouce" (from the dust in the roughing and hackling departments).

Wages

If conditions of work were bad, did good wages in any way compensate for this? The evidence points clearly towards bad wages as well as conditions whether measured against present-day standards or the then cost of living. The skilled trades in shipbuilding and engineering actually received higher wages than those of their counterparts in Britain. However, operatives and unskilled labourers were always paid considerably less than British workers. Taken overall, the "wages bills" of Belfast industries (except for shipbuilding) were nearly a quarter less than the UK averages. Belfast had another advantage for employers because, as Isles and Cuthbert describe, "Even where higher rates than in Great Britain had to be paid for skilled workers, the average labour costs per unit of output could still as a whole be kept lower than in Great Britain by employing a higher percentage of women and unskilled men".[10] Women, who in 1935 represented 46% of the labour force in NI (as against 26% for the UK) received only 57% of the average rate of male manufacturing workers. This was also a period of generalised wage cuts across Belfast industry. The *Ulster Yearbook* for 1932 carried out a general survey of industrial wage rates and found only two cases of wage increases compared to twenty-two cases of wage reductions, nine of these occurring in the textile industry. Between 1920 and 1930 employees in the weaving mills lost 40% of their weekly pay packet through such cuts. Anne McKenna remembers how:

> "Wages was ghastly. I believe railway workers were very badly paid. Anybody who was on construction, if it rained, they weren't paid . . . When I went to work in 1936, I had six shillings. I know I only came home with five and tenpence. When I went in I was on short time. My first wages was three and ninepence ha'penny. We were on short time for a long time . . . I think we started from nine to twelve, then we had an hour and a quarter for lunch and we stopped at four o'clock . . . When you went into the clothing industry you went in at a set pay of six shillings. Then you were taught and then you went on to piece rates. I was in a very vicious circle because I should have been paid 5 pence for a gross of button holes – I was a button-holer – but because I was under age, they only gave me half. So I got, 2½d. for a gross of button-holes and out of that I paid for my thread and I paid for my needles . . . No wonder when Charles Hill died, he left £103,000 [Clarence Clothing Co.]."

Holidays of course were not paid in those days. As Bobby Hurndall tells:

> "In Harland's when I served my time there was no payment for holidays – it was a lockout. You were locked out for a week at Christmas, a week in July and two days at Easter – no money, no holiday pay. During the slump there were *deductions* in wages negotiated nationally – there was no question of the shop stewards getting together, going in to meet the management, putting forward claims on behalf of the workers for more money."

Ida Patterson likewise remembers how:

> "We didn't get paid holidays or anything like that, not then. You got off for Easter, for Monday and Tuesday. On the twelfth of July you got your week, and you saved a shilling a week all year for your week. We didn't get a week's pay at Ewart's until I went

back after getting married and we thought it was great then. This was the forties, after the war. . . . "

Authority at work

Apart from the bad wages and conditions there is a more intangible elemen about work in the 1930s sometimes referred to by socialist writers a: "factory despotism". Authority at the workplace was vested in the manage and delegated to the foreman. Nearly everyone we spoke to had harsl words about their particular foreman. Florrie Addley worked in the mills:

"The managers and foremen, as we called them, we were terrified of them and you would never have thought of rebelling, that was unheard of, they were like God to you, especially when you were young."

Alice Quinn adds:

"If they took a dislike to you they could give you the sack. Or if they thought you were a wee bit slow. At that time there was no week's notice, you were just out."

Belle O'Hara saw authority in the workplace rather differently:

"A spinner was the best job, you had more money. I was in no trade union in them days, nobody bothered. I couldn't say nothing about the doffing mistress we had. Any doffing mistress I worked under was all right."

Ida Paterson, for her part, agreed that "nobody seemed to want a trade union – everybody seemed to be satisfied". Clearly, those immediately above workers had to maintain some kind of good relations if productivity was not to suffer. Florrie Addley shows there was no contradiction between decent behaviour and supreme authority. "In York Street: the men that were over us were all gentlemen, they really were, but they were this authority that you never thought of defying."

In the shipyard the authority of the foreman was usually displayed more aggressively. Scotty Best recalls some incidents:

"I remember Mr McDonald, the head time keeper – he was another tyrant. I've seen us being two minutes late in the morning and the time-keeper locking the door and locking us out. The foremen, they weren't proper foremen, they were proper tyrants. One of them, in fact, half stood over me while I was checking a plank with a wood chisel. The wood chisel slipped as it was getting dark and it stuck in my knee and he started to laugh."

Bobby Hurndall gives a similar picture:

"The foreman in those days had complete authority, he had complete control, his word was law. If he said work tonight at eight o'clock and you said 'No' you got your cards, you were sacked. If he didn't like you, if you had done anything to offend him, he had to give no reasons for dismissing you, he just dismissed you. If he wanted rid of you you were out – there was no redress, there were no industrial tribunals, no redundancy payments, nothing."

Tommy Patton adds:

"It wasn't easy to be a trade union official because the foreman had the first and last say. Foremen had a lot of power. If the foreman didn't like your face: 'You're going tonight and your going tonight' and that was it. That went on for year after year up until the war came and changes were made. In those days you had what was called a market where the men stood in the morning looking for work and the foreman would have stood in the hut and pointed out the men he wanted. I know people who were kept out of the shipyard for thirteen and fourteen years because the foreman didn't like their face. They might not have done anything, but some way or another the foreman had taken a dislike and once he took a dislike that was it; you might as well have got out of the shipyard if you possibly could, but you had nowhere else to get a job in East Belfast."

Jim Salmon gave a slightly different response when asked whether management were fair and considerate to workers:

"Well I would say that most managers would be anxious to get the job done. The manager would give the orders for the foreman who would then pass it on to the men, so what I'm saying is that the foreman plater could have maybe twenty men under him, but he would be responsible to a manager."

We asked him if in general the tradesmen, their apprentices, and the labourers were treated well by those above them. He replied:

"Oh yes. Well I'm speaking now of the steel department, which I knew, and the fitting department which I had to go into regular, they were treated well because its in the interests of the foreman to treat the men well to get the job done. If you were nasty to the men, tell them to go to hell or something, then they wouldn't rush the job because you weren't too pleasant."

We asked if by and large he any had complaints about them while working under them and his answer was a definite no.

In a sense the situation would dictate the amount of authority exercised by a foreman. Jim Salmon told us that:

"As a manager, if I saw somebody having a wee drink of tea I'd close my eyes to it. Other people would say 'I'm not having that', but you see that's different mentalities. My view would be, if they can get a wee drink of tea they'll work harder after it. A good lot depends on what attitude you would take."

The foremen were not above joining secret societies to increase their near monopoly over job openings. Tommy Patton:

> "I heard it said that men would have joined the Masons or the Lodge because the foreman was a member. Foremen got backhanders to give people jobs and I remember a very prominent foreman riveter getting the sack over this."

William Patterson remarked cryptically:

> "Well the foremen some of them were all right and some of them were all wrong and they weren't great tradesmen some of them I can tell you. They belonged to some wee crowd or other that got them shoved in most of them."

When asked what he meant by "some wee crowd or other" he replied, "There was one fellah used to work for us, our gaffer, and he went to wee functions. He was a foreman." He would not however specify what the "wee group" was. He went on the say, "I knew some big men who went to Sunday school for to keep in with the gaffer." Alec Salmon added,

> "That happened everywhere. If the gaffer would have been a Christian there'd have been a brave lot of Christians along with him. They'd still have their pints and their bookies but they'd never let on."

Another organisation operating alongside the Christians was, of course the Orange Order.

Workplace sectarianism

People are sometimes reluctant to talk about sectarianism at work but it nevertheless forms an important part of the "world of work" in the 1930s. One common reaction was simply to deny that there was any workplace sectarianism. Florrie Addley, for example, said, "I don't think there was any sectarianism in the mills, maybe in the shipyard. . . . " John Hyde gives his view of the shipyard thus:

> "You see, people say if you were a Roman Catholic you had no hope in the yard, but this was not so: men served their time with me were Roman Catholic. There were pay-offs when I was paid off and they weren't. But it never annoyed me that Paddy was kept, I knew Paddy well, we'd carried on when we were apprentices, but sure Billy beside him was kept too. Maybe I was more annoyed because Billy was kept because I knew that Billy couldn't work as hard as me. It didn't annoy me. I didn't think of it. The only time I began to think of that was when they started to tell me that men couldn't get a job in the shipyard because they were Roman Catholics. There were shipwright trades, there were Black trades, but *nobody* could have got in there, nobody could have got

in with the Blackmen [Royal Black Preceptory].

The complex nature of sectariansim begins to come out in Bobby Hurndall's recollection:

"When I was in the shipyard the question of Catholic/Protestant didn't loom very large; as far as the shipyard was concerned there were a number of Catholics worked there – some of them were well appreciated – but they were strictly in the minority. I knew some of them personally. I don't think there was any policy to keep them out, not that I knew anyway. Although some of them – like McGinty a swimmer, a shipwright – when trouble arose he was warned to take some time off. He never came back. During the war there wasn't this antagonism. As far as the union was concerned, they didn't employ Protestants and Catholics – our union had platers and welders, shipwrights and blacksmiths, that's all. I wasn't aware of any antagonism. At one stage – when there was periodic trouble – there were certain people shot and then of course everybody reacted and certain people were warned to stay out. But usually within a short time things died down and they came back. They were warned away probably for their own safety."

More common than an active sectarianism seems to have been this passive acceptance of religious divisions within the working class. Perhaps the unions did not discriminate between Catholics and Protestants but they never really took the offensive against a social and economic system based on this division. The other side of the coin is that, effectively, sectarianism was not always present. Most workplaces probably did have amiable relations most of the year round. But the divisions were there and there was always a latent hostility. This would become more open around the Twelfth of July. Alice Quinn recalls:

"It all just seemed to start. Every now and again there would be trouble anyway – every five or six years there would have been a wee spurt. Every year round the Twelfth – the mad month. No matter how great you were with anybody, even in the mill, when the first of July came there was trouble and then St Patrick's Day if you put on a green jumper or blouse or some thing, they nearly thought it was an insult. The Protestants started wearing a brooch with a big Union Jack, and the foreman, though he was a Protestant he made them take it out. Of course they were nearly all Protestants, the foremen, in the mill then. . . . A Catholic never got an overman's job, even in Jennymount". [The main thing was] "you always knew you were a Catholic; you were let known that you were a Catholic one way or another."

She remembers one incident particularly vividly:

"We were the only Catholics in Jennymount Street and one night about twenty gathered outside the door and they started to sing 'No pope, priest or holy water', and that was the first time I ever heard that. There they were outside the door and we didn't know what to do. The next day everyone in the street was coming apologising and saying that wasn't them, but my ma said 'If it wasn't you how did you know what door to come to?"

Betty Sinclair tells of her more unusual experience of sectarianism:

"My father would never allow any talk against the Catholic people and although I worked in Ewart's mill I think there was only one Catholic employed in the whole of the Ewart's complex. We never took part in any anti-Catholic sentiments and my mother's nearest friend, Mrs Annie McKee, who was a Catholic, was always welcomed in our house – although my mother, she always had a wee bit of antipathy towards the Catholics. But, father would never allow anyone to express any anti-Catholic sentiments in our home. He wouldn't allow us out on the Eleventh night, when we were young, to go the the bonfire. He had orange lilies growing in the back yard but he would never allow us to put one on our breasts. He called himself Labour and he remained that way all his life, never, never interfering with any of our political activities, our reading, our actions. So that stood me in good stead."

This upbringing helped make her a radical which in turn led to political discrimination at work:

"Later I got a job in Wolfhill mill and for two years nobody spoke to me, neither Catholic or Protestant. Actually the Catholic workers, in the ruling room, went on a deputation to the ruling master to ask him to pay me off. He told them to go away back to their work. I was a communist. Then the thing broke down. They started coming in to ask me to look at their pay sheets, which recorded the number of bundles of yarn they put in and one thing and another. Oh, there were times when none of the Catholics would speak to me and times when none of the Protestants would speak to me. There were times when none of them would speak to me. After two years it was all over and I was generally accepted."

Competition over jobs seemed to be at the root of most sectarianism in the industrial world. Anne Boyle tells of one fruitless job application after gaining a secretarial qualification:

"I carried that certificate round all the works and nice places, all the offices to try and get a nice job for clerical work or secretarial work or something like that and I couldn't get in anywhere. . . . I went to the Northern Publishing Company and they had an exam for theirs and I did the exam. I was called into a room and whenever I went in there were four of us just – we must have got the top marks in the exam, the four of us. They were from Methody College (it was another college then, it used to be a commercial college then) and the man asked me what school I went to. My father had told me to tell him I went to Saint Jude's in Oxford. I was to say that you see in case it came up. They didn't know what I was talking about so they came right out and asked me what religion I was. I said that I was the old Church of England, and they didn't know what to do then and they didn't ask me what the old Church of England was. They just wrote that down and said that they would send for me. . . . I never got any word about it. They knew rightly that I was a Catholic, they knew enough to know that."

Jim Salmon seems to point to job competition as well when discussing sectarianism in the shipyard:

"They were afraid, that was the attitude of some of the Catholics, they were afraid that some of the Protestant ones would disturb them or go for them, and there were some of them left actually because if there were troubles in the city and you're a Catholic in the shipyard and there's nearly all Protestants round you. The odd Catholic that would be in would feel 'They'll have me down there if I go' and most of them withdrew actually. I don't remember seeing any bad incidents with them but I knew some of them that just like left the job rather than face it. The Catholics, they were afraid to come down. If they weren't there then somebody else got their job, that was all. We were going through a bad period and eventually they would come back, but not maybe for months until the whole thing had quietened down."

Tom Boyd believes that the trade unions played a role in reducing workplace sectarianism:

"In 1935 in my memory there wasn't anything like the widespread violent attitude that there was in the 1920's. I think it was not only the leadership that was given by many trade union leaders and others, but that people generally had achieved a stability that they lacked in the 1920's, there wasn't the same fear abroad. . . . In 1935 I don't recall any large incidents or that happening in industrial works."

On the other hand, sectarianism could play a disruptive role when trade unions were forming. Saidie Patterson tells of one such incident:

"We would have had practically every factory in Belfast unionised, all the linen factories – we were fairly well organised. When Joe Devlin died in 1933 Bob Getgood, who was looking after our affairs, he went to Joe Devlin's funeral as any Christian would. Bob was a Protestant and Joe Devlin was a Catholic but that didn't make any difference, they were both good men. The

> *Belfast Telegraph* that night had carried a couple of headlines of; 'Bob Getgood Chief Mourner at Joe Devlin's Funeral'. I went round to collect the union contributions on the following Saturday and my Protestant friends refused to pay because Bob Getgood had been to a Catholic funeral."

As a result some Protestants left the union. Ironically, many Protestant workers admired and respected Joe Devlin but in public it was another matter . . . .

Trade unionism

In spite of all the obstacles caused by sectarian divisions, workers did organise in trade unions and did fight for better wages and conditions. The 1930s was a difficult period for the trade unions in Belfast. The militancy which followed the First World War had collapsed in the bloody civil war or pogroms of 1920-1922. The legacy of mass expulsions of Catholics from the shipyard and the linen mills was a heavy one. Wage-cuts and speed-ups also demoralised workers and weakened the trade unions. In his history of Irish labour Clarkson says that: "these two years of frightfulness have left their mark deep on the labour movement. Not only have wages plunged downward with amazing velocity, but hope of restoring any degree of mutual confidence between Catholic and Protestant workers has sunk to an extremely low ebb. . . . In industrial action nothing of importance has been achieved or even attempted in the last five years".[11]

The 1926 General Strike in Britain found no repercussion in Belfast, unlike the effect of the 1919 engineer's strike "across the water". The effect on trade union membership was of course noticeable. In 1927 only 28% of Belfast workers were trade union members compared to 41% for the UK as a whole. Not surprisingly, the editor of the *Northern Whig* could boast that "there is no part of the Empire where the relations between the employers and the employed are more intimate or more harmonious".[12]

The figures for trade union membership given in Table 1 show that the decline of membership beween 1932 and 1934 was reversed in 1935 and 1936 with a considerable jump in both male and female union memberships.

As to strikes and stoppages measured in the conventional form of "working days lost" we see in Table 2 that 1929 and 1933 were the highpoints. However, if we go on to analyse the share of each industry in the strike rates in Table 3 we find that shipbuilding accounted for the vast majority of "days lost" between 1929 and 1931; the 1933 rail strike provided most of the "days lost" for 1932 to 1934, with the figures for 1935 to 1937 showing a fair spread across industries. If we considered the overall figures *without* their individual peaks we would see how limited labour resistance was in the 1930s.

TABLE 1: Numbers in trade unions in Northern Ireland

Year	Men	Women
1929	56,077	7,674
1930	57,675	7,253
1931	61,434	6,971
1932	55,182	6,322
1933	51,181	6,168
1934	57,363	6,645
1935	61,058	10,402
1936	63,973	11,372

TABLE 2: Working days lost in disputes in Northern Ireland

1929	228,328
1930	5,210
1931	64,470
1932	21,960
1933	240,752
1934	20,072
1935/7	60,237

TABLE 3: Working days lost in specific industries in Northern Ireland

1929/31		1932/4		1935/7	
Shipbuilding	222,515	Railways	228,000	Bleaching/dyeing	12,640
Textiles	34,010	Building	41,697	Shipbuilding	11,304
Building	27,398	Textiles	6,023	Textiles	9,547
Furniture manufacture	4,360	Shipbuilding	1,300	Engineering	9,080

Source: *Ulster Year Books*

At Harland and Wolff's the management had always prided itself on its "humane" industrial relations policy. The biographer of Lord Pirrie, managing director of H & W until 1924, tells of how:

> "Harland and Wolff had been accused by other shipyard employers of fostering a crusade against Trade Unionism. . . .

> As a matter of fact his firm had always refused to be hostile to the men's Unions. The old days of settling labour problems, he insisted, were out of date for the difficulties of 50 years later. . . . He always urged on his men to remember that Capital and Labour were each dependent on each other; the interests were identical, and should be in union. The employers should be interested in the men and they in the employers, and proud of the work they turned out. There should be no suspicious feelings in a well ordered industry."[13]

The essence of Pirrie's philosophy was that "labour troubles should not arise if both sides approached problems in the proper spirit". This attitude was an intelligent policy akin to co-optation rather than a misguided philantropy as some fellow employers thought. It aimed at bringing the trade unions in behind the aims and objectives of the company. Its success can be gauged from the following quotes from John Hyde, a shipyard worker and, later, trade union official:

> "Men should be able to sit down with their employers. If you force anything out of an employer after hard driving and slogging by union representatives, the time could come when the men have to put their coats on and go back to the streets. This is wrong, totally wrong in this time and age. Both workers' representatives and the employers should have the knowledge enough and the free discussion among themselves of the whole facts that they can settle this without asking the men to come out into the streets. Who wins, who wins? The men lose something they will never get back. You don't win in a strike really . . . At one point we allowed shipwrights and pattern-makers to come and do work normally done by joiners, we relaxed on that. And this is always available, the openness and openhandedness with the employer, and he deals with the mens' representatives and puts the matter to the men, the difficulties and all, lets them be involved in it. Generally the men will accept a situation that allows them to have a fair wage and accept a number of conditions. They certainly worked hard, they always did. What was told to me by the owner once was, when there was disputes across the water over wages, stay you at your work here in Belfast, and if there's a rise across the water you'll get it, and you always got it and you got a little more. The result of this was that we were always a little in the region of three shillings more".

How had this co-operative attitude come about? The shipyard unions had begun organising the crafts from the mid-nineteenth century. Their craft or sectional consciousness was highly developed, but this meant essentially protecting their own position in the labour market. They could and did take industrial action but preferred to foster the corporatist outlook pioneered by Viscount Pirrie. Tommy Cochrane, a shipwright born in 1901, puts it succinctly:

> "The trade unions in Northern Ireland, the shipwrights', the boilermakers' the lot were conservatives. They wouldn't go against what they call the state; it didn't matter how rotten it was."

There were many obstacles to unionisation in the plants and mills of Belfast industry. In the linen mills, for example, the level of organisation was much lower than in the shipyards – Boyle estimates that "by 1910 less than 12% of the workforce was organised, and those who were, were represented by ten different unions. Nine of these catered for the sectional interests of the various skilled groups, and accounted for about 60% of the union membership."[14]

Frank Hughes tells of some of the obstacles encountered by union activists in the 1930s:

> "I was so fond of the movement as far as the betterment of the workers was concerned that I was made the shop-steward in the particular shop that I worked in; that was in Lindsay and Thompson's mill. The foreman had his friends inside that he talked to on various occasions, and he learned everything that was going on in the shop whenever he wasn't there. This was the kind of tactic that was used to keep you under subjection and naturally he had a thing on me because I read out the *Daily Herald* to the shop. I only read out the salient parts of the news, that is to do with trade unionism, to do with things as they are in parliament and that kind of thing, and he took umbrage to such an extent that he eventually sacked me. Now if a hackler is sacked, or a flax-dresser as he was commonly known, it usually was because of the fact that he done inferior work, and the foreman can accuse you at any time of doing inferior work and naturally in those days you had no redress. The only redress that I got from the union when I went and reported what had happened to me, they were able to give me victimisation benefit and I got that victimisation benefit for twelve weeks until I was able to get another job."

Sectarianism was undoubtedly a factor weakening the trade unions as Hughes recalls:

> "I was against bigotry, and bigotry was personified here in Belfast, particularly against the Catholics. It can't be cured within the establishment – it can be cured within the people, and unfortunately people didn't join trade unions, they didn't want trade unions, they didn't have time for trade unions. This is the awful thing you see; we were only about 40% *(sic)* of the whole working population who were unionised, but if it hadn't been for tradesmen who were compelled to be in trade unions it wouldn't have been 15%."

Was sectarianism a problem within the trade unions?

"It was a problem yes, but it was a problem that never was able to rear its ugly head because you had so many people who took a deep interest in the trade unions and they were able to down all these people who tried to have Protestant unions. . . . There was a man and his name was Bell, and he decided – he was a tram-driver – and he decided that he would form a union of Ulster workers and he tried to make the backbone of that union the people who were in transport, that is the Belfast Corporation and the Ulster Transport Board and people like myself got our sleeves rolled up and we beat this fellow Bell. That was in the early years of the war, about 1941, '42. But then there was another movement earlier in the 1930s – a man, I can't remember his name, who tried to have a Protestant union again. He started a breakaway union and organised some textile workers and organised particularly shipyard workers, he had them all in, and his union eventually fell because it was on quicksands actually, because the man, number one he hadn't a clue, number two he couldn't get anybody around him who was a trade unionist, who knew something about the trade unions. So that we did have sectarianism, we had it in the unions, at the branch meeting we had to shoot these fellows down left right and centre, it was shocking. . . . "

Harold Binks, who became a trade union official, says simply:

"The textile industry was an exploiting industry, 100%. The boss used to announce periodically that the first man to join a trade union would be immediately sacked. Very few were union organised."

When asked to account for the failure in organising across Belfast industry he told of how:

"The girls in the place I worked were all older than I was, but they weren't interested in the union. The union was a bad word to them. The unions were only troublemakers in their eyes."

Anne McKenna complements this account when discussing her time in the clothing industry after 1936:

"There was no real trade union organisation there though there was some semblance of it. You see, the men were in the union and they would have said to the women 'You should all be in the union'. Now the women at that time would have said 'Well, like, our learning's not good'. That's the way they would have put it. One of the men becomes the shop-steward for us. There wasn't any of us who was prepared to do that. Because what you had was people very, very young. The average age in the factory I worked in was nineteen years of age. We didn't have anybody old. We called people old who were in their late twenties or early thirties.

The majority of us were in from fourteen. You got girls coming in at fourteen, by the time they were eighteen, they were married and away having babies; they didn't come back. So you had this turnover of labour all the time. It was hard to organise because of the rapid turnover of labour."

Management, of course, was keen to dissuade people from organising. For Anne McKenna:

"Most managements opposed trade unions. Some did it openly, some did it through junior management, who reflected what senior management was saying. The whole attitude was 'Why do you need a union? My door is always open. You can always come and talk to me'. But you were made feel ridiculous because of the standard of education of the boss and the standard of education of the worker. Most workers, even now, are inarticulate when they go in to ask for particular things. There's an old trick that the bosses always play. You started out looking for your request, and he'd talk about everything and right before you know it, you're out through the door and you've never had an answer. Bosses don't like unions. I would say that there's good bosses but in a time of depression there's no good bosses."

Paternalism was one approach taken by employers but the threat of the sack was always there to back that up. William Patterson said that "the management did not have much time for trade unions. There wasn't really such a thing as a shop-steward. There wasn't really a shop-steward until coming up to the war nearly. If you had have been a shop-steward you would have been sacked that night . . . ." Florrie Addley told us of one incident where the very real fear of losing one's job rapidly stopped a potential labour dispute:

"We would have had a price for a cut – there was a great big web and when you weaved a certain distance there was a mark in it and that was a cut – and you were paid for that. Now we found out the York Street factory and Brookfield were under the same management and somebody brought into work that Brookfield was getting more for a cut of work, this same work whatever it was, and we all downed tools. I must have been very young for there were women a lot older than I was, but you were told to down tools and we went and saw the foreman who had to do with us and he told us we could get our cards then. We all scuttled back to work then for we were too frightened of getting our cards."

The level of unionisation amongst women was extremely low – around 7% according to most accounts. Rightly or wrongly several people saw the "conservativism" of women as a factor in the possible unionisation of the linen industry. For Tom Boyd:

"The traditional role of women in the home seemed to have been very strong during that period as it was previously, and it's only since I suppose the war period, and the paradox is, I think, that the war liberated women in many ways because they became involved in the services and even in the auxiliary services that were arising out of the war situation."

We said Saidie Patterson told us that most of the women who were in outside employment worked in the linen mills, working from 6a.m. to 6p.m., and then had to come home to do housework. He agreed:

"This was an aspect of it which meant that mostly any women that were active were single women. In addition to Saidie herself who played a very effective role in the trade union movement in organising women, there was the late Mr Bob Getgood who was very active in organising women at the mill, and to my knowledge he held many dinner-hour meetings at the mill trying to get the people, the women, into the unions, but I suppose over the centuries the women have been stronger in the conservative outlook, the preservation of the family and so on, than they have been active politically."

Saidie Patterson herself proves that women were active in factories as she recalls:

"There was a little union called Mary Galway's Union that came into being about 1917 or 1918 when there was what was known as the tenters' strike – the tenters were the skin section of the weaving trade, and the journeymen, they had a strike, and they lifted a bit of support and women in different factories joined. In those days Mrs Dunbar and Miss Galway, they fought according to their lights, and they collected their money round the doors, but I didn't think that was militant enough. It wasn't that I wanted to take a gun in my hand to anybody but I think that bosses ought to be told and see that you're active. We had tried for some considerable time to organise the textile workers because after the First World War, right up to 1924, the factories were very busy because the world was starving for materials and all the things that the textile industry produced. We were busy working from six in the morning to six at night. Many of the spinners would have had from seven to nine shillings a week; the weavers were a little better off, they would have earned about fifteen shillings – it was a different job, it's mainly piece work, while the spinning trade was 95% time workers and 5% piece workers, it was vice-versa in the weaving trade. It was dreadful wages we were being paid so we felt something ought to be done to get our wages raised. We talked amongst ourselves about the injustice which was done to us.

They built the mills and they built the workers' houses

around them, and therefore you got a house belonging to a mill or a factory. You didn't speak out when an injustice was done because if you got the sack you could have lost your job, lost your home – it was a very real thing. This is one thing that always was at the back of textile workers' minds. If we would join a union we would be classed as an agitator or a communist and then you're out. But you had to break that down. We tried to get them organised after America came off the gold standard in 1929, and the bottom fell out of the textile industry after that."

If women were under-represented it was largely because of male prejudice:

"They didn't play the role that I would have liked them to play but men were to blame for that. At the turn of this century men were the head of the household; the men had their meal by themselves and they got it first, the children got what was left then, and if there was anything left the mother got it. There really was that feeling that the man was the boss. It was the same in every street in the city where Labour MPs were shocked when they talked to women who said they had to wait until their husband came home. It was most difficult to get women involved because it could have started a row in the home; it was absolutely impossible to organise them in the trade union movement."

The linen mills were particularly important to the Revolutionary Workers' Group because of the mixed workforce and the chance to put their "class against class" line into practice. It had a number of members in the textile mills, amongst them Lily Magill. At the Jennymount mill they organised a factory cell and published a plant newspaper. It was through activities like this they recruited a young Protestant mill worker who had been laid off – Betty Sinclair. She not only shows the active role of women in the labour movement but explains some of the obstacles to more widespread participation by women:

"Well women's employment didn't conduce itself to unionisation – they were in low paid jobs. I worked in the mills for thirteen years, and the men who worked in the mills practically all of them were in trade unions but they never made an approach to the women to join the trade union. I got quite a number of women organised. For some it was actually, although the weekly dues were only thruppence a week, it was a big consideration. Then others raised canards, there were three unions organising mill workers, some of them women . . . Mrs Dunbar's union, our own union, Flax and Other Textile Workers' Union and the Transport and General Workers' Union whereas there should have been only one union for all textile workers. Canards were raised about those who were trade union officials, the women had fur coats . . . it always tickled me because how any person taking on a job like that could get a fur coat if you were only paid thruppence a week. Then in areas where Catholics were only employed there was this lack of unity. There were people who were always against trade unions, employers frowned against it and if they could if they found anyone who was a member of a trade union they were usually paid off. There was great repression among the women and in that decade the unemployment was so terrific the women who were married, their husbands were out of work and they were afraid to do anything that would lose them their jobs. It was a very, very difficult period. The first break came when Short's aircraft factory opened up. It was the first opportunity of easing the unemployment situation. But the textile industry was going down and down. You were in and out of work signing on the bureau, getting a few bob a week or else you were working for very low wages. I always remember the highest wage I ever had was 8 shillings and 4 pence one week and I was charmed with myself. It was very, very badly paid and very hard work too, in all sections. . . ."

A few people pointed towards a certain difference between Catholic and Protestant attitudes towards trade unions but we were not able to confirm this. Lucy McErlane, who worked in Gallaher's, thought that Protestants were hostile to trade unions whereas Catholics supported them. When asked why this might be she responded, "Goodness knows. I think its only Catholics rebel against things, you know, and want to be in trade unions. But by degrees all went for it, they had to." Whatever the case may be it is probably true, as Dohrs concludes, that "the greatest single factor working against successful trade unionism in the linen industry is religious sectarianism".[15] Also, given the fact that the owners, directors and managers of the mills in Belfast were predominantly Protestant it is likely that "to agitate against them, Protestant workers [had to] overcome [their] religious affinity before any action [would] be taken".

Looking overall at trade union organisation in Belfast during the 1930s there were internal sources of division such as demarcation disputes which should be considered. For John Hyde:

"Taking it by and large the workers in the shipyard were strong trade unionists, always one strong body, always tightly knit."

Did this unity apply across the different trades?:

"Oh yes. There was always the demarcation problem, but my own union, the joiners' union, had a written demarcation agreement between them and the other wood-working trade, the shipwrights. This was negotiated about 1914 and the code within it was adhered to strictly and fairly. There might have been the odd time, but taking it by and large, these two particular trades had this agreement which worked. There was always the possibility of friction but we never at any time, to my memory, walked off a ship or struck over a dispute with the shipwrights or they with us. If it may have been, it was very short, an hour or two. We had two demarcation men elected by my union, and two elected by the shipwright's union – these four men met and discussed the problems and came to an agreement. The result was there was absolutely no trouble with the shipwrights – in the end there was the right for arbitration, and the arbitration decision was final. There was one union there worried a wee bit about the arbitrator, but taking it by and large the arbitrator was generally accepted."

Hyde went on to describe the rivalry which could develop between different sections of the shipyard workforce:

"My union was, in the old days, the Amalgamated Society of Woodworkers, and the majority of the members of my union worked in the building industry, but we were in every type of work you could mention, mills, factories, shipyards and aircraft, when they came into being. So basically we weren't considered a shipyard union. We were an old union, established long before there was any such thing as a plater or a corker or a welder. If we wanted to strike we had to get the sanction of our executive across the water to do that, we had no local power. But the others, they could have locally downed tools just like that. They had that right. The result was that their pay, their bonuses, not their basic rate, their bonuses, was rising above what we called the craft unions. We had platers coming in with battens to lift lines, they put on these long thin battens of wood, the lines that the joiners laid down in the loft off a plan. The joiner's skill was vastly superior in my opinion. There was basically more responsibility, more education, required for the training to become a corker, a driller or a welder but we found these platers coming in and they were actually earning pounds more. It didn't matter how the line went there, or why it went there, all they had to do was lift it on the batten. We were the ones, the joiner was the man, the loftsman was the man, and yet they were being paid pounds a week more. This was always a source of annoyance with our people. If we had pulled our people off, the plater could have stood there with his batten all day, and it wouldn't have made a ha'penny worth of difference. The work wouldn't have been done. But it never developed into this."

Though unionisation was uneven across the Belfast industries in the 1930s the unions were not that weak objectively. Tommy Patton says:

"Trade union support didn't mean anything because there were too many outside looking for a job. The trade unions hadn't got the power that was required at that particular time. There was trade union representation, but nine times out of ten the shop stewards were more likely looking after themselves than after the men they were representing. They weren't going to stick their neck out . . ."

Bobby Hurndall says that it was not an absolute weakness of trade union organization, but the context of Irish unemployment which was the most important element:

"There was good trade union organisation in those days, but it lacked the power that it ultimately had. It was when the workers were prepared to stand together and act as a body that the trade unions made headway. It was difficult in the early days because they were always so many unemployed, there were almost as many people outside the gate looking for a job as what there were inside. Even the nature of work in the shipyard then was of a casual nature. When I came out of my time I was working for a few months, then paid off."

Hurndall also points to the weakness of the shop-steward structure as a factor preventing militancy:

"You had shop-stewards but they were mainly concerned with demarcation disputes. Wage negotiations were really carried out by the full-time officials. We had just two yard delegates for the shipwrights who had to follow strictly rules, regulations and procedures. Lightning strikes were unknown in those days."

Tommy Cochrane, ex-shipwright and trade union official gives his views on Belfast trade unionism and its problems in the 1930s:

"The trade unions were weak. I'll tell you a story about that, about the shipyard. There was a big coal boat, what you call the deep water coal boat, big steel hatches on it. I worked on it with the second head boss, Joe Parker. There was thousands and thousands of feet of wood, nine-by-two-and-a-halfs, had to go on the tank tops and sides to protect the steel, thousands of feet, maybe fifty thousand feet, maybe more. Anyhow, it was a big job. And there was four of us down in what you call the after end of the ship, where the propellors are. We got the work sheet this Friday and I see the sheet and I says: 'They've only paid us fifteen shillings a hundred feet'. You see, it was 21 shillings it was supposed to be for this after hold because it was tapered, it wasn't straight. I went up and I said to the counter, 'You haven't paid us enough. That's 21 shillings'. We had a piece-work book, you see, which laid it down in black and white. The forward and after holes was 21 shillings, the rest was 15. It was quite clear, but he wouldn't pay us. I had to go up and see the delegate. Now, he came down and got it fixed up. They couldn't deny the books. That was through the week. We had to finish the job. We got the sack on Friday. We said, 'What are we getting the sack for? Sure there's plenty of work'. He says, 'Aw, you're getting the sack'. I went up and I says to the others, 'We're getting the sack for looking for a rise. What are you going to do about it?' Not a thing, damned all was done, and we got the sack. That was in the thirties. That's what happened in the shipyard then. There was no leadership. The delegate was as weak as water. I called him an old bastard and so he was. Nobody liked him. It was the easiest thing in the world to give a man the sack."

Tommy Cochrane's story sums up the "world of work" in the 1930s. It was hard to get a job and once in one people tended to "keep their heads down" as unemployment outside the factory or shipyard gates mounted. Workers in Belfast were relatively well organised in trade unions – in that sense they were not *objectively* weak. The sheer arrogance of Cochrane's bosses shows how well they had assessed the subjective weakness of "their" workers. That was caused partly because the workers' representatives were "weak as water"; fear of unemployment did the rest. Through all this, there were people like Tommy Cochrane who could feel angry enough to fight back.

John Hyde – A Shipyard Worker's Life

John Hyde's testimony of an "Islandman" tells of his apprenticeship days in the 1920s, through the decline of the yards in the 1930s to the revival on the eve of the Second World War. His life story tells us about craft pride, the changing labour process, the mystique of the "labour aristocrat" and of a latent sectarianism.

"I was born when Ireland was all one, when it belonged to Britain, and the '21 was real troublesome, but at that particular time it had been going for years; it all depended on what history you got at school and at home, or whether you like Hibernian music or what have you. I left school when I was twelve years old. That was the general age for leaving for boys in my day and I worked in the Baltic Timber and Cooperage, a firm on the Ravenhill Road that made barrels, coopers generally, timber, firewood of all kinds. A considerable number of the young lads on the road at that time obtained employment there. During that time I applied to serve my time in Harland and Wolff as a joiner. I got a letter from them to go down; I was fourteen years of age. It was the common procedure for craft apprentices when they went to the trades in Harland and Wolff that they went before the age of sixteen, and when I went down I was sent to what was known as the stationery department. I also worked in the filing office. I generally did messages and what have you throughout the shipyard and obtained a pretty good idea about the yard and the different shops and slipways because you delivered letters on to the ships that were being built on the slips at the time.

Then, with the time learning about the yard ended, I moved in to learn my trade as a joiner. I went into the yard in 1921 and I went to learn my trade in 1923, and at that time Harland and Wolff weren't the only shipyard there – Workman Clark's also did some considerable shipbuilding at the time. They had two yards: one was known as the Workman Clark's south yard and the other was the north yard. Their south yard, and some slipways, were on the Queen's Road as well as their engine works. It was at that time that the shipyard was going full steam. Taking both yards into consideration, there was anything between twenty-four and twenty-five thousand men employed generally.

The wages were good as the depression hadn't really started to be felt, but the signs were beginning to show, and the first sign was the reduction in the wages that had been built up during the '14-'18 war with war bonuses. These began to be taken off the men, and they had to accept this if they were to continue in employment.

I worked on in the shipyard until 1928, completed my time, and was now a fully-fledged shipyard joiner. The wages at that time, when I came out, was £2.17.4. and that was for a fifty-six hour week – ten past eight in the morning, half past five at night, and ten to twelve on Saturday. We had a dispute once in 1928 when they were proposing to reduce the wages by a further three shillings in the shipyard, and my union refused to accept this, and the result was that we went on strike. We weren't working in the shipyard for nine months. At that time Harland's were not members of the Confederation of Shipbuilding and Engineering Employers, but after the joiners' strike they joined the rest of the British shipbuilders in their organisation. I don't know if this was of benefit to the shipyard workers in Harland's or not, because we did at least have negotiations with the firm locally, but now we found ourselves having to deal with a situation at a national level. In other words, wages and conditions were more or less discussed or negotiated on the other side of the water with all British shipyards representatives in attendance.

Following our return to work the clouds that had begun to show throughout the world really closed over the top of the Belfast shipyard. It started about 1930 and for at least four years from then there was no work in Harland's or Workman Clark's. It wasn't till 1934 or '35 that some orders were obtained, and three vessels were ordered for the Blue Star line, a refrigerated company that carried foodstuffs from Australia to Britain. These provided handsome work for us for each of these ships took an average of about 230-240 of our particular trade. Then the Northern Ireland government of the day advanced a loan to the Union Castle line, something in the region of seven million.

Of course we asked for the ships that were to be built with this loan to be confined to Belfast, which was one of the most hard-hit areas. They felt the depression right across Belfast because of the spin-offs which the shipyard provided for small work in the different engineering firms and different suppliers. This work continued and the work had, to a certain extent, brightened up.

The advent of 1939 in Europe, with the threat of war looming up under Hitler forced the British government to order more ships. We got the cruiser *Belfast,* which provided a considerable amount of work for the engineering men, and by the way, Harland's engine works had the reputation of being the finest works and having the turnout of the finest engines that was possible. They made engines for ships that were being built across in Britain and even foreign ships, where they built the hulls and the engines were made and supplied by Harland's of Belfast – always on time. They had a great reputation. The war arrived on the scene and there was no question of unemployment. But the good days were ending then. In shipbuilding generally things were changing – a terrible lot of the requirements, craft requirements, that used to be needed in the old days, pre-war, were no longer required.

As far as I would be concerned the shipyard was rough, it was tough, but they were a type of people in the shipyard that you met and they were a type of humour that you met that I have never met anywhere else. There was always the joke, even when things were rough, even during the thirties when I have seen two to three hundred joiners standing outside the back gate of the joiner's shop, waiting on the hopes of getting a job and only twenty men were required. Some of those men, at the end of the day stayed around the shipyard hoping to see someone that they knew could possibly say the word for them and get them a job or at least give them some hope of a job, yet the jokes were still there. They had to joke, what else could they do? There were jokes about managers, about what happened in the shipyard. They played different tricks on different people. I'm sure there were some of them heard the jokes about themselves and laughed at them. There was 'Can o'Muck', 'Paris Bun', 'Oily Waste' or 'Oily Rag', there was 'Air Raid', the 'Bomber', each had a different name. And these men were recognised by these names.

It was rough work, crippling work, in the shipyard and yet we have seen those men coming out after a very hard day's work, going home, and coming back the next morning and complaining about how long it took them to get home. They'd have fell in with somebody and gone in for a drink, and fell in with somebody else, and the talk went on and the drink went on, and they weren't home to all hours, and then there was a row when they went home, so they had to discuss it the next day, and some of them weren't in too good a form.

It was a breed on their own: you served your time in the shipyard and you were a shipyard man, and although we had men come in who had served their time outside, in the building trade and other work – joinery work I'm speaking of now – they made splendid joiners, they made splendid shipyard men. The shipyard was a way of life, and you didn't want out of it. Very few looked elsewhere. You had your stories and your laugh, and you've had you hard times too, but then everybody seems to be able to remember their hard times and you can treat even some of the hard times as a joke. It was a hard life, and the money wasn't great."

You said that the shipyard men were rough and tough. Well, we were talking to a woman who worked in a mill, and she said that you got out of the way when the shipyard men were going to or coming from work as they'd knock you down. Did they think the road belonged to them as she suggested?

"But so it did, as far as I was concerned. I seen the points man at Station Street having to watch for his bare life as they came out, charging out on bicycles, motor cars, tram cars, a solid mob and him in the middle. Nothing to it; hanging on the backs of trams, climbing up the backs of trams to get up on the roof. You would have seen a driver driving an old tram down the road and them all crowded around him, half of them paid, half of them didn't. Then religion arrived on the scene; the Reverend Nicholson came, and they marched across the road, thousands of them, and they knocked the pillars of the church down, they were all getting religion. He came from America, an evangelist or something. They marched up that road and the centre pillar was pushed off its base from wanting to get in."

You were unemployed for a while during the thirties. Did the shipyard men resent not being able to do the job they knew they were capable of because of unemployment?

"But there wasn't any work. Everybody was out, all the joiners were out, there was a very little building work going on. There was a depression, it was the day of the soup kitchen and the Poor Law Board of Guardians. There was a time when we blamed those that were running the country; we blamed Stormont and the Board of Guardians, we blame the unemployment panel sitting in Corporation Street. We blamed all these, but afterwards when you thought about it, if you really wanted to understand the thing and read about it, then you also had to read about the Jarrow marches, the conditions in Scotland, England, Wales, and to know there were riots in America. But then, who was wanting to look? It happened in this house and thousands others. They weren't worried what was happening in the South of Ireland, or in Canada or in England; they were worrying about what was happening here and in particular in their own home, and in this they didn't want to think that the people at the top here were to blame. It was only afterwards for anyone who gave any considerable thought to the thing and tried to separate those politicians who were telling you one thing because they wanted in and wanted you to vote for them, and you had to actually separate the truth from the half-lies. It was financiers, it was the people who decide when money would be invested, they can cause this, and they don't belong to any country, they are based in their own wee circle. They decided to hold on to the money. But this might cause unemployment and misery throughout an awful lot of the world, but when all is said and done, these are the people who decide what way it goes; this is money, and if it's not invested the shipyard folds."

When you said that the people blamed the government and the Poor Law Guardians in the 1930s, they wouldn't ever have voted against them, would they?

"Well, maybe a different problem might be introduced that would take men's minds away from their own particular problem. It could be anything; there would be some peeler shot, this could happen. Or there could be some raid up the country, or a riot somewhere, a small riot say at a football match – it didn't matter, it could spread, and then attitudes could change. It could change. It could be mob thinking, but afterwards even within the mob, cooler heads, it would die down and then they would wonder why, but it could happen again the following year."

What did you think of the 1932 Outdoor Relief strike?

"Well, it was something that was being forced, things were getting worse, there was no doubt about it. You can't starve people, well you can for a while, but you can starve some of the people some of the time, but then don't starve them all of the time. If they seen nothing in the future for them, then there's only one way, break out, this is your reaction to it. Nobody seems to have an answer to it, so here's an answer – somebody has called a meeting, a group of men has called a meeting and, I wouldn't place my finger on it, to tell you the truth, I couldn't tell you; you viewed it with a certain amount of suspicion, all types of politicians, even trade union leaders, this is so, we understand that."

Are you saying you were suspicious of the motives of the unemployed workers' movement?

"Well, the motives might have started out all right but then got lost. The men that produced the motive weren't all living together, they weren't all moving about together and they all split up, each to his own particular side and all that was necessary was to say that the money collected and the bread that was bought, it all went only into one section."

FOOTNOTES

1. Messenger, B. 1980:xviii
2. Ibid: xix
3. Coe, W. 1969:91

4. Ibid: 93
5. Messenger, B. 1980:23
6. See "Cyclical Variations in the Linen Industry", in Isles, K. S.; Cuthbert, N. 1957
7. Davis, M. 1975: 17
8. Ibid.
9. Armstrong, D.C. 1951:245
10. Isles, K. S.; Cuthbert, N. 1957:361
11. Clarkson, J. D. 1925:372 and 382
12. Davis, M. 1975:17
13. Jefferson, H. 1947:205
14. Boyle, E. 1982:54
15. Dohrs, F. 1952:146

4. Socialists and Communists

At the first Northern Ireland elections in 1921 no Labour candidates were elected although the party had won one-fifth of the seats on the Belfast Corporation the previous year. In the 1925 Stormont elections three Labour candidates were returned: Jack Beattie, a Protestant shipyard worker, for East Belfast; William McMullen, another Protestant shipyard worker, for West Belfast; and Sam Kyle, a Protestant trade union official, for North Belfast. They were all fiercely anti-partitionist in outlook, but this outlook waned when the last two moved to Dublin in the 1930s to become the leading figures in the ITGWU and the ATGWU respectively. In the 1929 elections to Stormont (after proportional representation had been ended) only one Labour MP – Jack Beattie – was elected. With the 1933 elections he was joined by Harry Midgley, a Protestant joiner and trade union official who was elected for Belfast Dock ward. In 1938, as Jack McGougan recalls:

> "There was an attempt to throw up candidates under the Labour ticket, and I was a Socialist Party nominee, but stood as a Labour candidate in Oldpark. The Nationalists were boycotting Stormont, and the Labour Party thought it could sneak in; in South Down Nationalists put a candidate in and the Labour candidate lost his deposit; Tommy Boyd fought in Victoria; Jack Beattie held Pottinger, but at that time was out of the Labour Party – he was in and out like a Jack-in-the-box, very much the lone ranger was Jack – and Harry Midgley lost Dock. He blamed the Spanish Civil War on it – some of us blamed the lack of support for his constituents during the pogrom of 1935, the riots down in York Street."

Midgley went on to become a member of the Orange Order and Minister of Public Security amongst other things in 1943.[1]

Overall it is safe to say that Labour did not command a stable, sizeable vote in Belfast. In many ways the labour movement was still torn by the Connolly-Walker controversy of 1911. William Walker, leader of the Belfast branch of the Independent Labour Party, counterposed a "gas and water" socialism to Connolly's republican socialism. When the Northern Ireland

Labour Party was formed in 1924, based on the trade unions, it attempted to somehow remain "neutral" on the constitutional question, although many of its members were firmly against partition. By the mid-1930s Midgley had become the undisputed maker of party policy, however, because Beattie had been expelled from the party when he refused to move the election writ on the death of the Nationalist MP Joe Devlin. The result was that the party swung firmly into an anti-nationalist position on the one hand, and rejected its earlier concern with unemployment in favour of more staid parliamentary questions.

Obstacles to organising

There were immense obstacles for the development of a socialist movement in Belfast during the 1930s. The ideologies of unionism and nationalism held sway over the bulk of the population. The employers and the state were sophisticated operators with regards to exploiting these divisions. Those in power were also ruthless in their exercise of that power. There was as always the fear that a radical confrontation with the régime could lead to a loss of job, house, and even one's life. Tom Boyd describes an election campaign which the labour movement contested:

> "In 1933, the Trades Council had maybe a dozen candidates, and this of course brought out the reaction from the Unionist Party; the old party cries were brought out. If you were looking for an increase in the outdoor relief, according to the unionists you were almost a republican and wanted to overthrow the state – this is the feeling that was created, a resurrection of the old party divisions . . . The election was fought on a restricted register; in the main only householders were entitled to vote. I do remember at that time we hadn't any microphones or loudspeakers or lorries; the procedure in those days was to go into a street and knock on a door and ask for the loan of a chair, and at times you would hope that you wouldn't get a chair at the first house because if you had to go to a dozen houses to get a chair then everyone was curious as to why you wanted the chair, and you started the meeting out in the middle of the street. I wouldn't say there was a great deal of physical hostility during the election but there was just a great deal of indifference, and of course there's always a great deal of fear among people, fear of authority, fear of being pinpointed perhaps as something of an opponent of the established order, and the usual things happens for men and women, to keep their heads down and not be noticed as people who are against the so-called establishment; there's the fear too that prevents people from expressing their opinions and their feelings."

Later, after 1936, there was the growing problem of fascists (and, of course, the Ulster Protestant League) in Belfast. Fred McMahon tells us how:

> "They would wreck a meeting and start rows in it – Labour meetings, propaganda meetings. I remember one meeting they draped a Union Jack over the balcony – rather provocative to people who were actively involved with the Labour movement, and most of them with leanings towards a united Ireland. The favourite ploy in them days when you were a young socialist was that you wouldn't stand for the King. You'd do it now of course, stand for any national anthem, but that was the done thing then. They behaved like hooligans, always have and they always will. There weren't many of them, but like the communists they'd a lot of influence. They'd a very close-knit band of activists and courageous, they weren't nancy-boys by any means. They were prepared to chuck their weight about. There were some in the Labour movement were prepared to chuck their weight about at that time too. On one occasion we were having a meeting down at the Ulster Hall and Job Stott, he was a fascist involved with the Ulster Blackshirts, had organised a crowd to wreck the meeting and Hugh Gemmell organised a crowd to defend it."

In the Protestant areas of the city the Unionist establishment made it difficult for Labour to organise. William Patterson spoke of how: "In the early days if you had've said you were a Labour man they would have done you up . . ."

His friend Alec Salmon adds:

> "In the early days my father, I wouldn't say he was a great Unionist but he was an Orangeman, he had the lodge and the two big drums in the house of ours. When it was coming to an election there was a big field in Templemore Avenue not all that far from our house, and when a Labour man would come to have his meeting them drums came round from our house, and they'd take out the wee window in the kitchen to get the drums out and go round beside the Labour man and nobody could hear him because they drummed the whole time until the Labour man went away; he never got staying. That was in the twenties and the thirties."

Fred McMahon remembers this type of incident from the other side of the fence:

> "The meeting was to be held in Templemore Avenue with banners like 'Give us bread or we'll turn red' and a bit of singing and that sort of thing. Then, just between Bridge End and Templemore Avenue the lambeg drummers came out – by arrangement they came the other way. The police at that period were certainly not pro-working class, they were anything but, and the police charged

the marchers. I think the march might have been proclaimed illegal. A riot ensued and the Lambeg drummers were well protected, and many a sore head was felt by the marchers and their supporters."

It is not surprising in this type of sectarian atmosphere that workers would support the patently conservative Unionists. William Patterson recalls one incident which is revealing:

"There were a couple of officials of the boilermakers went to the Midland Hotel and asked Sir Edward Harland, they actually asked Sir Edward Harland to represent East Belfast in the election; two officials of the boilermakers did that. Sir Edward Harland went up for East Belfast and won it and represented East Belfast. In your opinion who would he be representing, Harland and Wolff or the workers?"

He answers himself:

"In my view, any man that worked the way we worked there has something wrong with them if they didn't vote Labour. These people had their brain washed. I heard a woman saying when there was a house there and they were going to go for Labour, that they broke the windows in. They couldn't get a house for the Labour man as his base so he had to get a wee cart, and they wrecked it . . . I mind them coming round in a wee horse and cart and I've never forgot this man asking them a question and none of them could answer, and he told them, 'Do you know what I think, I think the horse is the most intelligent one among you' and he was right."

For Tommy Cochrane, a shipwright and later a trade union official, this is explained because of the basic conservatism of the "island man":

"Of course, our union was conservative. There's not a more conservative union and maybe still is, in many respects. People should know the shipyard people was brought up in the environment of Unionism. They were good trade unionists, but they couldn't see that Unionism, as they were taught it, was opposite to their views as trade unionists."

Cochrane told us that Billy Grant was the president of his union for thirty-two years. Though a founder member of the Ulster Unionist Labour Association, Grant was actively involved in the 1919 engineering strike in Belfast. This one-time shipyard worker was an Orange Order member and a Unionist MP from 1921 to 1949 – during which time he often voted against the government on social and economic issues. William Patterson and Alec Salmon both recall Billy Grant:

"Oh, the boss shipwright . . . I don't think he did very much work . . . He was in the Ulster Unionist Labour Association . . . But the UULA was just the Unionist Party. I never knew any group in the shipyard belonging to any of the parties although all of the men voted Unionist I would say, nearly all the men were Unionist, but there was never any organising in the shipyard. Although he was an MP and a member of the government he never brought it to the shipyard. He got it through working in the Unionist Party, it wasn't the shipyard men that put him there . . . he wasn't a representative of the shipyard."

The Nationalists were also an employers' party, as Harry Diamond explains:

"All the time opinions were changing, as between the old Nationalist Party . . . Younger people were getting away from the older movement's ideas and the labour and republican vote was growing and challenging the Nationalist Party which had mainly fallen under the control of the vintners' organisation . . . They [the publicans] were the principal people with substance or money in the Catholic community and that was how it came about. They were called all sorts of things. They were called the Cumann na Bung Party."

To a large extent Catholic votes for Labour were simply anti-Unionist votes because, as Fred McMahon explains:

"In Belfast religion has a bearing on nearly everything political. In the old days I never regarded our vote as a socialist vote, it was an anti-Unionist vote, and no matter who you had put up they wouldn't have voted Unionist, they'd have voted for the anti-Unionist party. The Labour Party was the best party for the working class, and still is naturally, but there were an awful lot of contradictions in it."

For Tommy Cochrane, the basic conflict was between Ulster unionism and trade unionism:

"Oh, there's a clash all right. The Labour Party, you see, in the trade union movement, the people that are supposed to be the officials and all that, they're Unionists . . . I can't after years of trying to work it out, couldn't see, as I told a chairman of my branch for years and years, a fellow called McClure – he was a great trade unionist, but he was an awful good Linfield man, an awful good Unionist. It's hard to reconcile, but whether you like it or not it's there. It was in me to be the same, I don't know how I changed, it was just circumstances."

Militants

In spite of all the obstacles a labour movement existed in Belfast with a handful of people keeping the working-class traditions alive. Bobby

Hurndall remembers one of these:

"A boilermaker called Samuel Brown who had been introduced as the best read man in Ireland. He used to give lectures on Robbie Burns, he gave me endless quotations from William Morris and various poets. He used to bring in the old ILP paper, the Glasgow *Forward*. I don't know if he was a member of any organisation but he was certainly a socialist. He told me that although the shipyard was full of ships, Harland and Wolff's was going down the hill and there was nothing but disaster facing them. I could see no evidence for that but as the ships were launched one by one the slipways were allowed to lie idle, his predictions came true. He himself was also paid off."

Frank Hughes tells of another activist:

"I remember there was a man from the Falls Road and he eventually became one of the Poor Law Guardians, Phil Wilson. Phil Wilson was a man who worked at the same trade as I did, he was a flax dresser or hackler and he worked in Linsdsay and Thompson's on the Crumlin Road, with me. And I always remember him, every Tuesday morning, taking off his apron and folding it nicely and brushing down his clothes to go down to meetings of the Poor Law Guardians, which started at eleven o'clock. Poor Phil, he was trying to do his best but he was trying on very difficult circumstances. In fact, I would go as far as to say he was battering his head against a brick wall because the people who were Poor Law Guardians in those days, they thought that those who weren't working didn't want to work. Not only did they think they didn't want work but they thought they were the scum of the earth. So therefore how can you get money off people whose thinking was in that particular vein? So I always had great sympathy for Phil Wilson. He was an uneducated man, he tried to do his best against these people who were pushed in by the establishment and the establishment's job was always well and truly done."

Wilson went on to become a member of the RWG and in 1930 ran as a representative of the Unemployment Movement in the Markets.

But there is one man we spoke to who is better placed than most to talk of the personalities and activities of the twenties, John McWade. His story is not only his own, but that of many activists, some of whom have been completely forgotten about by most people who look back on these pioneers of Belfast working-class struggle.

"We got together, about half a dozen of us; there was me, Phil Wilson, Jack O'Hagan, John O'Mara and Selma Sigerson, and a fellow from the Shankill area called Pennycook, a joiner. We then and there formed the Irish Revolutionary Socialist Party. We used to have meetings in a little place up off Rosemary Street. It got to be that Jack O'Hagan and Charlie (sic) O'Mara used it as a bloody debating society between the two of them. None of the rest of us got a word in edgeways, and there was no way we were trying to organise anything.

But that then led us to another fellow, Gaffikin, a shoemaker. And a few more of us got together and went to a little room in Hastings Street and formed a branch of the Labour Party. We had to get into something, and we all said to each other: 'We're selling our birth-right for a mess of pottage, but we have to do something.' We formed the West Belfast division of the party, and we had a room from the Hibs [AOH] on King Street. We attracted people like Hughie Gemmell, who was a black pudding maker over on the Newtownards Road. Hughie was a Scotsman who ran away from Glasgow at the time they were trying to conscript them. And Billy McMullen came along. Sam Hazlett came too. And Jimmy Grimley. We drifted up the Falls Road and got a room above the Clock Bar. Then we began to hold open meetings. We went down now and again to Corporation Square where the North Belfast Independent Labour Party had a branch. We had speakers there. Harry Midgley was one. Another was Slumdom Jack, Jack MacMurray; he was deaf as a bloody post, but he could read out John Stuart Mill like no man's business.

Things got very bad in Belfast. Before we started the Unemployed Movement there was no such thing as outdoor relief granted by the Belfast Poor Law Board. The Unemployed Workers' Movement wasn't started until about 1925/6; that was after the main unemployment movement started, our own movement that had the first march in 1924. I think it was 24 March 1924 but I can't give you the exact date. We went up to the workhouse and I passed a note in. An arrogant note, but it was how we felt: 'We your masters demand that you our servants receive us in deputation. Answer yea or nay'. We got no answer. Apart from myself Phil Wilson was involved, and the only trade union official who turned up to do anything for us was Jack Milan of the ETU. Paddy O'Connor from North Queen Street was with us, and Paddy Devine from off Leeson Street, George McBride, Winnie Carney. We organised and kept organising. We got the use of the Gaiety Theatre in North Street, the Alhambra in North Street, a picture house in York Street run by a sympathiser of ours called Gerry Loughrey, and a couple of cinemas on the Newtownards Road, and the Clonard on the Falls Road – we got it free and we were so successful that we even got nationalist councillors getting up and talking. One fellow said in the Alhambra, Matt

McCloskey, I think it was, a chemist: 'If demanding bread for the poor and justice for the people is communist, then I'm one too'. A bloody nationalist!

We went to work politically then and we had these four elected to the Poor Law Guardians – Billy McMullen, Jack Beattie, Phil Wilson and a fellow called Jimmy Mackin, who seems to have disappeared from everything a couple of months after he was elected. Then we got Billy McMullen and Jack Beattie elected to the Council. Then Billy and Jack got elected to Stormont (*sic*) and Sam Kyle and Harry Midgley, when the parliament used to meet at the Presbyterian College.

I remember we were organising a march on the parliament on 5 October 1925. I won't forget that because Dawson Bates banned it. The crowd gathered round at the back of the City Hall, in Linenhall Street. I got up and advised them to go home. I told them: 'The Cossacks of the RUC are around the corner with batons drawn ready to beat you down. You've suffered enough without waiting for that'.

Things went on from that. We had meetings all over the city, Labour Party meetings mostly, and unemployed meetings. And in the West Belfast Labour Party we formed a pipe band, if you please! It was the first time I remember a pipe band playing the 'Red Flag'. They were dressed in red kilts and a dull saffron shawl.

When the Unemployed Workers' Association was formed, the two leading members were two fellows from the Shankill, George and Sammy McVicker, two brothers. And there was Betty Sinclair, and Billy McMullen and Jack Beattie. We had very little relation with the trade union movement. Their attitude to the unemployed was: 'We'll use you'. We had Sam Geddis and Bob Getgood and Sam Hazlett and Dawson Gordon – all that crowd. They used our platform for propaganda, but as far as participating in the Unemployed Movement – no, they gave us no assistance whatsoever.

I wasn't active in 1932. By then I had a job that carried me all over the thirty two counties. I watched how things were going in Belfast between 1932 and 1936, and I found they weren't to my liking at all. I reckon I did my bit during that period when it needed to be done."

By the 1930s the labour movement had become firmly established. Tom Boyd recalls the lack of resources which still plagued the movement but also its commitment to an improvement of social conditions:

"Now, the Belfast Trades and Labour Council at that time, was styled a labour council so it operated politically at times but afterwards they changed the organisation to what was purely a trade union-type of operation. They decided to contest the Poor Law election of 1933 and candidates were selected, of whom I was one. My trade union put up the magnificent sum of ten pounds towards election expenses, and the AEU, the engineering union, they put up ten pounds for a much older man called Hanna, whose christian name I have forgotten, and we contested this Victoria ward in which I am now sitting. We had no election address as we could not afford that, but we had a hand-bill which had been produced by the Trades and Labour Council advocating schemes of public works such as the improvement of a local river, the Connswater; the scheme hasn't been completed as yet but we couldn't get any movement then."

A number of women were involved in the labour movement in spite of the traditional culture of the times. Jack McGougan recalls: "There was one woman by the time I came along, an elderly woman who had a great sharp brain, a Mrs Margaret McCoubrey – she represented Dock ward on the Corporation I think for a very short period."

He adds:

"You must remember that eighteen-year-olds, as well as being socialists, were interested in such things as chasing lassies and so forth . . . there were quite a number of girls attracted into this, I suppose it was the presence of a large number of youngish fellows that brought a number of girls in as well. . . . "

Tom Boyd argues in a more serious vein that the under-representation of women in the labour movement:

"reflects the traditional attitude that has persisted for centuries. There were only a few women who were prominent politically and played a part within the labour movement. There was one woman, a Mrs McCoubrey, she was quite active in the ILP and in the Socialist Party and in the co-operative movement, and its true to say that women were behind the Belfast Co-operative Society and took a leading part in the organisation of those societies elsewhere. I also recall a very effective speaker, the wife of a trade union official, a Mrs Ida Boyd, and she supported me a lot in the 1938 Northern Ireland election when I fought a seat against Sir Dawson Bates. There were one or two but its true to say they were exceptions. The traditional role of women in the home seemed to have been very strong during that period as it was previously, and its only since I suppose the war period, and the paradox is I think, that the war liberated women in many ways because they became involved in the services and even in the auxilliary services that were required arising out of the war situation."

Nationalism

So far we have dealt with general problems faced by most labour movements. In the north of Ireland there was also of course the “national question” and the contradiction between those in its ranks who supported Ulster unionism and those who backed the cause of Irish nationalism, and the nuances in between. Harry Diamond had a hostile attitude towards the official Labour party:

> “I fought Willie McMullen in the Poor Law elections and defeated him. What I resented was, he was coming along and he was trading on James Connolly and Wolfe Tone, and that was becoming a habit with Protestant labour men. They couldn’t get elected in their own districts. They were coming up the Falls Road and our people were so funny that way, so tolerant and broad-minded, that they supported them. But he was fighting for the Northern Ireland Labour Party and I was always opposed to them because I reckoned them to be the poor man’s Unionist party.”

The NILP may well have been “the poor man’s Unionist party” but it did not usually go around dressed in Connolly’s colours. William Patterson recalls Harry Midgley, who later set up the Commonwealth Labour Party in 1942, as follows:

> “He used to come round with a Union Jack and he’d sing ‘Land of Hope and Glory’ and he beat them in their own ward here and they made him Minister of Labour and away, Bob’s your uncle. . . .”

Alec Salmon then added:

> “I don’t think there’s much difference between the labour man and the unionist. . . . There’s been no communist to vote for here; a labour or a unionist is no use to me.”

Others had an equally sceptical view of politicians. Alice Quinn recalls:

> “Old Harry Midgley, you’ll never see an old twister like that. He was a real raver. It was more for the outing; when Harry would have been there, we would have charged along York Street and all went up to where the Newsboys [the Newsboys Club] were and we’d sing at the top of our voice ‘Keep the red flag flying here’. Then the first thing was Harry got a job with the Ministry of Education or something, the unionists. You didn’t care – it was just an outing for you since you’d no money for the pictures.”

Leo Boyle appreciated non-sectarian politicians but was scathing about Harry Midgley:

> “Joe Devlin and Tommy Henderson were very good to the poor. One was a Protestant and one was a Catholic. Both of them could

have swapped their districts. One could have gone up the Shankill and the other could have gone up the Falls, changed positions and they still would have been elected. Dock Ward made Harry Midgley, but he was a traitor to the cause. He finished up a unionist, chairman of Linfield and lived private in Bangor."

Even the more radical socialists within the labour movement were split over their attitudes towards the nationalist/unionist question. We have already heard Fred McMahon say that "most of them [had] leanings towards a united Ireland". He added that most had republican tendencies – "How could you not have?" Harold Binks, who became a trade union official, said, "In the 1930s the IRA was on the side of the workers. I knew a trade union official who lived in West Belfast who took some kind of sectarian attitude and he was warned, threatened that he would be shot if he did it again." McMahon believed that amongst republicans "there was of course a social ideology. It would be left wing if anything, but recognising the necessity of trade unions even more so than today. It couldn't be anything else; most of the republican ranks were from the working class." Jack McGougan summed up this positive appraisal when he said, "I look upon republicanism and socialism as two joint aims". This did not stop him from saying that they looked upon the IRA as sectarian:

"They were very much Falls Road oriented. We never really had any alignment with them whatsoever. Around the late thirties we had alignments with people that had been formerly IRA and had drifted towards a socialist standpoint. That could be represented by Peadar O'Donnell's group, people up here like Sean Mulvenna who tended to be somewhat oriented towards the Communist Party; we had various associations with them. . . . "

Other socialists were even more critical of republicanism. When Tom Boyd was asked if he had any contact with republicans during the ODR campaign he replied:

"None whatever. All these operations were discussed openly at the Trades and Labour Council and it was planned in that way. There was no attempt made to co-operate with extremists of any kind that I am aware of; quite clearly people were so concerned at alleviating their own poverty and the poverty of others among their neighbours and friends that they forgot about and ignored these so-called constitutional issues."

As far as he was concerned:

"I belonged to a union in which we had a number of Catholic people and they held office in the trade unions along with other people who were extreme unionists and they all worked together happily for the common objective. . . . "

Frank Hughes when asked for his attitude replied:

"I naturally was against the whole republican movement. My

contention was that we could better serve the people – number one, if they all became trade unionists and number two, if we had men being trained to look after the people generally and that is, I'm talking about MP's. Now this was the tack that I certainly would have followed in those days. I feel that you got rabble rousers like . . . I was plagued by people who hadn't a clue about what they wanted to do – all they wanted to do was to kill the establishment. Now, the establishment was rotten but at the same time, you can't make progress if you're fighting the establishment on the one hand and trying to feed the people on the other hand. You can't have it both ways. You've either to cure the establishment of the ills that you see . . . it was capable of curing."

He was aware of sectarianism:

"You had this bitterness, you had the Protestant population as it is today, who hated the guts of the Catholics and you had the Catholic population, who hated the guts of the Protestants. Now this is not a likeable spectacle, in any country, no matter where it is. These are the things that I was very much against, I was against bigotry and bigotry was personified, here in Belfast, particularly against the Catholics."

His attitude was to change the sectarian situation from within the system.

Reformism

The labour movement in NI was thus not only torn apart by the national question – it could be accused of being simply a reformist rather than a revolutionary party. Tommy Cochrane:

"I was in the Labour party for years up the Shankill, West Belfast Labour Party. They used to sit at Downing Street, above where the amateur band played. July came round and we were trying to get people from the Falls to come down to our meeting and to go up to theirs, to try and mix. I knew what they were then. They weren't socialists. They were half-boiled Tories. That's why I left it."

Fred McMahon was equally sceptical about the trade union side:

"There were some, the activists, naturally on the side of the workers, and the majority didn't give a damn just, as long as they'd a smug job and they were working. . . . The trade union leaders at that period, still are as a matter of fact, they were on a hell of a good wicket. They'd a far higher standard of living than the average worker. They were upper-middle-class smug citizens. There were some very good men, but most were what we call reactionaries. . . . In the trade unions, you get to the top by virtue of left-wing attitudes in the movement, on their feet shouting, active, then when they become leaders they're forced into leading a different sort of life: they've more money, and they've moved to a different locality. It's prosperous to come on through the movement to that stage. . . . In 1932 I'd say there were definitely a lot of them in the Socialist Party but as it became less profitable they left."

This sceptical outlook was reflected in the attitude of many socialists towards the ODR strike. For Frank Hughes:

"The whole thing was motivated by a few individuals who were trying to get a forum set up for themselves. I thought they were all a lot of fools. I thought that the struggle could be far better serviced if it was in the homes, in the workshops and with the people – all without having to recourse to going on the streets, I never was in favour of that."

Jack McGougan thought people viewed the ODR strike through rose-tinted spectacles. As far as he was concerned:

"The Irish Unemployed Workers Movement was, of course, a front of the Communist party, and as such a lot of people on the socialist side kept out of it and stayed on the sidelines. There was no real support amongst organised workers, trade unions and what have you, for the ODR people. The main objective if you were in a job, myself included, was to stay in it, because of the consequences of losing your job. I lost mine in 1938 and I didn't get a job until the war broke out, because I was very well labelled as a street corner soap-boxer and so on, and when I tried to start a union in 1937 for accountancy staff, it got me the sack."

The official labour attitude towards the outdoor relief issue, and one which was supported by most of the trade union leaders, was that it would be best to wait until the 1933 Board of Guardian elections to vote in a Labour majority. Right up to the beginning of fighting in the streets of Belfast, Harry Midgley as leader of the NILP was putting forward this position, which did not even call for an abolition of the means test but merely asked that it be administered more "humanely".

Fred McMahon remembers the ODR strike but:

"just as a looker-on. I went to the communist meetings at the Custom House steps, and I'll always remember Jack Beattie appeared there, and the commies used to say, 'Where are the leaders of the Labour Party tonight?', always upbraiding them for their absence, their non-participation. But Jack Beattie spoke from the Custom House steps."

In fact the hostility towards the communists did decline somewhat during the ODR strike as Tom Boyd recalls:

"In 1932, 1933 it's true to say that these divisions broke down. There was one, I think his name was Geehan, who was a member of the Communist Party and he fought a very effective fight in the Shankill area in that Poor Law election. There was a kind of unsigned agreement not to conflict too much with anyone who was against the terrible suffering that the people had to endure."

Tommy Boyd, who was a brother of RWG member William Boyd, recalls one incident which showed him the reformism of the socialists:

"One night in 1932 there was a meeting called in the ILP hall at the corner of Frederick Street. They got the choice, would they take the people out on the streets, along with the people that I was with, or not. It came to this point – them that wants to stay to go to the other side of the room, and the Labour Party walked away to the other side, they didn't want nothing to do with it. . . ."

The lack of interest in the ODR strike by the socialists was quite remarkable. John Lowry, when asked if the Socialist Party took any effective action or saw it as a chance to further socialist principles, replied:

"No, I can't recollect anything like that. It was an economic struggle, it was largely run by the strike committee and it seemed to me at that time that the leading figures in the agitation were Geehan and his friends. They were, of course, not in the Socialist Party. But, on the other hand, in the parliamentary field, you had the various few Labour people, who were elected at that time, did their best through parliamentary representation and Jack Beattie did address those meetings on the Customs House steps."

Perhaps surprisingly in this context Boyd (and the RWG?) had a favourable view of Jack Beattie: "We'd a great respect for Jack, my father and all that knew him, a very straight fellow". Even of Harry Midgley he said:

"He was a great labour man, I was reared not far from him, well he swung over to the Unionist Party, he was the Minister for Education then [1952]. He done more good then than when he was in the Labour Party. A whole lot didn't know that but Billy McMullen and me and the brother knew this, he done a good job that he couldn't have done in the Labour Party. He was still with the poor people, he wasn't a conservative, but that was Harry Midgley's form."

Of course reformism, as always, works to the extent that reforms can be granted and in NI it was only the Unionist side which was in a position to grant reforms and make improvements simply because it controlled the government.

Socialist activities

How then did socialists organise in Belfast during the 1930s and what activities did they engage in? John Lowry tells how he was attracted to the socialist movement:

"I was only sixteen at the time, but I remember seeing an advertisement in the press that Mr J.T. Dorricott was going to give a lecture in the Labour Hall at 48 York Street. And that was some time in 1932, I went along to that meeting. I found out that the premises in 48 York Street were occupied by the Northern Ireland Socialist Party. I also found out that this was a merger of former members of various branches of the Independent Labour Party, which had existed in Belfast since before the First World War. Now, in 1932, the Independent Labour Party, which up to that time had been a constituent party of the British Labour Party, dissaffiliated from the British Labour Party. Leading figures in the ILP, who were amongst the Clydeside brigade, James Maxton, and Kirkwood and people like that and also Brockway, who is still alive. So really, the ILP movement disappeared in Belfast and a new organisation was founded. So I went to various meetings in the Labour Hall. They had meetings every Sunday night. Incidentally, Jack Dorricott, who gave a lot of lectures on general affairs, was the Northern Ireland organiser of the National Council of Labour Colleges. This was very much a Marxist organisation – but its function was to provide educational classes for trade unionists. The Socialist Party was composed of members of these former organisations, the ILP branches and also people who attended meetings, many of them were from various trade unions, Amalgamated Transport and General Workers Union, Woodworkers, the AEU, that is the Amalgamated Engineering Union, and so on. Some of these meetings were quite well attended and some not so good. Speakers were brought across from England and indeed from Scotland as well – but as time went on attendances seemed to be getting smaller and it indicated that there wasn't that degree of working-class consciousness or any great desire for social change in Northern Ireland."

Jack McGougan speaks of the relative prosperity of the socialists and their youth:

"In 1935 I was in the Socialist Party and most of the people in the party were not on the very lowest rung of poverty. Some were indeed still working, though mostly in poorish jobs. We had a young membership and closely knit – climbing, rambling and so on. We used to go to youth hostels, they started here about 1933 and we were in it from the beginning and used it quite extensively, groups of 16, 17, and 18 year olds. They'd run along with their jerkins with 'Socialism is the Hope of the World' across them and some of the people in it eventually became quite substantial people in their own right in due course.

The Socialist Party was attacked because it became the platform around which all of the pro-republicans gathered. The young people were very much het up about it. Of course the Spanish Civil War was a very traumatic affair with the younger people, some of us indeed tried to get enrolled to go to Spain."

Fred McMahon recalls the participation of women and the cycling clubs of those days:

"There were about nine or ten or twelve perhaps, very, very good women . . . Then there was the Clarion Cycling Club. I was a member of that cycling club. We used to go to meetings in country towns and I can remember the club going to Carrickfergus. I can remember going to one in Dromore Town Hall. It wasn't just a cycling club it was also a socialist propaganda organisation as well. The motto of it was 'Socialism all over the World'."

Fred McMahon also remembers:

"At that time there was a meeting every Sunday night in the Labour Hall in York Street. From this Northern Ireland Socialist Party, the Guild of Socialist Youth started, and we used to meet every Thursday in the Labour Hall, and we'd play deck-tennis and that sort of thing and throw darts and had an odd lecture. Then we started, the Clarion Club. There was a Clarion Club in England, and I believe it was the first socialist paper, the *Clarion*, edited by Robert Blatchford. We had about twenty or thirty members and 90% of them socialists attached to the labour movement in some way."

Socialists, then as now, had a great thirst for knowledge and so the bookshop was important. John Lowry tells how:

"Davy McLean's bookshop started around 1928 and it was really a great centre of activity on Saturday night. He had all sorts of radical publications. I can remember Tom Paine's *Age of Reason*. But Davy McLean did a lot of good work in having that bookshop, which was really the only radical bookshop at the time. Later [in 1935] the communists opened up a bookshop in Skipper Street."

Jack McGougan tells of some of the activities at the York Street socialist offices:

"I was the secretary of the Socialist Party at the time, and we owned the hall, 48 York Street, we were the tenants. With being the successors of the Independent Labour Party we had inherited a building fund, the nucleus of which came from compensation paid for the loss of a Labour Hall in the Oldpark which was destroyed in the 1922 troubles. There was an ordinary sub-committee meeting or something on there always. York Street at that time was a social centre for dances on Saturday night, the sixpenny hop, which paid the rent for it, and it was always packed, and then there were nights during the week when there was ping-pong, table-tennis. . . . "

He estimates the membership of the Socialist Party at around one hundred and fifty during the 1930s but adds:

"It would be up and down, the turnover in membership was fantastic; you'd get a good speaker and you'd hand out forms and you'd get it filled up and get a tanner to join, and you'd never hear of them again. We used to bring speakers from across the water and from Dublin. Sometimes we got a good attendance and sometimes we didn't."

The party kept up the tradition of public meetings:

"Every Sunday, for donkey's years, the ILP held a propaganda meeting on the Custom House steps, going back to the twenties. There was a man called Hugh Gemmell, who kept a black-pudding shop on the Woodstock Road, he was the activist in that. Eventually he had a row and left the Socialist Party. I was never clear what the row was about for I wasn't in the inner circles at the time, but we held meetings right through the thirties with different speakers. I served my apprenticeship there. We had three meetings, there was always heckling, and then it became a barrage and dangerous. There was a man called Rittman, and he used to mobilise, in a semi-military way, mobs of men and women, old harlots that were around the end of the Shankill Road and so on, and they just kept up a barrage of abuse. It was borderline at times with pushing and shoving, and on more than one occasion the speaker was pushed off the platform. Eventually a decision was taken to abandon the meetings as they were having no useful purpose and some people held were bringing the party into disrepute, and the party itself was getting smaller, with too many disagreements. Internal problems had a lot to do with it. . . . "

Socialist politics

At this stage we should try to assess the politics of Belfast socialism during the 1930s. First of all it is necessary to stress that they provided the life force for the Northern Ireland Labour Party which was really just an empty shell. Fred McMahon recalls:

"At that time I was a member of the Northern Ireland Socialist Party. The Labour Party in those days was practically a nonentity. It had an executive and affiliated bodies, but it didn't act as a party as such. The nominations for the elections would come from the Socialist Party and be endorsed by the Labour Party – it was just a committee really – it had no branches."

Tom Boyd supports this view:

"The Northern Ireland Labour Party only afterwards set up divisional organisations in each of the Stormont constituencies, and the most of those who were active politically belonged to what was known as the Northern Ireland Socialist Party. The Northern Ireland Labour Party in the first instance was mainly trade union affiliations but we were individual members of the Northern Ireland Socialist Party. I was a member of the Independent Labour Party, but when the division occurred we had to set up an organisation that could affiliate to the Northern Ireland Labour Party without any difficulty."

Belfast socialists were undoubtedly revolutionary in their outlook. According to Fred McMahon the socialists would regard the Labour Party as "pale pinks" and McGougan says that the "Socialist Party looked upon itself as well to the left, it was sort of the, I suppose you would nearly call them, the Bennites of the day". John Lowry recalls:

"In those days the idea that we had was that the capitalist system was manifestly breaking down. There was a very strong feeling that this was the deepening of the crisis of capitalism. You'd unemployment throughout the world, in '32, '33 and it did seem that capitalism simply wasn't producing the goods. And there was a need for a [better] system, and of course we at that time felt that social ownership was going to be the answer and that, obviously, productive capacity was there, it just wasn't being used. If that productive capacity had been used then there would have been a great growth of wealth and a lot of poverty could have been subsequently avoided. We hadn't thought, at that time, well perhaps some of us were thinking it, of the danger of state capitalism and the danger of bureaucracy . . . the danger of a lack of initiative, a lack of flexibility in state organisms and perhaps it wasn't just as simple as that."

Jack McGougan reflected on the rather elitist socialism of the early 1930s, "We had the pure milk of socialism, and being associated with anybody else would have contaminated it." He was aware that "the Communist Party was floating around at that time" but rejected any alliance with it because "it was a conspiratorial body then". Those who believe they have the "pure milk of socialism" are rarely successful in the real world of politics. It often leads to a revolutionary "purism" which makes difficult the compromises and alliances which are always conducted by the workers' party on the way to state power.

Again and again the socialists were divided over their attitude towards the unresolved national question which made "pure" class politics in the North of Ireland impossible. McGougan remembers the case of Jack Beattie:

> "He was very active in the Socialist Party, slightly older than the group that I was associated with; as a matter of fact he was a person that we looked up to at the time. He was a very elegant speaker and a terrific wit, but he was very inconsistent in his politics – from being, in the early '30s, a constitutionalist following the British Labour Party he swung right the other way indeed. At a later stage, after a lot of us had left the Socialist Party to go different ways, he was the main person in turning it into the Socialist Republican Party . . . associated with Harry Diamond, and it was very much a militant nationalist organisation rather than a traditional labour party. But people like myself were always uncomfortable in the Northern Ireland Labour Party, but we were able to . . . abide it as long as there was freedom of conscience on the constitutional question. In other words, the party walked a tightrope and the people had their own views on the ending of partition. . . ."

The key words here are "inconsistency", "freedom of conscience" and "walking a tightrope" on the national question. What it amounts to is the general failure of socialism in Ireland since the death of James Connolly to take up the struggle for national unity as a means of achieving socialism. It is interesting to add that John Lowry believed that "there weren't many Catholics in the Socialist Party [though] there certainly were a number".

There is a certain ambiguity amongst labour activists as to the extent of sectarianism in the trade union movement. Tom Boyd says that:

> "In 1932 there was absolute unity between all shades of religious and political opinion at that time, indeed, although I was a supporter of the Northern Ireland Labour Party at that time within my own union, we had the co-operation of people who could be regarded as unionists. I was a delegate from a union to the Trades Council: that was the United Patternmakers Association. But as I say the thing was so severe that people of all political shades of opinion were suffering together, and there was a kind of unity then; although in my union we had elements who were opposed to the Labour Party, they were behind this. They were unionists, supporters and members of the Unionist Party but they forgot about that during the troubles."

When asked about the Unemployed Action Committees he replied:

> "The Trades Council appointed a chap called Bob Rainey and he endeavoured to organise an unemployed workers' association, and the rest of us gave whatever help we could in helping with that, but it too disappeared in time when the divisive elements got

to work again among the working people."

When asked what he meant by "divisive elements" he replied:

"I mean what happened about 1935 and so on. You see once bombs are used, or once guns are used, and it doesn't matter in the first instance who uses it, it starts off this chain reaction and until we have something constructive like we suffered during the thirties we're going to continue going the way we're going."

For John Lowry:

"The bigoted Orangemen, you just didn't come up against that, not in twenty years. You found that it's a great mistake to see all unionists as such and such a crowd. It just doesn't work out."

Spanish Civil War

In spite of the political divisions at home, Belfast socialists were able to unite in support of the major international cause of the 1930s – the republican side in the Spanish Civil War which broke out in 1936. John Lowry recalls the participation of the socialists:

"After 1935, at the beginning of 1936, there was the outbreak of the Spanish War, the Spanish military rebelled against the legally constituted government and, of course, there was a great deal of feeling in the radical movement about the need to support the Spanish republicans. A fair amount of work was done, at that time, in the Socialist Party. I can remember a film being shown in 1936, *The Defence of Madrid*, and there was a large banner on the front of the building and this film was shown on a number of occasions and attracted very considerable crowds. But the problem that arose from the Spanish Civil War was that quite a number of the Catholic people who had been going along to various meetings began to become less enthusiastic about the Spanish Civil War."

He tells of one meeting:

"We organised in Dromore Town Hall after the Spanish War and I went along with Midgley and John Campbell, he was a councillor, and Dromore Town Hall was packed. But it soon became clear that it wasn't so much the Spanish War that the people were interested in, it was economic conditions, particularly among agricultural labourers. Talking myself about the conditions and the low wages that agricultural labourers were getting and it was a very successful meeting."

Jack McGougan adds:

"There would be the odd meeting, or a few leaflets given out, during the Spanish Civil War there certainly were some: I remember addressing them in Dromore. The meeting was held in

> the Orange Hall, but it was held under the auspices of the Dromore Homing Pigeon Society, they wouldn't have given it to the Socialist Party. And there was a chap who came from Dromore and was a socialist, Bob Fairleigh he went to Spain. . . . "

Fred McMahon says that in relation to the Spanish Civil War "the average trade unionist tended to be apathetic. There were a few of the keen trade unionists, the shop steward type who were pro-Republican". He agrees that many Catholics began to oppose the Republicans because of the Catholic church's support of Franco. He says – "there were quite a few Catholics and Protestants, but mainly Catholics, who were pro-Republican at the start, and then the media thumping into them about the patriots, and thumping the atrocities by the Republicans, which undoubtedly took place, they take place at all wars, and glossing over the atrocities by the fascists and some of the vicious bombing, Guernica particularly, the most sickening bombing before the war, the most sickening massacre". One must also bear in mind that "the *Irish News* is a Catholic paper, and it represents the Catholic majority, and it called the insurgents, that's Franco's troops, patriots. Most of the Catholic population, and the church certainly, was pro-Franco, and very violently so. And yet, peculiarly enough, I met some church men behind Republican lines: I met a couple of Redemptorists, and they were very pro-Republican".

McMahon himself says simply "I was an anti-fascist – that's why I went to Spain – I was violently anti-fascist".

Jack McGougan did not actually get to Spain but remembers how their efforts at organising solidarity were "more or less diverted into aid for an ambulance. Two people went, Fred McMahon and Joe Boyle, both from the Socialist Party". It is ironic that socialists, communists and republicans were able to forge a common front against fascism in Spain yet remained divided against another enemy – imperialism and unionism – at home.

The Republican Congress was one of the main organisations active on the question of Spain. John Lowry recalls:

> "Peadar O'Donnell coming to Belfast and there was a paper started, I can't remember the title of that paper but O'Donnell was a leading figure in that paper and there was some contact between O'Donnell and some members of the Socialist Party. At the time of the Spanish War O'Donnell had courage enough to stand on the side of the Spanish republicans and I remember there being organised in the Ulster Hall, where a Basque priest, called Father La Borda, was pro-republican and he addressed us, I'm not sure if he spoke English. But O'Donnell was there and it was a very good audience that listened to him."[2]

Communists

Apart from the socialists there were of course the more "extreme" communists who were part of an organised international movement pledged to support the Soviet Union and to carry out their version of the 1917 revolution in that country. We have in previous sections examined the role of the Revolutionary Workers' Group during the 1930s in Belfast. Here we will look behind its direct participation in politics to see what its members were like and how other people saw them. It is Betty Sinclair who has come to symbolise Belfast communism so we shall let her tell her story:

> "School taught me a lot, a church school, St. Mary's, because there were boys and girls there, sons and daughters of people who had businesses. They always seemed to be well dressed. I often wondered why these things were happening. So in this quest I had already left the church when I was eighteen years of age. They had no answers to the things that I was questing about and by 1932 I was ready to become active in the movement.
>
> My eldest brother was a member of the Revolutionary Workers' Group and we used to have lots of political arguments, especially coming up to the 1920 election. My father and two brothers used to be discussing the role of Ramsay McDonald and whenever I asked questions I was told to shut up because I knew nothing about those things. From '29 until '32 I was asking questions all the time, wanting to know why these things should be happening, why were some people rich and others poor, why one couldn't get work when people needed goods. I was working in Ewart's mill at that time as a reeler. Of course, one didn't know what money was being brought into the house, but we always seemed to be on the verge of poverty, not very high up in the social scale as far as well-being was concerned.
>
> Connolly had a very big influence on my father. The only argument we had was he used to make reactionary statements and I fought him on that and he said he was only doing it to try and draw people out and I said it wasn't an honest way of dealing with people. One should let people ask questions and then answer. You didn't convince people by saying that so-and-so was no good, when you knew they were good. It was better to allow the discussion to develop to the point where you could point out that so-and-so, whether it was a personal circumstance or an action. So it was one morning I was taking his breakfast up to bed – he was already unemployed – he just laughed and after that he never took this approach and we got on very very well together.
>
> [The ODR strike] was my first baptism of local politics and it taught me quite a lot about the whole political set up in Northern

Ireland. So I remained with the Revolutionary Workers' Group. I later went to Moscow, I arrived there in January 1934 to study at the Lenin School and when I came back in June 1935 the whole of Northern Ireland, particularly Belfast, was in an uproar, in the midst of a pogrom. I was very young in the early 1930s and had lived through that whole period of pogroms and I always knew that one of the last weapons in the armoury of the unionists was the pogrom, you know, the setting of the Catholic and Protestant workers apart. Where I lived in the Ardoyne, I was able to observe it for myself. There used to be slogans put up, 'No Pope Here' and I used to ask my father what does this slogan mean. Well, he said he'd be a bloody fool if he lived here. So that was the first piece of political advice I got.

We used to have meetings over the town and on Sundays at the Customs House steps and they were generally broken up by the Ulster Protestant League. They made things very difficult for us. That was before the pogrom broke out. The first attack was on the Independent Labour Party Hall in York Street, and then they began to attack us but then the whole campaign went in its usual way. They began to attack the Catholics, so it developed into a pogrom. It was a very serious one, not as serious as the one that broke out in '69, but it was very, very serious. Hundreds of Catholics that were employed lost their jobs and hundreds and hundreds lost their homes. They had to fly away wherever they could get some kind of succour – very frightening.

We campaigned against it, demanded that the authorities cease the activities of these ultraists. Then the British soldiers were brought in, in full strength. You know they always had a garrison of two and a half thousand, but they brought in more. The right hand side of York Street, going down to the railway station, it was cordoned off, protected by the soldiers and the people couldn't get in or out. Those who worked couldn't get to work and who were unemployed couldn't get to the labour exchange to claim their benefit. Harry Midgley was their MP but he took himself off to his house in Groomsport, never came near the place to help the people. People said he lost his Dock seat because he helped the Catholics but I said at a public meeting, that he didn't lose his seat because he helped the Catholics, he lost his seat because he deserted the Catholics, whose vote he depended on. He knew there was going to be an uproar about that."

As to the membership of the RWG Betty Sinclair says that:

"After the ODR strike was over we had a terrific membership. We had hundreds of members but after the strike was over, these men were great at fighting but, the hard everyday slogging work, most of them were unemployed, didn't appeal to them. So they just drifted away, they hadn't any disagreement with our policies, it was just they weren't working, they were in no trade union movement, how could they continue operating, that's one big lesson I learnt."

When pressed on the actual strength of the RWG in Belfast and whether it would have been, say, 500, she replied:

"Oh, it would have been more, going upward of a thousand. After the strike it decreased . . . we didn't have the apparatus to deal with it, you see, we had no full-time people who were able."

Perhaps one of the most remarkable facts regarding the communists was their basic hostility towards the republicans. Betty Sinclair, when asked how she felt about republicanism in the 1930s replied:

"Well, I considered myself an Irishwoman and from my reading and what knowledge I was given I didn't call myself a republican, I called myself a communist. That covered everything because I believed that Ireland should be united, free and socialist . . . that became my objective."

Asked whether the RWG had liaised in any way with any republican groups, like the IRA or Cumann na mBan, she told us:

"Well the interesting thing I found about the republicans was that coming up to the relief workers' strike we asked people who had come from the republican side of the movement and who had joined the Revolutionary Workers' Groups. They asked the republicans to give protection to our meetings, not to indulge in any warfare, but to be there and they said no; they were only interested in a united Ireland. They weren't interested in such questions as unemployment. People like Sean Murray and others who had been in the republican movement in the early days. Sean Murray came from the Glens of Antrim, he was our general secretary at the time, and he knew many people who had been or either still were in the republican movement and he and others made overtures to the republicans, but they wouldn't have anything."

Did the Republicans not get involved in any way: even as individuals?

"No."

What about the time of the ODR strike, did they not set up things like food kitchens in their own areas?

"No, no we had to do all that ourselves, the joint committees of our party and the Unemployed Workers' Movement."

So there was no IRA involvement at any level, formal or informal, official or unofficial?

"No, their ideal was to get a united Ireland and then people could do what they wanted to do. They had no political or social policies beyond that."

Did you ever have any direct contact with them yourself?

"No, no I didn't."

Betty Sinclair's account certainly minimizes republican support for the ODR strike – which though not organised nevertheless existed – and emphasises their negative stance towards social and economic issues. It seems that the fledgling communist organisation in Ireland saw the republicans as a rival movement and not as a body to draw into a united front. With emphasis placed on working-class unity there was also little understanding of a movement which had as its focus – albeit imposed by circumstances – only one section of the population, the Catholics. All in all there was little meeting of minds between communists and republicans in Belfast.

But how did other people view the communists? On the one hand attitudes were coloured by the dominant "anti-communist" ideology of the times. For Leo Boyle:

"The government's idea was, when you oppose the government, for instance the ODR riots, you were branded a communist. Even if you voted Labour, they tried to make the labour people communist. If you fought against their so-called society, you were branded a commie. Our clergy helped the government by branding them as communist."

Here, "communism" acts as a scapegoat for an oppressive system and something with which to frighten people. Jack McGougan as we mentioned above thought the communists were:

"a conspiratorial body, they were nearly underground; they used to hold demonstrations and so on, and they were experts at throwing up front organisations, of course that's been a mark of the Stalinists all over the world."

McGougan also answers firmly "No" when asked if they were a big grouping in Belfast. He remembers:

"Tommy Geehan, he came to the fore in the 1932 affair, but he faded out afterwards; there was a Loftus Johnston, he was a woodworker, and Betty Sinclair of course was beginning to appear on the horizon; she went to Russia for quite a while and came back. She was very intolerant in those days. . . . "

Tom Boyd tells another story which shows the extent of anti-communism in Belfast. He says that the socialists:

"were regarded as entirely communist by the establishment. If I might quote this instance: during the May Day procession in '33 I was giving out these hand-bills, which the Trades Council had prepared, to shopkeepers down the Shankill Road: it so happened that the communists came and just tagged along at the end of the May Day procession and no one was troubled to say that they

> shouldn't be there. I was opposite them when I was handing a bill to a shopkeeper standing at his door, and he said to me in a few rough phrases what he thought of me, and when I walked further down the street there was another shopkeeper standing in his door and I gave him another one of the bills and I referred to this, and he said, 'Well you know, if it wasn't for you people what would we do?' So you even had a division of opinion among small shopkeepers. But I afterwards found out and realised that the first chap thought that I was part of the communist procession and of course its true to say that his shop had been looted and he put this down to the communists. I found this out afterwards although I can't remember the man's name. Indeed through a friend of mine who lived on the Shankill Road, when he realised afterwards and was told about it, he sent an apology for his attitude. These things only illustrate the stresses and strains that people suffer through the bad economic and industrial conditions."

It also illustrates the need for a scapegoat when things get bad – in Belfast in the 1930s the communists provided just such a handy scapegoat to be added to the eternal one of republicanism.

Tommy Boyd, a docker and the brother of RWG member William Boyd, has vivid recollections of the period:

> "[In the 1920s] the brother had to get out of the Midland Railway; he was chased away to Greencastle by boys with hammers – they came down like wolves and they beat any man they got the hold of and kicked him all round like a football. He had to run all the way down to Greencastle to wee houses there by the football ground and he had to hide there till the mob went by. Then he had to make his way home as best he could when it had quietened down. It was a rough time . . . [In 1926 William] stood as a communist at the Markets, but he never counted. I was out one night, me and another fellow and the brother and we put up bills about the Indian Mutiny round by the Markets and as far as the Ormeau Road. The peelers came to the scene – they were coming for us we thought – but they just said 'Good morning boys' and never did anything about it. He did stand and everybody was going to vote for him that knew him – dockers and all – but he didn't count, the old sting was there you see."

Tommy Boyd spoke of the efforts at organising the unemployed on the Shankill Road and the difficulty of holding meetings over the din of the Lambeg drums. He told of how the outdoor relief men "ran jumble sales and all [to raise money]. They hired a pub in Union Street – McErlean's – they had their meetings in different places". William Boyd had a duplicating machine, which belonged to the party, and which they used to produce all the leaflets. Then his brother was arrested – "he was arrested out of bed that morning. Willy's wife was having a baby . . . My mother of course was away seeing about it." His opinion of the Outdoor Relief strike was "that's the first time we even got close to the Protestant people and our party – my brother's party – was the first to bring them to live together." As to his brother "he died – he was a tallyman at the dock at the finish, he worked along with me – he was a worker and he got arthritis and he was on a stick and they had to give him a job with a pencil you know."

His opinion about the other communists was quite mixed:

> "The brother sent me on a message one night up to Tommy Geehan's house because I was under no suspicion or anything you see. Tommy was the top man like, although there were other smart men there you know. Tommy was working down in Duncrue Street there at the buses. We used to call him 'Molotov' – he used to have his hand in his waistcoat pocket when he was making speeches at the Customs House. . . . Arthur Griffin was another fellow but he wasn't too deep into the thing. His health went down and he got sent out there [the Soviet Union] to a rest centre and he died there – he didn't want home. . . . Betty Sinclair came down to the Customs House in a white blouse on her – she was quite a young girl and she made a speech 'You've nothing to lose but your chains' style of speech, but we didn't see much of her . . . After the troubles she got a suite of rooms down the town provided to her. We'd no suite of rooms, my brother or them, oh no – but the party got her a suite of rooms . . . [There was also] Sean Nolan – he came down and spoke at the Customs House steps – and Bob Stewart came from Glasgow – he'd put you in mind of James Connolly, moustache and all like Connolly."

To sum up, the Communist Party of Ireland (as the RWG became in 1933) was a tightly knit group of dedicated women and men. Until 1932 – and the recruitment of some radicalised Protestant workers – it attracted mainly Catholics into its ranks unlike the Socialist Party. Its disciplined membership played a vital role in the ODR strike and other working-class actions. One reason why it did not achieve wider acceptability amongst the Belfast working class was its conspiratorial methods so that the unemployed movement was generally regarded as a communist "front" or "splinter group". Another source of resentment was the well-founded suspicion that the communists followed an international line. The switch from "class against class" to "popular front" strategies clearly followed directives from the Communist International rather than changing local circumstances. This subordination to "foreign influences" could only repel radicalised republicans and deepened the traditional anti-communism promoted by the clergy. The communists play up their number in the 1930s – fifty members is a more realistic estimate than Betty Sinclair's 1,000. It is true that many would have been attracted to its ranks by the 1932 events and in this Sinclair is correct in saying that the party had not got the structures adequate to cope with the new sympathisers. The narrow organisational priorities of the communists did not allow them to build a united front with either labour, socialist or republican forces. The Republican Congress could potentially have played this role but they allowed a premature split over a semantic debate on its objectives.

In 1933 there was a move to set up a united front based on a number of demands including the repeal of the Special Powers Act, assistance of the striking railwaymen, and against the menace of war. Harry Midgley was elected to chair this front but it came to nothing partly because no meetings were called – Midgley seemed to have been worried by Geehan's defeat of Murtagh Morgan in the recent elections for the Court Ward seat on the corporation. The communists themselves soon lost interest in the front as well, though. That same year they had declared their critical support for the republican candidates in the NI elections, but at this stage the republican movement as a whole was moving to the right with Frank Ryan, for example, being removed as editor of *An Phoblacht*. William McCullough, secretary of the Belfast branch of the CPI was thus exaggerating in his 1937 report which claimed that "the Party had achieved successes in the struggle for the unity of the working class movement". (*Worker,* 6th February, 1937.) In fact by 1937 the party had largely dropped unemployment from its work, partly no doubt because its members were entering work, most markedly at Short's aircraft factory. The CPI had now become adapted to the parliamentarianism of the NILP and it had ceased to pursue a militant line on the national question (in the 1938 Stormont elections it even called for an alliance with the "Progressive Unionists"). In 1941 the CPI marked its tacit acceptance of partition as it split, its southern branches remaining neutral and the "Communist Party of Northern Ireland" throwing its weight fully behind the war effort.

In this chapter, we have examined the obstacles in the way of socialist organising in 1930s Belfast and some of its early unsung heroes; the reformist tendency of the socialist current and their big split over the national question. The more revolutionary communists, who were key participants in the events of 1932, had the strengths and the weaknesses (political sectarianism) of a highly organised international movement. On the issue of the Spanish Civil War, socialists, communists and republicans could unite, but in Ireland they failed to form a strong united movement for revolutionary change. Nevertheless, given the weight of clerical reaction, the ruthlessness of Belfast's capitalists and the international divisions within the working class, their accomplishments were considerable.

John Nicholl – Becoming a Socialist

John Nicholl describes his family background and his time in and out of work; how in the 1930s he hesitatingly embraced the cause of socialism and participated in the events of 1932. He describes the atmosphere of "popular sectarianism" and ends with a declaration of uncompromising faith in the labour movement.

"In our house you were never allowed to be sectarian. My father wasn't connected with any organisation. My mother was very understanding. She had worked in the New Northern mill among Catholics and there was no sectarianism. I can remember as a kid in the twenties them burning the Italian ice-cream shop at the corner of Downing Street and my mother bringing the Fusco children in. There's not one of our family of seven that I can think of who was sectarian. There's not one of my brothers that's connected with the Orange Order. I had uncles connected with it, but generally speaking there was a fairly non-sectarian attitude. If some scare was raised, all right, that would maybe draw the horns in a little bit, but there was no question of going out and getting somebody because they were Catholic. I am speaking on my own family's behalf, there was quite a lot of sectarian things happened about the Shankill Road. I chummed with lads who were terribly loyal lads, fellows who beat the Lambegs and all that type of thing, and were very anti-Catholic. The kids were maybe at a disadvantage that there was no liberalism at home. Usually you found it coming from a family that hoped to retain the establishment, helped to retain it by their attitudes. But I can never remember in our family that there was any sectarianism in it. I was always able to go about the Falls Road, different dance halls and all that type of thing, dance with Catholic girls.

I started work in 1924, and if you take it I was born in 1911, I was thirteen. In fact, I had been working before that for a company called W.J. Reid, at the corner of Berry Street, the Paragon House, a gents' outfitters. They required me to take a fellow's job who was going out on an advance party for the Church Lads Brigade who were camping at Southport. He wanted to go out on the advance party, resulting that he asked me if I would take his job and during this time that I was doing this job for the fortnight, this traveller came in and he noticed the new boy and he started speaking to me, asking me what I was doing there, what had happened to Tom, the fellow I was taking over from. And then he asked me after I gave up this job would I take a job with him. It gave me the incentive to start putting pressure on my mother to let me leave school. After a lot of debating and arguing, I eventually succeeded.

I got my leaving certificate, so therefore I was about thirteen when I started. My birthday was in July and it was around July that I had this job with the Paragon House. I started immediately after that with this traveller . . . As far as I can remember, the minimum school leaving age was fourteen, but if you had reached seventh standard you could put some pressure on it. . . . I worked for this man Davison who unfortunately turned out to be an alcoholic. It wasn't only a question of working for him, it was a question of nearly going up and looking after him. After a limited amount of drink he was sent home in a taxi.

I was with him from 1924 to 1929 and the depression was getting worse. Large outfitters like Kyle and Chain were closing up, the premises were being sold to some of the English monopolies. Cavendish's took over the Kyle and Chain, they were one of the leading outfitters in Belfast. There was Marshall's in High Street, those type of places, all first-class outfitters, were closing, resulting in Mr Davison telling me that he was bringing his nephew in to work, he had to dismiss me, pay me off. I was on the dole for quite a while. As far as I can remember, my first dole was 15/- a week. I think I was paid for twenty-six weeks at that rate. You needed ten stamps to renew your benefit for another six months. There was a man called McMullan who owned a bar on the Shankill Road and he would employ men for ten weeks at a time to get their benefit renewed.

I did search for work. I went to the shipyard every morning in the week with a lad called Davey MacGrath who had served some time in the army, three years in the army, and nine years reserve. He and I went down, and there were hundreds of men looking for work. You had no chance unless someone knew you. Both he and I had never worked in the shipyard, so it was absolutely impossible to be acquainted with anyone. The point of going down was to satisfy Davey's father who thought he wasn't trying hard enough to find work. Don't forget you had to answer the investigators on the dole if you had been looking and seeking work in order to qualify for benefit. If you said No, they would ask you what you were playing at. We went down every single morning for a couple of years and we were never called. One of the reasons I stopped going was that I got a spell of relief work about 1934. This wasn't the same kind of relief work as in the 1929-1932 period where people were given chits rather than cash. The first job I got on relief work was in Montgomery Street. It was preparing the road to lay wooden bricks. Business people were demanding these to keep down the sound of the carts. A big lot of deliveries were made by horse and cart. I think the noise upset the office work. The work wasn't too bad. It was heavy enough for me to develop physically as well. This was one of the good things about it. What I did pick up was the frustration of men who were skilled men who couldn't get work at their own particular trade. You got a wage for it, I think about £2.9.0 a week. About 1938 they sent me to work on the Blackwater overflow scheme. It went from Lavinia Street on the Ormeau

Road, right up McClure Street into, I think, Lower Crescent.

Even from what was called the Protestant people of the Shankill Road you were getting labour men coming to the front in 1932, coming out openly and arguing politics. This question of defying people at every nook and cranny. You had to take off your cap when 'The Queen' [*sic*] was played at picture houses. You would have walked out and you wouldn't stand for 'The Queen' at picture houses. You just pushed by and made your presence felt rather than the way it was previously when if you didn't stand it would be too bad for you. The Colonel Eager Band and the Ulster Amateurs both practised, on different nights, at the corner of Downing Street in what was known as the wee Mission Hall above Jackson's oufitters. Coming back from a parade, they usually stopped at the corner of Downing Street and played "The King" and quite a number of boys at our corner would have stood with their caps on. There would have been people protesting, shouting at them and the lads would have been shouting back. It was a manifestation of frustration, of bad times.

I can remember as a kid, Joe Devlin, my mother really respected that man, notwithstanding the religious aspect. From the politician's point of view, she thought he was the be all and end all of everything. . . . I would say Joe Devlin, particularly among the mill workers, had a fair amount of support on the Shankill. I personally felt a bit of a rebel. One of the frustrations was this question of not taking your cap off to 'The King'. It was purely in a protest. You mightn't really have known what you were doing, but you were rebelling against something really. You were denied opportunities . . . I think people kind of talked to you in the sense "Be thankful for small mercies", you know, and if you were working, all right, you were lucky, and if you're not, as long as you're getting that wee bite of food, well then, to be content with your lot. Nothing seemed to be man-made, it seemed to be heavenly made, you know, that it was a question of being poor was sent from heaven . . . divinely ordained type of thing, and be content rather than rebellious type of thing.

In the 1932-34 period I was on the dole. I remember coming from the dole and looking in the window of the Progressive Bookshop in Skipper Street. At that time I was reading the like of A.J. Cronin, *The Stars Look Down.* I was also reading biographies and some Irish books. I read Connolly's *Labour in Irish History*, pamphlets by Billy Gallacher. I remember reading one small history book which gave me an insight very early on, Boyd's *History of Ireland.* I don't remember where I got it, whether it was in the library or got it given me. But I remember it gave me my first idea of politics, a new insight into the Irish question, from the point of view that I had never known that as history. My history was different. The history that I was taught in school was British history rather than an Irish history. I wasn't really aware of it. I was astounded at the things I didn't know about. . . . I was reading newspapers a lot, quite a number of newspapers.

Some of the newspapers, on the question of the soviets in the early days, that they were nearly eating their babies. That never seemed to appeal to me. I was always looking for some further information. Just the same as Boyd's *History of Ireland* revealed something to me that I hadn't known, I was looking for some alternative opinions to deny or substantiate what was being reported.

I kind of a way lacked confidence to join a working-class movement in the sense that I very often went to Skipper Street on my way back from the dole and I looked through the window in the paper shop. I seemed to be a wee bit over-awed about it, not a wee bit, a big bit, with the type of language on the book covers, the question of dialectical materialism seemed to be away above my head. And for a number of years afterwards notwithstanding that I was always actively participating in elections I was asked by the Labour Party on different occasions to work for them and I always did. But I never joined the Labour Party. It never had the policy for me. I just can't say what it is. I couldn't say what it was at that time . . . I felt anti-establishment enough. I worked for Tommy Henderson, an independent unionist, and I worked for old D.J. Nixon who was anti-establishment too, but I always felt a bit conscious about him because he had been a leader of some sectarian grouping at one time. . . . Peculiarly enough, I always had this anti-establishment feeling. I can't remember anybody advising me to do it that way or anything, it seemed to be just spontaneous.

Now at that time, particularly in '32, you found that men from the Falls Road were able to come up and participate in the struggles on the Shankill. And maybe men on the Shankill Road went to the Falls because the local police mightn't have known them on the Falls or the Springfield Road and the Catholic lads weren't known on the Shankill Road as well. I think basically that people were beginning to have sympathy for each other rather than bringing the religious question to the fore. You know that, well, you're not the only one starving, I'm starving as well, type of attitude. I didn't know it was an organised movement. I had the feeling that, all right, people were beginning to get frustrated and really uptight about the thing. There was a statement from a woman called Coleman, Mrs Coleman, at the time. She said that if they worked as hard as they do under the blankets. This was the inference, now I don't know if those are the correct words or not. If they looked as hard for jobs as they worked under the blankets, they would soon find work. Which meant that it was wrong to have children while they were unemployed. I took that personally because there was three years and three-and-a-half years between my youngsters. People were hurt about it, particularly people who were very anxious in looking for work. As an organised force, if there was one at that time, I wasn't just completely aware of it. I was aware of the protest that was going on.

The corner of Agnes Street used to be a Mecca for meetings. There was gospel meetings and all at Agnes Street, you know. Each had their own night and then on Sundays everyone settled on the Custom House steps. I remember the time when I went to the Custom House steps, that there was I would say thousands of people. . . . There was different meetings going on. I remember Doctor Moore, the black doctor, I think he used to sell medicine down there, you know, but he didn't sell it as a trade name, he sold it as a mixture. There was all sorts, there was old Townsley, the old tram driver, who was known by his famous sayings: "You're going to hell," and yet in many ways was an old socialist at heart. There was another, I can't remember his name, there was another tram driver who was a great old socialist, who preached down there every Sunday. I can't remember his name. He lived about Silvio Street on the Shankill and was driving a tram until he was a very, very old man. But from that on you were becoming more politically conscious while maybe not being organised and when the troubles had started itself on 11 October (1932), then you were participating. . . . I not only seen it because I had a daughter who was just three days old at that time. She was born on the eighth and the baby was born at home. They usually had the midwife coming rather than get you into hospital. I was partly glued to the house the first couple of days, but then when it started, and part of it started just outside our door, and I participated in it pretty actively. Well, we were protesting and then the police charged and then there was rioting started and you were participating just as wild as the next one, you know. The police were, in my opinion, very very heavy handed at the time. There was very little compassion from policemen. They usually defend the system, anyhow, it doesn't matter what system it is but they usually seem to defend it. What angered me most was the question of the role that was played by a big lot of the B Specials who came out after working all day and became active at night doing the role of the police and just were as heavy handed as the police were at that time. An uncle of mine never spoke to me for about nine years and warned my mother that it didn't matter about him being an uncle of mine he would arrest me if he caught me doing anything more. Him and I never spoke until he was home on leave from the Second World War. We had a drink together and I can remember his words distinctly in the Mountainview Bar. He says to me: 'You know, you're a fool.' He says, 'Why don't you get into the Masons?' And he says: 'You'll never be without a job'. I said: 'No, I'll never be in anything other than the working-class movement'.

FOOTNOTES

1. cf. Walker 1985
2. According to Cronin (1980:87) Fr Ramon La Borda had been in Dublin for the Eucharistic Congress in 1932. George Gilmore met up

with him some years later in the Basque country and invited him to come to Ireland to speak on behalf of the Spanish Republicans. He came in January 1937. The NILP organised a meeting for him in the Ulster Hall, but during that meeting he was frequently interrupted by shouts of "Up Franco" and "What about the murder of nuns?" On Irish involvement in the Spanish Civil War, see O'Riordan, M. 1979.

5. Republicanism

Modern republicanism – the Irish Republican Army – was born of the Easter Rising of 1916 when the Fenian Irish Republican Brotherhood joined forces with Connolly's socialist Irish Citizen Army. After the failure of the rising there was a widespread revival of Irish nationalism culminating in the 1919-21 war against Britain which achieved a nominal independence for the 26 counties which became the Irish Free State. From 1922 to 1923 the republican forces were pitted against the new state – a battle they finally lost.[1]

The North was left out of the 1916 Rising and later the IRA was engaged in a fierce rearguard action between 1921 and 1922 as six counties of Ulster became the new state of Northern Ireland. The IRA in Belfast was decimated in its battles against the incipient Orange state and its panoply of repressive forces, but also due to the civil war in the South. A writer in *An Phoblacht* (10.9.32) noted how "There is a great deal of truth in the statement that there was too great a trek southward of leaders in 1922 to 1925, which should have been stopped by the Volunteers. . . . It is shameful to relate that many of those North-East Ulster Volunteers sold themselves to the enemy of the Republic, and are still among our most active enemies . . . What a difference there would be if the political and military leaders of 1918-1922 had stuck to their posts at any cost!"

The republicanism of the 1930s is generally associated with socialism and internationalism – the Republican Congress and the Connolly Column's fighting for the Spanish Republic. In Belfast, however, the pattern of politics did not change very radically in spite of the 1932 Outdoor Relief strike. The Belfast IRA remained a small persecuted band dedicated to a narrow "a-political" nationalism and acting effectively as a Catholic home guard. Our aim is to bring out the social and political outlook of Belfast republicans in the 1930s and the nature of their movement. This understanding takes us behind the rather simple personality terms in which the IRA historians such as Bowyer Bell[2] have posed things. Our account begins with the reorganisation of the IRA in Belfast after the difficult years of the 1920s. It looks at the participation of republicans in the 1932 unemployed movement, the 1933 rail strike and the 1935 sectarian riots. Likewise it examines the attitude of Belfast towards Saor Eire and the Republican Congress, both political organisations designed to radicalise the IRA. It looks at the thoughts, the doubts, and the activities of the IRA in Belfast, focusing on debates which have a contemporary ring to them.

Reorganisation

Liam Mulholland was active in Ardoyne in those years:

> "The IRA was practically non-existent right on up to 1924 when the army was re-organised again. A GHQ man came to Belfast. He held a meeting and he talked about organisation and the difficulties of organising and he was of the opinion at the time, that it would be almost an impossibility to reform the IRA because of the dangers, and because of the attitudes in those years. So, he was asked at that meeting, if the IRA was reformed in Belfast, what would be the objectives of the IRA, and he said it would be a period of training and organisation, but then he said, when that period would be over, and we were armed and trained again, we would resume the war in Ireland, and that would be against the South and all – that was the army's attitude in those days. He suggested we should reorganise under the guise of Gaelic athletic clubs in areas where we would feel there would be nervousness and so on, from people who would be potential members. It was agreed that we would re-form the Belfast Brigade, although it wasn't at brigade strength.
>
> We were fairly well armed: we could have armed about two hundred men, with different kinds of rifles. The arms had been dumped in various areas and people had moved out of the city . . . people didn't know where they were, so you were going round trying to find out where the arms were, North Queen Street, Ballymacarrett, Ardoyne, Oldpark, places like that, and we'd find out and we'd go to the people and ask could we search the house with the arms in them and generally we got permission to do it and we lifted a lot of guns that way. There were others that had been put down by people who didn't like us very much and wouldn't divulge where they were!"

We asked if the majority of Belfast IRA went pro-treaty and if one would not have expected Belfast to be the strongest anti-treaty area. He replied:

> "You had to look at the situation in Belfast at the time; the Catholics were nearly all unemployed, especially working-class Catholics – they had been chased out of work, so when the Civil

War came they were getting White Cross – they were getting thirty shillings, single men were getting ten shillings, a fortnight. When the Free State army was formed there was one special unit called the Special Light Infantry. Their role was keeping open means of transport and communication, guarding the railways and you were given twenty-four shillings a week if you joined it. The White Cross was stopped in the Civil War and men had nothing.

The Army offered railway passes to go to Dundalk or Dublin to join up, and large numbers of them took it up. The money was the big attraction . . . I wouldn't say they were terribly involved with politics . . . It wasn't so easy to join the republican movement, or what we called the Anti-Treatyites; as soon as you crossed the border and went into any of these towns, you came under the attention of the Free State. If they thought you were up to join the IRA you were put in gaol, Dundalk was full of them . . . People were starving and I'm not making excuses, I stayed on the republican side, but the vast majority went and republicans daren't open their mouths – if there was a bit of a debate and you took the republican side, you'd have got a dig on the nose and there was nobody to defend you, until the Army was reorganised again. After it was reorganised we got a fair amount of support. I went to a meeting up where the picture house was, and all of Sinn Féin was there, Cumann na mBan, the Army, the Fianna, were all there, and out of the whole lot there wasn't forty; that was what was left. That would have been in 1927. But then in 1930, '31, '32, there was an awful resurgence in the movement. Whether it was brought about by the success of Fianna Fail I'm not quite prepared to say. That was '32, but prior to that Fianna Fail had been making great inroads and the Army had become active again in parts of the South, had shot informers down in Tipperary, a fellow called Ryan, a superintendent in the Guards and others, and they had banned Orange meetings in Cootehill and places like that, and the Army had gone over to enforce the ban. At the 1933 Bodenstown march I remember there were thousands of Volunteers on parade – that's without counting the Fianna, Cumann na mBan and Sinn Féin."

Across the city, in Ballymacarrett, Jack Brady was also helping to reorganise the Republican movement:

'I joined the IRA in Ballymacarrett in 1928/29, just the end of 1928. I was fifteen, and I remember it well because I was in my first suit with long trousers; I was serving my time as an apprentice cardboard box cutter. A school pal at that time, he joined the IRA, that was Jim Straney. Later, in the 1936 Spanish War, he joined the International Brigade and was killed in Spain along with another Protestant friend called Liam Tumilson from Templemore Avenue.

The IRA at that time was only forming in Ballymacarrett because previous to that there was one company and men from different areas went on to the Falls and then it was decided in an organisational effort, to branch out in your own districts, so it was that it covered the Ballymacarrett and Markets areas. In the IRA at that time, it was decided to form a branch of Sinn Féin, and we formed our branch called the Roger Casement Cumann of Sinn Féin – it covered the Ballymacarrett and Markets too.

We met in Tynam's Hall, that was a hall belonging to Tynam's, the drapery shop below it, and above that and to the rear, shared by us: actually the tenants of it were the Saint Malachy's Pipe Band, and they sublet to us too. We used to run a ceilidh every Sunday in the Tynams. From that then Sinn Féin expansion went on – the main club was in King Street called the Wolfe Tone Cumann, then there were branches in the Falls: the Austin Stack covered the Lower Falls, the Sean McDermott Cumann from the Bone, they had their own hall and run ceilidhs in it, at a hall in the rear of the old City Bakery in Ardilea Street and the Rory O'Connor Cumann in Springfield and Clonard area, they formed the whole nucleus of Sinn Féin Cumainn."

We asked if these Cumainn corresponded to battalion areas, or if they were just held in convenient places. He replied:

"They were really district areas, and there was an IRA unit in these areas probably too. At the time Sinn Féin was actually the political wing of the IRA. That continued up to about 1936, and then, following the events of the Republican Congress split, a kind of a social conscience creeping over everybody, and unemployment and poverty, that a political movement, especially in the North, needed a better appeal than the national policy of Sinn Féin at that time. Our policy then was abstention because the Dáil Eireann and the Ulster parliament were the result of the treaty and Lloyd George's threat of 'immediate and terrible war'. They came out of that with the claim that the Dáil was still the legitimate government body in all of Ireland, and the survivors of it were the actual Dáil Eireann and it would take an all-Ireland election to change that position. After that then, and after 1932 and events like the Outdoor Relief strike in the North [there was a] tide of new thinking coming out. . . ."

Republican activities

What were the day-to-day activities of the IRA in Belfast in the 1930s? It was, on the whole, low-key military activity – arms training, drilling, and such like. As Charlie McGlade says:

"We were very much a military organisation. We attended parades where you'd be drilled, and as well as that you'd be getting lectures on the different guns: rifles, grenades of course, Webley, Colt, Colt automatic, Thompson sub-machine gun. I remember once in the thirties we had a few people over in Leeson Street and I went over to give a lecture there. I was coming home that night up Conway Street where you turn up Lawnbrook Avenue and under my arm I had a 'peter the painter' and a Webley. The 'peter the painter' was a German automatic, and a very, very good thing – you put the gun itself into the butt which was hollow. I was just coming up to the corner and there were two policemen standing at the corner and the stunt they had in testing you was, this was about half eleven at night, one would move out onto the footpath and you had to go in between the two of them. So when I was coming up my heart nearly went into my boots. One of them moved out onto the footpath and that meant I had to pass between the two of them, and me carrying two guns that were useless to me because they weren't loaded. So I just strolled past not looking left or right and praying that I'd be all right, because it would have been ten years, and instead of going up Lawnbrook Avenue I cut across the road and went up the wee streets there as if I was local because if you'd gone straight up Lawnbrook Avenue they'd probably have thought that this is, you know, heading for Ardoyne - you always have to think of these things. But it was that sort of stuff we were mixed up in, training people and that sort of thing, and you hadn't much time to think about the unemployed or anything like that, you know."

Why did people join the IRA and how did they experience it? Barney Boswell tells us of his case:

"I joined in 1934, after the outdoor relief riots; it made me a rebel probably. I think it made a lot of rebels. [Another young man, Joe Cahill, also joined the movement that year for similar reasons.] Conditions were chronic, talk about conditions today. Nobody working, everyone on outdoor relief. I got a pound a week."

We asked how he actually went about joining:

"You'd be approached by a volunteer, that was the usual . . . You'd have known who to go to, but they usually approached you, they'd have weighed you up and all. They contacted me, a couple of lads. They'd tell you about the struggle and give you a wee bit of history and that. There were no cowboy types then."

What did you think when they asked you to join?

"Well I was always a republican in mind, I've always thought that Ireland should be a republic. I didn't want much persuading."

What did you think the IRA could do?

"It's hard to say, you see at the start you'd be enthusiastic and maybe get carried away, but when you settled down you'd see about fighting and getting organised to try and achieve what the '16 men failed to achieve. You were well tutored; you got a good grounding in Irish history in them days in the IRA. There was a period when you would be put through your paces when you'd be called to pass an examination. Because it was fairly open at that time we could have gone to the Pearse Hall in Belfast, every company, and paraded at different times. Your own O/C would put you through your paces. You'd be tutored in arms. You did most of that locally. Giles Quay was the camp. You would go there annually, but there was always somebody going there."

Did you ever go up Divis mountain or Cave Hill?

"We did, off our own bat, very often. There was a lot of trouble over the head of it, but we did it. We used guns and hand-grenades; the Thompson was the main weapon they had. You'd have to take a Thompson down and put it together again. With a couple of short-arms we'd go up the hill, and I remember there used to be an old milepost up the top of the hill and we'd whang the bullets off it; you'd have seen the hill scattering. We might get into trouble, you see stuff was very precious – they were hard to come by all right, many of them were brought by sea and one thing and another."

How did the IRA organise in those days?

"Well, you had a battalion, there was seven companies in a battalion, A to G, and the one battalion in Belfast. In later years, in Charlie McGlade's time, there was the Northern Brigade."

How many men would there have been in the IRA at that time?

"I remember at one time we would have had 800 men in Belfast. That's incredible, but that's what it was. That was with the auxiliary force which was set up in '38 or '39. In Belfast we could have pulled out 800 men but that would have been the peak. In '34 or '35 you would count it in the hundreds, it was very secretive but there were plenty of men."

What was it like being a republican in those days?

"You would be harrassed by the RUC. I did two months twice for wearing an Easter lily, in Crumlin Road, twice for two months. We refused to recognise the court. They fined us forty shillings and a month in lieu of bail. We never opened our mouth in court. I remember old Campbell bringing me back out of the cells and he said to the policeman, 'Is this man a mute?' and he said, 'No, I heard him speak in the dock,' well, 'forty shillings I want, and a month in lieu of bail.' We never took bail or anything; we never recognised the court. And the next time I got two months again, for wearing an Easter lily!"

What were local attitudes towards the IRA then?

"There wasn't a great deal of sympathy. It takes something like a hunger-strike to rouse them, doesn't it? They weren't unsympathetic, but they didn't get involved because people were afraid because if you were in the 'RA, when I was in the 'RA the door of our house was battered in day in day out when I was on the run. I never slept in my house, none of the lads did. You always were out and tried to get away in Ardoyne and everywhere. Nobody would give you anything. Any genuine sympathisers would give you a cup of tea or something and you'd stop in houses. You'd have got a bed for the night all right. We were badly messed about but you didn't care."

Republican politics

The outlook of the average IRA volunteer at that period was relatively uncomplicated: it was a question of securing a British withdrawal and "politics" could be left till later. Charlie McGlade was at that time a prominent Belfast republican. His views when asked his opinion about socialism are probably representative:

"Our ideas? We didn't stop to think an awful lot about that, some people did all right, it would be discussed. I remember one time, it was just Saor Eire, they were to set up some other thing, and we were to have weekly meetings or parades and we were to discuss the constitution that they were to have and to discuss different articles every week, but to be quite frank with you it was nearly a complete flop. The republicans, especially the young men, weren't interested apart from the odd one to discuss the thing at all. In fact, you'd nearly have to drag them along to a parade if they thought they were going to be discussing things like that. They really weren't interested, it was too dry for them. Their idea of joining the movement was to get trained and equipped and go out and fight to free Ireland. In fact, in our particular company we were more concerned about purchasing stuff, as we called it, and each man was encouraged to save up enough money to buy his own gun, and some of them did that. We concentrated on that more than anything else."

We asked if he would have seen himself as a straight down-the-line military man?

"Yes, and I'd say that 99% of the men in the IRA were the same."

How did the IRA feel towards communism and socialism?

> "Well, to tell you quite frankly, in the South here, and particularly in Dublin in the leadership of the IRA, generally were at that time, revolutionary. In the North, and particularly Belfast, the IRA were looked upon as being very much against communists and communism. I didn't like communism to be frank with you, I didn't like it. There was one thing always held against the commies and I discovered it was right. They'd call themselves an Irish Communist Party, but at the heels of the hunt they always had to do what Moscow said. There were lots of people in the republican movement, their idea was 'They're communists and we're against them because we're Catholics.' I would agree with that all right."

The attitude taken by the Northerners towards Saor Eire which was formed in 1931 as a republican political organisation was significant. The republican newspaper *An Phoblacht* (12.3.32) spoke of how when Saor Eire was launched "its programme appealed immediately to all who favoured a real revolutionary basis for a re-assembly for National Freedom and the ending of Imperialism . . . This programme immediately gripped all those who had an opportunity of studying and discussing it." This did not happen in Belfast, however, as a number of veterans recall. According to Jack Brady:

> "It didn't get much of a backing in Belfast because, to be honest, it was a kind of sop to socialist thoughts inside the republican movement, but I would say that the majority of Belfast IRA men, Belfast republicans and so forth, they were national republicans. That's not to say they were Tories or anything, they were national, there was no kind of dogma, they would vote Labour, and their sympathies would be wholly with a Labour government emerging in England. It was probably from the oppression; oppression made you be anti the system or anti the government. They called themselves nationalist; they wouldn't admit to membership of anything that was socialist."

Opposition to Saor Eire in Belfast was not purely a conservative reaction but had more complex causes as Sean Mac Con Uladh explains when asked why he did not join it:

> "For the simple reason it sprang out of the IRA and not as an organisation from the people. The people themselves until it was actually launched were always completely ignorant of the fact. It was always Army personnel that were conducting the thing in the country. It hadn't the popular support it was intended to have and it didn't get popular support because the church came out openly and banned it. Any popular support there was would fall

away."

But, supposing it *had* got popular support would you have fallen in with it or would you still have opposed it?

"Well, I didn't oppose it as such . . . I simply kept out of it."

Had the movement spread to Belfast?

"No, not very much . . . In Belfast at that time you couldn't have launched an organisation like Saor Eire for the simple reason that nationalist people generally in Belfast were on the poverty line. There had been from the twenties complete disregard for Catholics in work or anything else that went on and most of the Catholics . . . were hardly existing. There was no such thing as work. Take the like of the Sirocco Works, who had a blackboard nailed up with white writing: 'No Catholic Need Apply'. That was there from the middle of 1921 . . . ."

Did these social and economic issues not provide the basis for a radical political organisation?

"This was probably in the minds of the people who propagated Saor Eire, but that wasn't put over to the men in the ranks and it wasn't put over to the general public. Against what you're saying about what we should have done or what we might have intended to do, we here in Belfast had a physical force movement which liaised with socialists in West Belfast . . . We had complete liaison with a labour group. Now I'm talking about labour as distinct from being outright socialist. The Court Ward Labour Party met in rooms at the lower end of Tyrone Street . . . Paddy O Connor, McAllister, Alfie Byrne . . . they were closely associated with us from as far back as 1923 and when we were fighting the Falls/West Belfast elections that group undertook to appoint polling officers at the different polling stations in that area. There was also the West Belfast Socialist Party, the McVicker Brothers."

For what reason did the IRA have liaison with these groups?

"It wasn't a general principle of the GHQ. It was a local thing completely that those who were in the IRA here in Belfast, they couldn't pull enough support for a social and economic programme or workers in an election. It was a good thing to have a liaison with these groups and they were quite prepared to come in and work with us at an election time but they weren't prepared to touch us otherwise – the physical force side."

In 1932 Eamonn De Valera was elected president of the Irish Free State and his republican credentials made for a general revival of republicanism. Liam Mulholland recalls how:

"There was a resurgence of republicanism at this time – Fianna Fáil hadn't been tried and people thought they were going to redeclare the republic, which was far from their mind. De Valera got this idea to enter the Free State Dáil and to break the Treaty from within, and he convinced a terrible lot of people that he would do this. There were a lot of people still believed that Dev was republican. He had come down to Belfast in 1929 and opened the Ard Scoil down the road there. He had been arrested on the way in. I was in gaol with him, I was a republican and he was a couple of cells from me. He sat all day and wrote page after page of I don't know what. He never spoke to me the whole time he was there. The medical officer, a fellow called McAuley, used to take him out for walks round by the hospital, but he kept very much to himself. There was a certain amount of belief, even among the people in the Army, that Dev was going to bring in all these things. I would say there was great hopes among the Nationalist people that Dev was going to do something, that he would undo partition and all that. So that accounted for the influx."

By 1932 a left-wing element was firmly entrenched in the national leadership of the IRA, associated with names such as Peadar O'Donnell, Mick Price, George Gilmore and others. They looked hopefully to the growing economic crisis in the North to produce a breakdown in sectarian politics. Their social outlook was uncompromisingly radical. Mick Price, at an Easter Commemoration at Drogheda in 1932, (*An Phoblacht*, 2.4.32) spoke of how "Conservative minds in Ireland will allow no discussion on this plan [Saor Eire's] for social reconstruction in Ireland" and ended with the slogan "Long live the Irish Workers' Republic". George Gilmore spoke similarly in North Kerry (*An Phoblacht*, 30.4.32) of uprooting the capitalist system and building a new social system in which the "wealth-producing resources of Ireland are the property of the people of Ireland and not of the exploiting class." And Gilmore, in what would appear a criticism of Northern republicans, said that " in answer to certain people who are suggesting that we are 'sullying the flag' by introducing 'bread and butter politics' and that we should keep our movement on a higher and more spiritual plane I say that the spiritual life of a nation is not a thing apart from its material welfare but that it can be compared to a blossom growing from its roots."

The Southern leadership of the IRA looked to the North (*An Phoblacht*, 21.5.32) because "There are progressive forces in North-East Ulster, and economic conditions, growing rapidly worse, are forcing a new consideration of 1) the value of the close British connection, 2) the whole economic and social system, as revealed in the apalling conditions of industry and trade and consequent unemployment. Those who are really Nationalist should take up this question immediately. Conditions in N.E. Ulster have altered in recent times. To all it is evident the Six County political and economic structures cannot last." The following week Joe McCann of Belfast wrote to *An Phoblacht* supporting this view declaring hopefully that "Religious differences, while a great difficulty, must be no bar to unity of effort. Economic pressure will surmount the religious barrier used artificially by Imperialists in the past." When sectarian rioting broke out in Belfast in July 1932 *An Phoblacht* criticised republicans there because "much more concentration could have been put into propaganda amongst fellow workers and fellow-unemployed – this last year, especially – explaining to them that disloyalty to their own country did not pay, either in honour or in material necessities."

This orientation reached the peak of wishful thinking with the "Address from the Army Council of the IRA to the Men and Women of the Orange Order" on the occasion of the Twelfth of July celebrations in 1932 (*An Phoblacht*, 16.7.32) – "Working Farmers and Wage-earners of North-East Ulster! You surely must see that your future is bound up with the mass of the people in the remainder of Ireland. . . . The industrial capacity, and training of you, industrial workers of North-East Ulster ensure for you a leading influence and place in the economy and life of a Free Irish Nation." The response to this appeal was a furious rejection from the Orange Order parades and from a different quarter, the *Dundalk Examiner*, for whom it showed that "Catholicism counts for little" in the IRA. While the Orangemen were being wooed by the IRA leadership criticism of its Belfast Brigade was stepped up. Under the heading "Belfast Bigotry" *An Phoblacht* (20.8.32) spoke of how "we have those who speak of emulating Tone and uniting all Irishmen, 'Catholic, Protestant and Dissenter' in the country's interest. The intention is good. And they make it honestly. But it is not acted upon. Belfast Republicans, on the whole, are possessed of a bigotry that is all the more dangerous to the cause they have at heart since they themselves are unconscious of its existence." The writer was amazed that "the grass is growing in the shipyards . . . yet Orangemen are not being won over to the cause of nationality".

Outdoor Relief strike and after

We shall return later to this harsh verdict on Belfast republicans but we must turn now to their role in the 1932 Outdoor Relief strike. For Peadar O'Donnell:

> "1932 was the time of the ODR strike. I was a member of the IRA Army Council continuously from 1924 to 1934. There had been riots in Liverpool. And I said to the O/C in Belfast at the time: 'As sure as hell that'll spill over into Belfast'. But he pooh-poohed the idea. But it did. And it caught the republican movement quite unprepared."

Other reports mention the Belfast O/C, Davey Matthews, receiving a dispatch from GHQ on the strike and rejecting it as a "communist" line.

Whatever the case, the IRA in Belfast did not participate as an organisation though a number of individuals did.

Liam Mulholland from Ardoyne tells:

> "I was a prominent republican at the time, and I'd about one hundred and fifty men and I wasn't allowed to use those men, although I suppose it never struck me to use them. Any of them that wanted to participate, and there were some of them wanted to participate, could."

He was himself elected to an unemployed workers' committee and recalls:

> "There was another fellow who worked with me, a fellow called Ruari Fenton from Ardoyne, he was a Gaelic teacher, and he played a very prominent part in the committees and became associated with the Court Ward Labour Party, and worked very hard in that particular strike along with myself. Him and I worked together, encouraging the men in the various different areas that we had lived in to participate in the strike. We threw stones along with the rest, put barricades up, and everything else. That fellow Lavery, from the Falls Road, he participated in it as an individual too, Anthony Lavery, and another volunteer, John Reaney, from the same area – very active man in regard to attacking the police, putting up barricades in support of the outdoor relief. . . ."

Across in Ballymacarrett Jack Brady had this to say:

> "I was a staff officer of my unit in the IRA, and very much interested, but decided not to take part in anything like that. We had all the sympathy for the working-class people, but maybe through police intelligence they would take a photo or something and cry conspiracy or something like that. . . . They were very active, they used to go to meetings and they'd take short-hand notes and all of what was said. You had to be careful of the words that you used: if you said to people to join the IRA you could be arrested for sedition, but if you said to join the progressive movement, choice of words, nobody could send you to gaol for saying that, and the audience knew what the meaning was."

Was there a decision by the IRA not to get officially involved in 1932?

> "Yes, not to get involved . . .."

But were there any objections, or any permission given to individual action?

> "No, if you wanted to yourself and you were just an ordinary fellow."

Another republican, Sean Mac Con Uladh, was also asked if the IRA had any involvement in the 1932 ODR struggle and he said, "Not officially." But did they have any connection unofficially? He replied:

> "No . . . the IRA had never any part in the 1932 riots or the

ODR programme. . . . It has been stated over and over again that the violence on the Falls Road was all carried out by the IRA. That's wrong. The violence on the Falls Road, applying it now to the gunfire part, may have been done by members of the IRA in their own capacity, but there wasn't a directive on the part of the IRA."

But how would they have got the guns?

"Anybody could have had guns in Belfast between 1922 and 1932."

This is undoubtedly true and we would have to reject some of the wilder stories about the IRA sending a unit (or guns) over to the Shankill Road during the riots. There were plenty of B Specials amongst the Protestant unemployed who would have legally held weapons. There is a tantalising hint of armed involvement in a letter to *An Phoblacht* on 29 October 1932 from Eileen Delany, "late of Hawthorn St. Belfast". It tells how: "When the brutalities of the police became intolerable IRA men and UPA[3] men undumped their guns in defence of the workers and their reborn unity was cemented with their blood." There is little to back this view up however.

After the ODR strike was over some of the Belfast republicans began to reconsider their position on this type of "bread and butter" agitation. Jack Brady from Ballymacarrett recalls how "it was debated with hindsight that the IRA missed the boat" and people asked themselves "should we have got involved in it or not, gone on the streets and opened up with guns. . . ." Henceforth there was more republican involvement in trade union disputes. Liam Mulholland recalls:

"We participated in various trade disputes, union disputes. Now, the dockers approached us one time to blow up the mills, they saw that as a threat, the new grain mills being built down at the docks. We were prepared to do that and then they took fright too. They must have got in touch at local level first and then when they got in touch with their superiors in Dublin [the ITGWU] and they tabooed it. But any offers made like that, we were very, very much prepared to help. . . ."

Later Liam Mulholland was involved in the 1933 rail strike, probably the most important strike since the Northern state was set up:

"In 1933 there were two policemen shot, one shot in March, one in October. The one shot in March, that was during the railway strike, he was shot on the Grosvenor Road. The railway was operating transport, not passengers, from the transport place down the Grosvenor Road. They were carrying goods to various places, big lorries and that sort of thing. It was decided to intimidate those people who were driving the lorries and things like that. . . ."

Was this an organised decision?

"Very much so . . . I, along with other officers, was ordered to mobilise the various companies to sabotage. . . . Now we, if we had have been there a day early, we would have sabotaged the whole system. . . . We carried arms, grenades and things to the dockers who were to help if any effort was going to be made to transport things by boats. We supported the Irish union, the Irish Transport Union. . . . We carried arms to them for raids and to sabotage things that belonged to the railway. In 1933 we were very very much committed, I along with other officers of the time went along and we were instructed on sabotage. Actually the whole army was mobilised in Belfast, but the union called it off, the NUR. There were blacklegs – we beat blacklegs up. We went to their homes and intimidated them and threatened them. Protestant areas and everywhere. So, we were fully committed at that time to sabotage the whole railway system, if the union desired it, to put everything off the road connected with railway and transport. That policeman shot dead by the IRA was guarding the railway gates where the lorries were coming in."

The 1933 rail strike saw extensive co-operation between the unions and republicans but this was not the general type of confrontation that the ODR strike of 1932 had been. It was probably too late to build a strong labour-nationalist alliance.

Republican Congress

In 1934 the Republican Congress was formed by prominent republicans who broke away from the IRA, such as O'Donnell, Gilmore and Price, and some socialist and labour figures such as Roddy Connolly. In Belfast there were a few supporters of this new movement like Murtagh Morgan:

"We tried to organise it, but it didn't work out. That is one of the difficulties in Irish movements – there are always splits and splits within the splits. The first conference we had was in Rathmines Town Hall. I was there representing Belfast. We wanted to take a social aspect to the new Congress, wanted to concentrate on working-class affairs, social affairs, what have you. Peadar O'Donnell, Frank Ryan wanted the high ground of the Republic. Another split."

What was the strength of the Congress in Belfast and how many people were involved?

"Very few, very few. It was a one-man band practically. Two or three people. Roddy Connolly came up a few times and gave us moral support. He was a very radical type himself. There were some local people – they were probably disgruntled IRA people who wanted the IRA to do more for the workers."

But was the Congress able to cut across sectarian lines?

"No, all the Congress did do in the South was take part in rent strikes, that sort of thing. We tried to organise up here, but it was difficult. There was no basis for it here."

Peter Carleton was another who joined the Congress because:

" . . . it was revolutionary, it was working class and you can judge a political party by its activities and inside the first few months it had carried on great activities far from Cork to Belfast; it participated in rent strikes and housing programmes, all sorts of activities like that."

Did they participate in these kinds of activities in Belfast?

"Oh we did aye. We got round to organising a rent strike in Beechmount. There were houses in Beechmount that were built by subsidy and it was a Father Murphy owned them. There were other houses beside them that weren't built by subsidy and the ones that were built by subsidy had no bath and the other ones had and they were paying two shillings a week more the ones without the bath so they went on strike. Then the tenants association called a meeting and you had to produce your rent book to attend the meeting. They wouldn't let no press or anybody in and the meeting was in the Foresters' [INF] Hall at the corner of Forfar Street and Springfield Avenue. A deputation went to see the priest and they got a reduction of two bob in the rent. The Republican Congress organised the tenants and the credit goes to the tenants. They did the same thing on the Whiterock and got a reduction of two bob."

Betty Sinclair also remembers the Republican Congress and particularly George Gilmore:

"He didn't join the RWG, but he was always very close. He and Sean Murray [RWG general secretary] had a great attachment to each other, I had great respect for him. He was very keen on widening out the whole basis of republicanism, you know, to deal with the social and economic questions. But they weren't successful because the Republican Congress lost itself on the basis of slogans and the name. Other than reading the papers I didn't know of any active work here but there were people from Belfast, Protestant and Catholic, through our party who went down to the Republican Congress meetings but there wasn't the same approach. Connolly's daughter, Nora, she took a different attitude and others, who I learnt of later. They took a different attitude and the whole thing split which meant they had left the republican movement and they couldn't go back in again and start the fight again. . . ."

The mainstream of Belfast republicans were decidedly against the Congress. Charlie MacGlade:

> "It was generally accepted that the Belfast crowd and the Belfast staff were all just against the Republican Congress, but you'd find individuals who were in favour of the Republican Congress. I was very much against it."

On what grounds?

> "I thought it was weakening us completely, and I couldn't see them getting anywhere at all. Usually when you split a thing you weaken it, no matter how good your intentions are. I'd say that the effect of the Republican Congress in Belfast was hardly worth talking about, it didn't have much of an effect at all. It flared up suddenly and died as suddenly. It didn't create much of a stir at all in Belfast, it really didn't. At the time they were supposed to have had some people up around by the Shankill who supported them, but I always had the opinion, although I've nothing to back it up, that they probably did have about half a dozen up around the Shankill who could be classed more as communists than as republicans. That was always my feeling about it, that their communism would come before their republicanism."

Barney Boswell recalls:

> "They were a breakaway, they were a splinter group to me. It wasn't the right thing in my estimation, it was a cleavage in the republican movement and you want unity at all times without splits. I've seen more splits than enough in this town, and there was never nothing come of them, Saor Eire, Saor Uladh, disgruntled people."

Did he not think that it was a good idea that the Congress had a political and social message?

> "Sure the republican movement has that. Sinn Féin is the political wing of the IRA. They've a social and economic programme, Sinn Féin always had. They've a wonderful programme."

Would he have been opposed to the left-wing tendency in the Republican Congress?

> "Well, I wouldn't have liked that. I go on the philosophy of Connolly with the banner slung across Liberty Hall, 'We serve neither King nor Kaiser', that's my philosophy."

Surely the Congress would agree with that?

> "Aye, but they would have gone further. There are certain things that I would agree shouldn't be done. I believe they deviated from the principal course which shouldn't be done. I believe first and foremost in a military solution backed up by your Sinn Féin programme. It was about mining and the wealth of the country being distributed, and it covered everything. It was good, very good."

There was one famous incident when Republican Congress supporters from the Shankill Road attended the 1934 Bodenstown rally in the South. Peadar O'Donnell recalls:

> "After Dev had been elected, I decided that the IRA had no role of the sort they'd practised during Cosgrave's regime, and I raised the question of a wider Republican Congress, based as far as possible on the working class of the north-east, but involving all the discontented republican masses, for instance, small farmers and workers. It caught on considerably in the North among the Northern Ireland Socialist Party and people of that sort. In 1934 a couple of lorry loads of Protestant workers came down from Belfast, carrying a banner saying 'United Irishmen, 1798-1934', and took part in the parade at Bodenstown. The IRA, which by that period was pretty conservative, decided that no banners should be carried, it should be an IRA parade. And the Northern Ireland fellows carried the banner of theirs quite proudly. A company of the Tipperary battalion [of the IRA] were to see that no banners were carried. The Belfast fellows were taken aback when an attempt was made to seize their banner. For a moment they were confused, but they rallied to the defence of their banner to a slogan that never before was heard at Bodenstown and probably never will again – 'Up the Shankill Road!', by God!"

Liam Mulholland, however, recalls this incident differently:

> "I was at Bodenstown that year, and I'll tell you what happened. The chief steward ordered that there were to be no banners carried except with the permission of the national committee. Now, those people came down and they unfurled their banners. The South Tipperary Battalion was ordered to go and take them down. Now it was blown up out of all recognition, that particular incident. . . . Many of those Shankill Road men were in my company; I always had Protestants in the company, twelve, fourteen sometimes . . . a good lot of them Shankill Road men; volunteers from the Shankill Road, Crumlin Road, Agnes Street, Cliftonville Road, Antrim Road, all, you know, Protestants. . . . "

Whatever the exact nature of the incident at Bodenstown it became a symbol on the left of the IRA's antipathy towards socialism.

1935 riots and after

There were objective pressures on the IRA which reinforced this separation from the socialist movement. That was its traditional role as a "Catholic defence force" in Belfast, a role it was forced to reassume during the sectarian riots in the York Street area in 1935. Jack Brady recalls that:

"In 1935 when trouble broke out in the York Street area the IRA from Ballymacarrett was over there purely in a protective capacity, and the whole thing in Ballymacarrett was protective too. You used to go out to vantage points in case of any trouble and those were the orders . . . you'd have got court-martialled if you'd fired a shot on your own, if you fired at a Protestant area. . . . No way were you to provoke anything. Even, it used to be when the Twelfth of July parades were going by. Some of them were very provocative, on the Newtownards Road and going by Saint Matthew's chapel and Seaforde Street dancing and singing and yelling; it was tense, but you had to make sure that they got past . . . nothing at all to do unless people actually came in and invaded your streets.

When the riots broke out I was in Ballymacarrett and the whole IRA in Belfast bar Ballymacarrett was away training at Giles Quay. My unit had been there on our own and a woman came, a Mrs Kelly of Seaforde Street and Sarah Trainor came over and said, 'Jack, they're shooting in Lancaster Street'; it was the Orangemen coming back from the Field, and she said it was desperate. We went to action stations and got about thirty men rounded up with guns and so forth and went over. . . . All except my unit, even the York Street company, they were A Company, were at Giles Quay.[4] The only IRA unit in the town was Ballymacarret. So we went over and we had our headquarters in Trainor's yard, a big scrapyard in Lancaster Street. They were coming down the streets, shooting, down Corporation Street right down to Sailorstown by the railway. We were there in the thick of it for two days till an IRA unit came back from Giles Quay. We were still there when Jimmy Steele, he was the battalion adjutant in Belfast, came back and said 'You've done great work, but we'll take over from here'."

In 1936 the Northern leadership of the IRA and two representatives from GHQ met in a back room of 10 Crown Entry in Belfast for the purpose of a court martial. The police descended en masse and arrested everyone in sight. The background to this event began the previous year when the IRA carried out a successful arms raid outside Belfast. Mick Traynor remembers people transporting these arms over to the Falls Road in a horse and cart. This successful escapade led the IRA GHQ to suggest a raid on Campbell College where a number of arms were held for the purpose of training the young gentlemen who studied there. Mick Traynor went down to Dublin to seek more details from the IRA's intelligence officer but he proved to know less about it than Belfast. The raid went ahead nevertheless but arrests followed immediately. One man was known to be innocent so the Belfast Brigade authorised him to defend himself in the courts. Dublin GHQ stuck to the traditional non-recognition of courts but as Traynor says, "The Belfast men replied that if we let them away with this they'll have the whole crowd of us in jail". The Belfast O/C Tony Lavery was held responsible for this breach of orders and a court martial (largely a formality according to Traynor) was called. Before it could start the [B] Specials arrived. The republicans were charged with treason felony. Killeen, the A/G of the IRA received seven years, others five or six, the young Traynor received two years as did Lavery who was considered "the victim of circumstances".

Belfast republicanism: the balance-sheet

At this stage we can try to make a general assessment of Belfast republicanism starting from Peadar O'Donnell's frank criticisms:

> "Once I joined the Republican Congress – it was a moot question whether I was expelled or whether I withdrew – I didn't think there was any role for the IRA. It wasn't among the IRA in Belfast I looked for support. It was among the Protestant workers. I couldn't see any future for any movement in Ireland unless it succeeded in winning over a very considerable section of the Protestant workers in the North. We won some. We took two lorry loads to Bodenstown. There were some IRA men who did join the Congress, but it wasn't my mission. I never really put much weight on the IRA in Belfast. I never thought they could do much more than do little bits of things that would divide the workers in the North. I was often rather impatient that Connolly had laid down no guidelines on the North. It has to be said that the republican movement in Belfast never really gave the Protestant workers of Belfast a chance to join with them. I remember on one occasion – I think I was speaking to the Northern Ireland Socialist Party – the Easter commemoration had been banned. I said, 'Well, you may not agree with all the things in the Proclamation of the 1916 Rising, but after all, Connolly was a member of the group that was executed, so even if you don't commemorate him, you should protest against a ban on the procession that does commemorate him'. Eventually quite a few of them did agree to turn up and join the procession. We went along until the stage where the B Specials would allow us to go no further. Then the whole republican procession flopped down on its knees and began the rosary. My Orangemen could have afforded to risk getting their heads cracked with a baton, but they couldn't kneel on the Belfast streets to say the rosary. That was the great weakness of the republican movement in the North, that they never managed to hold their religious services apart from their political commem-

orations. I always maintained and repeatedly said it to the Army Council, 'We haven't a battalion of IRA men in Belfast; we just have a battalion of armed Catholics'. I was probably the only person on the Army Council so aware of the need to bring Protestant workers of the north-east to our side. They had no opposition to the existence of the IRA, but there was a lot of impatience with their idea that they could achieve it by force of arms. We were hoping to do it by propaganda."

There is a mixture in O'Donnell's recollections of genuine criticisms and some wishful thinking. The IRA in Belfast was narrow-minded politically and did not put forward clear socialist principles. But was it simply "a battalion of armed Catholics"? Were Protestant workers genuinely ready to join in the republican cause if only it forsook armed force and its advocates their Catholic faith?

One finds little evidence of sectarianism in the thinking of the Belfast republicans we spoke to. Charlie McGlade, a conservative Catholic by all accounts, could say:

"We looked upon ourselves that if any district was attacked we would defend it, but we never thought at any time of attacking the loyalists. While we were anti-British and we wanted the British out and we wanted Ireland to be free and united and all that, we never thought of going out to shoot down Protestants because they were Protestants – that was never considered, or anything like that. We'd be engaged in the fight against anyone who wore England's uniform. We weren't concerned as to whether he was Protestant or Catholic, we weren't concerned with that at all, he just happened to be fighting England's battles in Ireland, and he's just the same as an English soldier who comes over. The IRA felt that the country was partitioned and divided and you had all these things wrong with it due to the presence of England in Ireland. For instance, in the North we felt that bigotry and sectarianism was an end result of the continued British occupation, and that if the Brits were got out of the country it wouldn't die immediately but it would die; it had died in other countries, I mean sectarianism and bigotry."

McGlade's social thinking was undoubtedly conservative but there was still the acceptance that a new social system – "Irish socialism"– was necessary:

"In the 1930s, you weren't too much concerned with political issues, they came up all right and they were discussed, particularly before and after Saor Eire. There was a crowd who were that way inclined who eventually went to Republican Congress, but the vast majority of republicans at that time just wanted England out of Ireland. It was a simple thing. They honestly believed that our social and economic ills flowed from the English occupation of this country, they occupied the six counties, dominated the twenty-six."

Would he have supported a social and economic policy?

"I'm a strong believer in the social and economic policy. I believe that the workers will have to be ultimately in control. You don't have to be a communist to believe in social justice. I believe in socialism, but I believe in Irish socialism – we want socialism that suits the people and suits the country."

Liam Mulholland says of the IRA in the thirties:

"They were moving towards socialism, and you got the feeling that nationalism, pure nationalism of the romantic type, [was not what] the people wanted. It was felt that you would have to give them something if you hoped to get them. It was thought there was a mistake in the attitude during the 1920's truce of the Army towards people who were seizing lands and things, there was a big line of thought in that direction. Some of them would qualify that by saying that the Republic should have taken the land and distributed it, instead of men having to walk about and grab it. The Army was used in a good lot of cases to dispossess those people, and there was a fairly strong feeling in the Army at that time that it was wrong to do that. At the same time it was admitted that if it was allowed to continue that everybody would just grab it."

Yet he also goes on to say, apparently in contradiction:

"The strongest thing in Ireland is nationalism, I suppose it's the strongest thing in the world – there's millions of men have died for nationalism in various countries, in England, in Russia, in Germany, America, but very few have died for socialism. We have, from time to time, had a number of people in, and very socialist about this and that, and they'd think they'd be adding socialism to it, that its going to bring about a miracle, that there'll be a republic overnight, but my experience is throughout the world, what I have read and what I have seen, is that men are prepared to die for their country; they're not prepared to die for an '-ism', so few have died for an '-ism', so this is what dominated the republican movement."

Sean Mac Con Uladh shows a similar mixture of conservative thought and recognition of social and economic issues. He said he had opposed the Republican Congress and fought against it:

"On the grounds that it was something that sprang up in the minds of a few people. It was never openly discussed on any convention or anything else, and the people in the movement knew nothing about it until it was moved at an IRA convention in

1934. In my mind it cut across certain articles of the IRA constitution which said that the IRA would not lay down its arms until a republic was established in Ireland. The other one came along and it said that the IRA will not lay down its arms until a *socialist* republic was established in Ireland – two different things. In my mind it's the people of Ireland as a whole who should determine what social or economic programme will evolve on the establishment of a republic. That was always my teaching. After all, Connolly didn't try in 1916 to push his socialistic ideas down the minds of the volunteers who went out with him in 1916 or the members of the Citizen Army. He dropped his socialistic ideas in order to participate in the physical force side of the establishing of the republic which was a very logical thing. And that's the kind of thing that animated me in my thinking at that time. I know that there were good men in the Congress, men who believed in a socialistic Ireland, but what I wanted to know was why the hell did they let Connolly die for fifty years without anybody even having a reference to him except his son Roddy or his daughter. Anybody who wanted to talk socialistic ideas, they were talking about Marx and Engels and all this kind of stuff, and nobody wanted to refer to poor old Connolly. Connolly died as a socialist and a member of the forces in the GPO in '16. But Connolly wasn't out shouting on the steps along with Patrick Pearse 'This is a socialist Republic'."

If there *had* been any support shown for a socialist republic in the 1930s would you have supported it, or were you still opposed to socialism and communism?

"No. Why would I be opposed to it?"

Jack Brady provides the key to this apparently contradictory outlook. When asked whether the military or political side was most important to the average volunteer he replied:

"The military was the basis for their training for I remember one IRA officer at a training class, and he said to them, 'You're training to take the field', that was his expression, and always in your training was not to dissipate your energy in any local thing. . . ."

Did this mean that all the social and economic questions would have been secondary?

"They would have been secondary."

All the Belfast republicans knew poverty and unemployment and would be "latent" radicals. The republican-socialism of those such as O'Donnell did not appeal to them because it implied a run-down of the military side. The one overriding principle was the end of British occupation of the Six Counties. Everything else – even something as momentous as the 1932 strike – was seen as a possible diversion of energy from this aim. Republicans were instructed "not to dissipate your energy in any local thing". If the importance of social and economic issues was recognised – as presumably was the case for the republicans who participated in 1932 – this was usually seen as something which could destabilise British rule and not important in its own right.

In this context "socialism" could be seen as a deviation from classical republican aims and objectives – especially when many socialists were lukewarm on the national question. On the question of class unity in the North the local republicans were probably more realistic than O'Donnell. It was quite futile to appeal to Orangemen to be good Irish nationalists when the whole basis of their way of life and outlook was radically opposed to it. If the IRA had dumped arms in Belfast it would have left Catholics open to attack more certainly than leading to a flocking of Protestants to its ranks. It was hardly justified to accuse Belfast republicans of bigotry because they were forced to act as a local defence force for nationalists, who happened to be Catholics. The fact that some Protestants did join the IRA would indicate that there was not too much Catholic sectarianism in its ranks. Finally, why were so many Belfast republicans opposed to "socialism"? In part the Catholic Church's offensive against "communism" when Saor Eire was formed and later had its effect. More than that it relates to traditional republican thinking that first the republic can be gained and then the Irish people could freely choose the social system they preferred. This is but one aspect of a more general tendency in traditional "physical force" republicanism to neglect the properly political dimension of their enterprise.

Outside observers were usually hostile to the IRA though some did provide fairly accurate portrayals of the movement. For Harry Diamond, later a Republican Labour MP:

> "They didn't officially involve themselves in the Outdoor Relief struggle. Some of them were interested in the economic struggle but there was a split when what you would call the nationalist section of the IRA more or less expelled those that associated with the Republican Congress. They reckoned it was departing from the traditional national struggle. . . . It was a young membership and they were primarily concerned with the physical force struggle. In their printed programme they had a lot of stuff about social and economic matters, just like today they say they want a socialist republic, but that, to my mind, is secondary to the struggle they are otherwise waging."

Diamond confirms the growing strength of the IRA:

> "In the 1930s the IRA was organising very rapidly and after I left Belfast in 1936 they built up their strength considerably. They had parades carrying rifles in places like Raglan Street. There

> must have been hundreds of them, probably a thousand or so by the late 1930s."

This growth he sees as due to the emergence of a new generation after the defeats of the 1920s and a realisation of the effects of sectarianism. It contrasts with the situation in the late 1920s when "only the doctrinaire were in the republican movement and there were only a handful and the police knew them. They had no public support. . . . "

Diamond saw how Dan Turley, the then intelligence officer in Belfast, was found out to be an informer after several leaks were traced back to him. This led to his execution in 1936 and "subsequent to that there was another prominent old-timer called Hanna who was shot outside of Saint Peter's Pro-Cathedral. In fact, they discovered quite a few of them. The awful unemployment left themselves wide open to informing. . . . " Diamond also recalls a meeting in the winter of 1932-33 which he arranged between nationalists and republicans because he believed the cleavage between physical force and constitutional representation was divisive and should be ended:

> "It was a conflict over tactics and means and what have you. [At the meeting] I remember one phrase that Devlin used, and I suppose you couldn't argue with it. He said to them, 'I don't believe in people dying because they're angry'. Their struggle was so hopeless in the circumstances that it seemed a reasonable remark to make. . . . Of course Matthews [Belfast IRA O/C] and Turley were arguing that the means employed by Devlin and others never succeeded. In other words, the national struggle always had to be one pursued by the hillsiders as Connolly called them . . . "

This confrontation certainly captures the dilemma of republicanism/nationalism in the 1930s.

As a conclusion Diamond's verdict is accurate only in part. Certainly most of the Belfast republicans we interviewed would consider themselves as militant nationalists, divided only on the means to achieve the United Ireland from constitutionalists like Devlin. But republicanism cannot be reduced to physical force nationalism. Many of the testimonies we collected reflected a deep radicalism and hatred of all forms of oppression and exploitation. Notwithstanding the incomplete break from the Catholic church, Belfast republicans were undoubtedly a radical force in the 1930s.

Liam Mulholland – A Republican Life History

Liam Mulholland describes the life of an active republican in Belfast during the 1930s after the turbulent period of the 1920s. We learn of outlooks and activists, but most importantly of republican intervention in the 1932 events and the 1933 rail strike.

"I joined the Fianna in 1917 immediately after the first release of prisoners after 1916. There was a meeting held and I went maybe out of curiosity to a certain extent, but they were calling for volunteers, people who were over eighteen, and I wasn't anything near eighteen, so this particular fellow came and says afterwards, if there's anybody here under sixteen come up here after the meeting. So with a few others I went up and formed the Fianna.

In the Civil War we took a terrible hammering. After the order came to dump arms many had to go on the run and many more emigrated. The boat to America left from Cobh and you could see people walking there from all over Ireland – going away never to come back. We were losing people all the time, they were going away, getting married and that. . . . Some went to America, some to Canada, some to England, some severed their connections altogether and the result was that – this would be in the late twenties – it became a very small organisation. There were two companies and an independent unit; I belonged to the independent unit. There were five or six of us and we covered the whole of Ardoyne, Oldpark, in fact you could say North Belfast and we covered North Queen Street. There'd be no Army in North Queen Street, maybe an odd volunteer; the same thing would have applied to Ballymacarrett.

There was a big revival of republicanism in the 1930s. We became stronger in Belfast and by 1933 we had 700 men in the Belfast Battalion. During the thirties 'C' Company had about 150 men."

Were there any Protestants in the IRA at that time?

"There were . . . they weren't corner-boy types, they were the intelligent type, and seemed very very serious young men – I think we were proud of them. There were Protestants in a fair amount of the companies, odd ones you know, but there were Protestants . . . there was no such thing, to be honest about it, as sectarianism: you had people who were very good Catholics. Charlie McGlade was one of those, Charlie was always a good Catholic, he would have been a supporter of Davey Matthews who was a battalion O/C at the time of the '32 riots, although Charlie was only adjutant at the time. To be quite honest, our foremost objective was the freeing of Ireland – all others to us was merely means to an end, and that's just being honest. I have always said about the motives of an Irish republican, and I have analysed it in my own mind: an Irish republican is an extreme nationalist, one who is prepared to use extreme methods to bring it about. If you look up our constitution, you will see that our objective was to set free an independent Ireland. Other things came up, and other people wanted to add things to it, but that has been resisted all down the years, and every time we did go away from that, ultimately what we found was that we almost disappeared, and you would have a few left and you'd have to build up again."

Were you involved in the 1932 Outdoor Relief strike?

"We participated in all of their marches, we went to their meetings, and we took part in the parade up to the poor house, or the work house. They marched up there in hundreds, we marched up with them: we didn't get in, maybe we didn't want in, I don't know. To get into the city hospital at that time you must declare yourself a pauper. Even if you were in the city hospital with say a heart-attack, you must first of all go into the poor house, you had to declare yourself a pauper. They would have gone in there in hundreds, the wards were full of them, these were people who were participating in the strike, marching and demonstrating, whatever they thought would bring attention to their plight, the plight of the worker, you know. The marches were generally orderly, but they planned a demonstration, and one of the meeting places was Tennent Street, off the Crumlin Road and Shankill Road and that's where they made the onslaught and out of that came the resistance, physical resistance.

The Shankill men fought for a fair amount of time, but the Falls Road people came along and helped them, and some of the Shankill men participated, but very very few, you know, although there was a fairly strong group, and the Shankill Road was as hard hit as the Falls Road as regards poverty and things; they fought, but there were agitators, people going around whispering, you know, about republican participation, and in that particular area it was heard that De Valera had been seen in Albert Street. All these things were brought about by people, members of the Orange Order, you know . . .

I was out in a riot and we got chased, and we ran back and it was in Walton Street where we ran into a house, about three or four of us. We were sitting in the house, and the people of the house welcomed us; now, these were loyalist people, Protestants really, and they welcomed us and gave us shelter and helped every way they could, the doors were open for people, you know. This woman came into the house when we were sitting there, the police were running up and down the street with their batons, looking, you know, for a victim and some of these rioters, and we were sitting there cooling off, and this woman came in, a neighbour I think, for she was known to the people in there, and she'd come in because of the riot and she was scared I think. "Did you hear the word that's going about that DeValera's been seen in Albert Street?" She believed it and she was telling the others, scared you know, and they would feel that they couldn't participate in anything that the republicans were in . . ."

The idea being that Southerners were taking over?

"Yes, there'd be a take-over; that was the intention of the people who originated the stories, that would be their purpose in causing confusion and division. . . ."

Did the IRA send a unit over to the Shankill Road during the riots?

"No, there was no organised support . . . and I know that for a fact, for I was an active volunteer at the time. No, there might have been volunteers who went over as individuals, without arms. I wouldn't believe . . . Belfast is the sort of place where there's a lot of guns and there may have been some that brought guns into the area, so they'd get an opportunity to shoot, but definitely there was no intervention by the IRA, or participation as a body by the IRA."

Why did the IRA not get involved?

"The IRA gave it sort of approval in Belfast, like they weren't against it, but as regards participating as a body, no they refused to do that. I would say the IRA leaders would be met by certain people and asked for their support, and the IRA leaders would say we support you to that extent all right, but we're not going to participate as an organisation. There was no order against individual volunteers participating, and you'll probably find, in working-class areas where there was activity, that volunteers did participate, but just as individuals – you weren't ordered to do any particular thing, no order at all. I do know there was a certain amount of bitterness because they didn't participate in Belfast. But the overriding thing, the thing that made the people join the IRA, especially in the North would be the national question. You see, they were very conscious of the fact they were under the domination of England, and the domination of England as they saw it was brutal, and it was administered by the Loyalists: there was no secret made of the way the Northern government looked on the nationalist minority, as an unnecessary evil, and that was all – if they could get rid of them in any way, they would do it. If you take the speeches of the various politicians in all those years, about their attitudes to Catholics and republicans. I think they recognised during the thirties that the IRA were becoming a force that could be a threat, at least."

You supported the 1933 rail strike didn't you?

"Actually I remember I took a party of volunteers to disrupt that railway. . . . At that time there was a Ballymena railway that went on down through Antrim way, you know, but it was called off. Actually I was on my way when couriers came after me on a bike and that was the beginning of the end as far as that was concerned."

You were on bikes were you?

"That was the only transport then. Bikes suited us because we could have got into country lanes, and the only way they could get us . . . we knew all the areas very well, and we knew what we had to do, we knew the points of attack – it was all planned out prior to that so we would disrupt the railway lines. This was the policy of the movement at the time. . . . "

Were you in Belfast in 1935?

"In 1935 there was the sectarian pogroms in Belfast. Catholics were expelled from Corporation Street – we found them homes in Ardoyne which were still being built. Every company in Belfast was on the stand-to, positions were mapped out. We had no intention of attacking the Protestant people, but we were going to defend the Catholics. There was an ambush of the RUC at Lancaster Street – there is a song about it you know! The powers that be came to the conclusion that it was too dangerous to encourage the pogroms, and they cooled off a lot then."

FOOTNOTES

1. This period is covered by Griffith, K; O'Grady, T. 1982, and MacEoin, U. (ed) 1980.
2. Bell, J. B. 1979; see also Coogan, T. P., 1980.
3. The Ulster Protestant Association was a loyalist paramilitary organisation of the 1920s, but there is little evidence that it acted as an "armed wing" of the Ulster Protestant League, itself a rather shadowy organisation in the 1930s.
4. Giles Quay was the site of the IRA training camp. It was fifteen miles from Dundalk and two miles inside the Free State border. On the morning of 14 July, 1935, while the riots were raging in Belfast, about one hundred IRA men, probably all from the North, were training in the camp when they were surrounded by a squad of Gardai and detectives. Some shots were fired and twelve men, said to be "leaders", were arrested. One of these was Liam Mulholland. That night about seventy people picketed Anne Street Barracks in Dundalk where the twelve were held under Article 2A of the Constitution. Police fired shots in the air to disperse them. Whether it was coincidental that the arrests occurred precisely at the point in time when, as Jack Brady makes clear, the IRA was under pressure in the North is an interesting question.

By Way of Conclusion

The eighties are not the thirties. This obvious point must be made by way of conclusion for at least two reasons. Firstly, to initial appearances there are many similarities between the present Belfast and the Belfast of fifty years ago. At the time of writing NI's unemployment rate is officially 21% overall; some areas, especially west of the Bann and working class (and most noticeably, Catholic working class) areas of Belfast have much higher rates of unemployment. Moreover, a number of reports have recently predicted that unemployment will continue to climb in the foreseeable future. The spectre of 1932 seems to haunt us again. In addition, sectarianism is alive and thriving, with residential areas hermetically segregated, the recurrence of flare-ups of sectarian violence with their accompanying deaths and displacement of families, especially around the period of the July Orange marches, and the presence in the streets of armed and uniformed security forces supposedly keeping the peace between the two rival factions. In many ways things would seem to have changed little since 1935.

But this superficial view of similarity is too facile. Changes have occurred in the fifty years since the period of which our respondents have spoken. Gone are many of the places of employment spoken of in this book. The shipyard, although closed in the mid-thirties, revived afterwards but is now a mere shadow of its former self, with less than 6,000 jobs, all of them highly dependent on state support. The linen industry, already showing some slight signs of ill-health in the pre-war years, to all intents and purposes died in the post-war period, as did its successor the synthetic fibres industry.

These have not been the only changes. The trade union movement, not officially recognised by the NI government until 1964, is now a more legitimate institution than it was in the thirties. But one consequence of this legitimation is that it is now in many ways integrated into the state through various quangoes, legal arrangements, etc. The state itself has increased the range of its interventions into daily life. Present public expenditure cuts notwithstanding, the whole post-war period has seen the growth not merely of state support to business and industry, but of a commitment to some sort of welfare provision, however defined. People are not now ejected from employment into a life without any income at all; they get some income, albeit less than the official poverty line. The payment of many benefits is not at the complete discretion of a Board of Guardians; many benefits are, as welfare rights advocates have successfully shown, guaranteed by law, there for the demanding. In addition, the place of the Board of Guardians has been taken by numerous bodies existing ostensibly to manage labour relations, fair employment, sex discrimination, wage levels, unfair dismissals, etc. Whether the existence of these bodies, and indeed of all the institutions of the welfare state, have made life better for the working class is not the point here. What is important is that the hungry thirties and the hungry eighties are different.

As with employment and unemployment, so with sectarianism and political action. The unionist establishment suffered a severe blow to its prestige and sense of direction by the prorogation of Stormont in 1972 and the introduction of Direct Rule, forty years after that imposing building was erected on the outskirts of Belfast. Direct Rule encourages its own form of sectarianism based ultimately on the granting of a veto on political solutions to the Unionists by the British. But the Unionists themselves do not directly hold the reins of power as they did in the thirties. But, perhaps for that reason, and despite the subsequent divisions in unionism, militant populist loyalism (in the form especially of the UDA, but also represented by other loyalist paramilitary groups) has shown itself more than capable to thwart political solutions with which it does not agree, and to cause terror in Catholic communities through assassination campaigns.

And if the loyalists are stronger, better armed and better organised than fifty years ago, so too are the republicans. The IRA is at a point where, as even British generals themselves have admitted, it cannot be beaten by military means alone. This is a far cry from the previously weak movement that our respondents spoke to us of. Furthermore, the republican movement may have "missed the boat" in terms of its lack of a social programme at the time of the ODR Strike, but as recent developments in the rise of Sinn Féin as a political force in the North indicate, there is no reason to believe that they would be as inactive now.

In short, it is a bad analysis which rests only at the level of appearances. Proper analysis must cut below superficial similarities between different periods in time to see the specific factors that make up the uniqueness of each particular period. In other words, analysis must rest on accurate historical understanding and not on a method that abstracts from history in the pursuit of some timeless paradigm.

This leads to the second reason for stressing the differences between the thirties and the eighties. Analysis is not just a luxury reserved for academics. It is also a necessary tool to be used by political activists who would seek to learn from the past in order to prescribe programmes for the present. This book has deliberately avoided prescriptions and programmes. However, there is a necessity in these final words to stress one important point about such a task, that is, that bad analysis can easily lead to bad politics. Insofar as political programmes for the present attempt to build on the past, they must learn from real history and not from myth. Take, for instance, the following advice:

> "The NI working class is not immune to the crisis. On the contrary, it is experiencing 'peripheralisation' in a particularly acute form. However, the political responses are being forced along channels which developed in nationalist struggle. What is missing is non-reformist political leadership which can offer the class the models of change which were last on display in NI in the 1930s with the National Unemployed Workers' Union."[1]

For a start, the author is factually wrong; he misses the vital point that the unemployed in the North organised in the Irish Unemployed Workers' Movement, not the British National Unemployed Workers' Union. More substantially, as many of those who were themselves politically active in the thirties were at pains to point out to us, the ODR Strike was not a pre-revolutionary situation, even though it is often portrayed as such. And, following on their assessment, we have emphasised here all the factors which came together in the ODR Strike, of which an important one, but certainly not the only one, was the work put into organising it by the RWG. Further, we have rejected political assessments which see the few weeks of the ODR agitation as a socialist oasis in an otherwise barren desert in the twenties and the thirties. By extension, we would be willing to suspect that there were at least some elements of socialist activity and indeed socialist success between 1932 and the present.

So, we must reject this view that sees the ODR Strike as unique, and urges the introduction, like some *deus ex machina*, of the supposedly one key factor that would repeat that unique event, correct revolutionary political leadership. A "solution" such as the one advocated in the above quotation, resting as it does on the espousal of a seemingly timeless and ahistorical magic formula, does justice neither to the present nor the past. Conversely, we have based our arguments on the specific historical complexity of politics in Belfast in the thirties. We have emphasised the presence of two waves, as it were, both with relatively independent rhythms: socialism and sectarianism. The presence of both these elements in Belfast in the thirties is historically understandable. Some may be surprised at the extent of socialist activity in the period (and indeed earlier, in the twenties, although we have only referred very briefly to that decade) in benighted Belfast; but the total absence of any socialist activity in Ireland's main industrial city would be even more surprising and inexplicable. Moreover, given the origins of Belfast's working class in the divisions that rose out of the Plantation in the seventeenth century, as well as the way that those divisions were reinforced and institutionalised by partition, the extent of sectarianism in Belfast in the thirties should come as no great surprise, for all that it may be regrettable.

The way in which these two elements, sectarianism and socialism, inter-relate in the thirties (or in any decade for that matter) must be the starting point for any analysis and ultimately for any political activity which seeks to learn the lessons of the past. To try to brush aside sectarianism as a temporary aberration which exists solely because of conniving bosses and political leaders and which can be overcome by the introduction of correct political leadership is at best wishful thinking.

Finally, in attempting to cut through the myth to see the real historical Belfast of the thirties, we have had one indispensable source of information, namely, the accounts of events by people who experienced that decade and its political struggles. Oral history, we have argued, is not just a source of homely anecdotes spun by pleasant old men and women, but a vital clue to the complexity of a particular historical period. If we were tempted at all to wishful thinking or ahistorical abstraction, it was often the words of our respondents which pulled us back to history. So, it was ultimately from them that we learned that, in the political and not just the analytical sense, the eighties are not the thirties. Or, to put it another way: there is no way back to the thirties; there are only, possibly, ways forward.

FOOTNOTES

1. D. Byrne, "Theorising Northern Ireland", unpublished paper, Department of Social Administration, Durham University, 1980: 42.

Afterword on Ideology

The life stories of John Hyde, John Nicholl and Liam Mulholland have been presented without commentary. They stand as representatives of the skilled shipyard worker, and the socialists and republicans of Belfast. They are meant to complement our analysis made up of a patchwork of multiple personal experiences. The choice of which particular testimony to use as a "typical" life story depended on several factors: some narratives flowed better than others and were more comprehensive, their experience embraced more of the topics and incidents covered in our analysis. In no statistical sense could our chosen testimonies be considered typical, but there was a deeper social and historical sense in which they were.

Over and above some passive quantitative criteria we would argue for the representativeness of our life stories. Another aspect of the life story apart from its content is of course its form. Certainly the great lesson we learned from this part of our research was to confirm Daniel Bertaux's advice that, "one must not think of life stories as just dead strings of factual beads waiting to be taken apart and sorted back into different piles – hard and soft. The stories are themselves part of a living, social relationship: between teller and listener, past and present. So, far from being a drawback, this is a great strength: for as we discovered, the telling of the story may give as many clues as what is told."[1]

In recent years several writers have noted the empiricist bias of much oral history work. So, for example, Ronald Grele has argued that "our interviews . . . are far more complex than we usually assume. If read properly, they do reveal to us hidden levels of discourse – the search for which is the aim of symptomatic reading".[2] Althusser's "symptomatic reading" bids us look not only for presences (facts and comments) but also for absences and oversights to uncover the underlying problematic of a text. Writers on cultural studies have also pointed out that oral history generally, "reads language 'transparently', as a source of empirical and factual evidence, with little attention to the structural determinations exercised historically by specific linguistic forms".[3] The language of our oral history tapes is not of course "transparent" and we should in future pay more attention to the socio-linguistic dimension. The form of our data is as important as its content. Luisa Passerini has helped bring these concerns squarely into the "new" more critical oral history, noting that our raw material "consists not just in factual statements, but is pre-eminently an expression and representation of culture, and therefore includes not only literal narrations but also the dimension of memory, ideology and subconscious desires."[4] We shall now try to elaborate some of the key concepts necessary to develop a "discourse analysis" approach.

A possible starting point would be Derrida's method of deconstruction, already applied widely in literary criticism.[5] Deconstruction is a critical method of displaying the latent metaphysical structure of a discourse. It operates through an inworming or internal subversion of the text; as Norris explains; "taking a repressed or subjugated theme, pursuing the various textual ramifications and showing how these subvert the very order that strives to hold them in check."[6] Derrida is above all concerned to reject what he calls the "logocentric myth" of Western philosophy with its concern for origins, truth and presence. For him, language can be seen as a decentred play of signifiers with an infinite structure of possible meanings.

Another theorist who has developed "discourse analysis" is of course Foucault. His aim is to analyse discourses: "their conditions of existence, the systems which regulate their emergence, their functioning and their transformation."[7] In his work there is a break from the simplistic opposition between science and ideology typical of some versions of Marxism. Foucault can still be seen as a precursor of the materialist analysis of ideological relations and the formation of ideological objects. Foucault's theory of discursive practices also helps us break decisively with the history of ideas approach, generally used in previous histories of republicanism.[8] Whereas the history of ideas usually credits the discourse that it analyses with coherence, Foucault maintains that "a discursive formation is not an ideal, continuous, smooth text that runs beneath the multiplicity of contradictions, and resolves them in the calm unity of coherent thought. . . . "[9] So, following Foucault in the course of our "archaeological" analysis of republican ideology, "contradictions are neither appearances to be overcome, nor secret principles to be uncovered."[10] Foucault helps us reject the quest for a general theory of language and subjectivity as with Saussure and Lacan. He alerts us instead to the historical specificity of particular statements and re-opens the possibility of a historical materialist semiology.

Without wishing to neglect the "post structuralist" advances of Derrida and Foucault we should also consider the relevance of the Marxist theory of ideology. Following Althusser we can say that "ideology is a 'representation' of the imaginary relationship of individuals to their real conditions of existence."[11] From this definition flows a rejection of ideology as simply "ideas" or worse "false consciousness", which would be a poor guide indeed to our study of republicanism. Furthermore, ideology for Althusser has a *material* existence which determines the subject; it constitutes the "cement" which binds society together. Ideologies must be seen as real social relations, bodies of representations existing in institutions and practices. Ideology is the lived relation between people and their world represented in an imaginary way in their unconscious. More questionable is Althusser's conception of "ideology in general" which tends to become a transcendental subject above social classes.[12] Particular ideologies may serve the reproduction of the capitalist mode of production or they may challenge it. Eagleton has quite rightly criticized Althusser's conception of ideology as "a seamless web enmeshing all lived practice, a homogeneous structure to subject the subject", urging us instead to see ideology "as a heterogeneous, contradictory formation, a question of constant struggle at the level of signifying practices."[13] In short we need to reintroduce the class struggle into our discourse analysis which cannot be sustained simply by the science/ideology opposition.

All ideologies must "recruit" subjects and this process whereby individuals are constituted as subjects is referred to as "interpellation" (or hailing) by Althusser. It is Ernesto Laclau who has developed this non-reductionist conception of ideology furthest, arguing that "the class character of an ideology is given by its *form* and not by its *content*."[14] That is to say, ideological elements are "neutral" if taken in isolation; their class structure is determined by their specific *articulation* within the class structure. So, there is nothing "bourgeois" about nationalism *per se* for example: it takes on its different complexions according to its integration into class discourse. There are certain limits to this, because ideologies are not quite so free-floating: a socialist movement cannot adopt racist policies (however "popular") and continue as such. The general point is a sound one however, and will help us in a non-reductionist analysis of republicanism. It is worth mentioning in this context the work of Pêcheux for whom, "a meaning effect does not pre-exist the discursive formation in which it is constituted. The production of meaning is an integral part of the interpellation of the individual as subject."[15] Furthermore, a word or expression does not have a meaning "of its own", this is only constituted in each discursive formation: a same word or meaning may change its meaning as it passes from one discursive formation to another. Nationalism is a prime example of this, but the same would apply to democracy, socialism and other ideologies. In what follows we carry out a "case study" of one such ideology, namely Irish republicanism.

These thoughts do not immediately resolve our problems as to how to "read" an ideological formation. However, we can attempt to analyse some of the contradictions in Irish republicanism which emerge from our interviews. One way to avoid these problems is represented by the recent book *Curious Journey – An Oral History of Ireland's Unfinished Revolution*[16] which simply organises its account in terms of nationalist ideology. One of three questions asked of the same sample of prominent ex-republicans was: "Where do you hope all this blood and suffering will eventually take your ancient island home?"[17] The answers were predictably at the level of mythology with no attempt by the interviewers to challenge or draw out contradictions.

We found that our 1930s republicans were rather full of contradictions. One ex-IRA officer had been active in the 1932 Outdoor Relief strike (in spite of his movement's non-involvement) and expressed certain concern with social and economic issues:

> "We were moving towards socialism, the republican movement, and you got the feeling that nationalism, pure nationalism of the romantic type, that the people wanted [more]. During the [1920s] truce the Army [i.e. the IRA] was used in a good lot of cases to dispossess those people who had seized land. There was a fairly strong feeling at the time [the 1930s] that it was wrong to do that."

This same activist, who had a prominent role in the IRA sabotage action in support of striking railway workers in 1933, went on to say:

> "The strongest thing in Ireland is nationalism; I suppose it's the strongest thing in the world. There's millions of men have died for nationalism, countless millions of men have died, but very few have died for socialism. Men will die for their country: they're not prepared to die for an 'ism'."

Another republican, who had been out of work a long time and would look in the newspaper ads for wakes he could go to for a feed, agreed he was a "straight down the line military man" and said:

> "I didn't like communism. They'd call themselves an Irish communist party but at the heel of the hunt they always had to do what Moscow said. There were a lot of people in the republican movement who thought 'they're Communists and we're against them because we're Catholics'."

This orthodox and traditional nationalist could go on to say:

> "I'm a strong believer in the [*Sinn Féin*] social and economic policy. I believe the workers will have to be ultimately in control. You don't have to be a communist to believe in social justice. I believe in socialism, an Irish socialism that suits the people and the country."

Belfast republicans in the 1930s were subject to contradictory interpellations which forged an inevitably unstable discourse: they were nationalists, they were often practicing Catholics, but they were also workers and members of a revolutionary organisation engaged in armed struggle against the state. This complexity has to be analysed, not simply reproduced, if we are to move into a "post-heroic" understanding of Irish republicanism.

So, finally, what constitutes the unity of a discourse such as republicanism if its discrete elements are seen as relatively autonomous? The contradictory unity of a discourse is maintained through a system of displacements during periods of stability, but the opposite occurs in a period of crisis when the inherent contradictions are exacerbated. If we may borrow a term from Lacanian psychoanalysis, a full analysis of the republican discourse would examine how its various elements go through a process of "binding"; "binding of physical energy, binding of representations, binding of meaning, which finally confers a certain stability."[18] Thus the various sets of interpellations are bound up in the republican "movement" which has its mythical or symbolic side as much as its material reality.

Another area of fruitful analysis would be around the question of sectarianism conceived as an exclusionary ideology and practice on the grounds of religious/national/political affiliation. The Belfast shipyards were traditionally the site of a Protestant "labour aristocracy" seen as a prime motive force in anti-Catholic sectarianism.[19] Most of our respondents were at pains to deny any sectarianism in the shipyard:

> "People say that if you're a Roman Catholic you've no hope in the yard – but this is not so. Men who served their time with me were Roman Catholics. There were pay offs and I was paid off and they weren't. But it never annoyed me that Paddy [a Catholic] was kept. I knew Paddy well. . . . "

Yet at other times the employment discrimination at the yard was admitted:

> "When I was in the shipyard the question of Catholic/Protestant didn't loom large. There were a number of Catholics worked there – some of them were well appreciated – but they were strictly in a minority."

When it came to the expulsion of Catholics from the yard, as in 1935, it was admitted too, though in a strange way:

> "I didn't see any signs but I knew there was a bit of trouble while I was an apprentice. The few Catholics that were there, fellows would have gone down and said: 'Some wild men are about so you'd be as well to take some time off'. That happened at times. In 1935, a lot of the hotheads got together and would set out to beat them up or throw them out but their colleagues would have told them trouble was brewing and they'd be as well to go home for a few days."

For the skilled Protestant worker at the shipyard, Catholics were workmates and fellow trade unionists, but they also represented a threat: the objective threat of job competition and the equally, if not more important, subjective threat from (most) Catholics' commitment to the reunification of Ireland, and the severance of the link with Britain which ostensibly guaranteed their livelihood.

It is only the most recent work in oral history[20] which seems to be more aware of the complexity of consciousness, the contradictions which operate within our memories and the sheer inconsistency of much of the human experience. It is after all ideologies or fragments of ideologies that we gather in our interviews yet we look at them mainly for "facts". As the Popular Memory Group stress, we must not ignore "the cultural framing of 'fact' – all the symbolic and linguistic features through which human meaning is conveyed."[21] Our oral history testimonies are not simple records of past events but complex cultural products involving still untheorised relations between the "private" and the political, the past and the present. We must seek the "matrix of meaning" within a discursive formation, the system of social/psychological/subconscious relationships which make sense of our experience. We are looking at the relations between language and action, knowledge and situation.

FOOTNOTES

1. Bertaux, D. 1982 (b):96-7
2. Grele, R. 1975:137-8
3. Weedon, C; Tolson, A; Mort, F. 1980:215
4. Passerini, L. 1979:84
5. See Derrida, J. 1980
6. Norris, C. 1982:39
7. Foucault, M. 1978:23
8. See for example, Bell, J.B. 1979, and Coogan, T.P. 1980
9. Foucault, M. 1972:155
10. Ibid: 151
11. Althusser, L. 1971:152
12. See the discussion in Larrain, J. 1983
13. Eagleton, T. 1981:141
14. Laclau, E. 1977:160
15. Pêcheux, M. 1982:187
16. Griffith, K; O'Grady, T. 1982
17. Ibid: xxiv
18. Laplanche, J; Leclaire, S. 1966:178
19. See Reid, A. 1980
20. See Thompson, P. 1982 (b)
21. Popular Memory Group. 1982:225

Appendix 1: People Interviewed

Florrie Addley
Scotty Best
Tommy Best
Harold Binks
Barney Boswell
Tom Boyd
Tommy Boyd
Anne Boyle
Leo Boyle
Jack Brady
Peter Carleton
Tommy Cochrane
Harry Diamond
Tommy Fitzpatrick
Malachy Gray
John Hewitt
Frank Hughes
Charlie Hull
Bobby Hurndall
John Hyde
James Kelly
Geordie Loughrey
John Lowry*
Sean Mac Con Uladh
Norman MacNeilly
Frances Maguire
Lucy McErlane
Charlie McGlade
Jack McGougan
Anne McKenna
Fred McMahon
John McWade
William Monaghan
Murtagh Morgan
Liam Mulholland
John Nicholl
Peadar O'Donnell
Belle O'Hara
Ida Patterson
Saidie Patterson
William Patterson
Tommy Patton
Alice Quinn
Jackie Quinn
Alec Salmon
Jim Salmon
Paddy Scott
Betty Sinclair
Michael Traynor
David Wylie

*This is not the real name of the person concerned; he wished to remain anonymous.

Appendix 2: Abbreviations Used

AEU	Amalgamated Engineering Union
A/G	Adjutant-General (IRA)
AOH (Hibs)	Ancient Order of Hibernians
ATGWU	Amalgamated Transport and General Workers Union
CPGB	Communist Party of Great Britain
CPI (CP)	Communist Party of Ireland
ETU	Electrical Trades Union
GHQ	General headquarters
GNR	Great Northern Railway
GPO	General Post Office
H&W	Harland & Wolff
ILP	Independent Labour Party
INF	Irish National Foresters
INUM	Irish National Unemployment Movement
IRA ('RA)	Irish Republican Army
ITGWU	Irish Transport and General Workers Union
MP	Member of Parliament
NCCL	National Council for Civil Liberties
NI	Northern Ireland
NICSS	Northern Ireland Council of Social Services
NILP	Northern Ireland Labour Party
NUR	National Union of Railwaymen
O/C	Officer Commanding (IRA)
ODR	Outdoor Relief
RUC	Royal Ulster Constabulary
RWG	Revolutionary Workers' Group(s)
SVDP	Saint Vincent de Paul (Society)
TUC	Trade Union Congress
UAB	Unemployment Assistance Board
UDA	Ulster Defence Association
UPA	Ulster Protestant Association
UPL	Ulster Protestant League
US	United States
UULA	Ulster Unionist Labour Association
YMCA	Young Men's Christian Association

Glossary

Ancient Order of Hibernians (AOH): a conservative, Catholic organisation modelled on the Orange Order

Ard Scoil: literally "high school", a centre for promoting Irish culture (in particular dancing, music and language) in Belfast

Black trades/Blackmen: exclusive skilled trades within Harland & Wolff; name probably derives from connections with the Royal Black Preceptory, an elite within the Orange Order

B Specials: an entirely Protestant auxiliary police force in Northern Ireland, disbanded on 30 April 1970

Connolly Column: called after James Connolly; collective name given to Irish volunteers who fought in the International Brigade in the Spanish Civil War

Cumann na mBan: women's section of the IRA

Dáil (Eireann): the parliament of the Republic of Ireland

Direct Rule: government of Northern Ireland directly from Westminster, imposed with the prorogation of Stormont in 1972

Fianna: Na Fianna Eireann, the youth wing of the republican movement

Fianna Fáil: one of the two main political parties in the Republic of Ireland (the other being Fine Gael); formed by Eamon De Valéra in 1926, first came to power in 1932

Foresters: Irish National Foresters (INF), founded in 1877 as a nationalist benefit society to provide relief for members, who had to be Irish by birth or descent, and their families

Garda/Gardai: Garda Síochána, literally "Guardians of the Peace", the name of the police force in the Republic of Ireland

Republican Congress: a short-lived organisation formed by some members of the IRA Army Council and some trade unionists in 1933, supposedly to take up the same issues as the failed IRA initiative, Saor Eire; the lack of IRA backing was partly responsible for the demise of the Republican Congress

Roger Casement Cumann: a particular Sinn Féin club, called after the executed revolutionary leader of 1916

Saor Eire: left-wing organisation sponsored by the IRA in the early 1930s, later superceded by the Republican Congress

Saor Uladh: republican group formed in 1951 which recognised the southern state but began a military campaign in the north in 1955

Sinn Féin: political party formed in 1907, but later to become the political section of the republican movement

Sinn Féin Cumann/Cumainn: local Sinn Féin club/clubs

Ulster Volunteers: Ulster Volunteer Force (UVF), a unionist paramilitary group formed in 1912 in opposition to Home Rule for Ireland

White Cross: a republican organisation to aid financially dependants of prisoners; precursor of the Green Cross

Bibliography

Althusser, L., *Lenin and Philosophy and Other Essays*, New Left Books, London, 1971
Armstrong, D.C., "Social and Economic Conditions in the Belfast Linen Industry, 1850-1900", *Irish Historical Studies*, 7, 1951
Bardon, J., *Belfast: an Illustrated History*, Blackstaff, Belfast, 1982
Beacham, A., *Report of a Survey of Living Conditions Made in a Representative Working Class Area in Belfast, November 1938-February 1939*, Presbyterian Church in Ireland, Social Service Committee, Belfast, 1939
Bell, J.B., *The Secret Army: the IRA 1916-1979*, Academy Press, Dublin, 1979
Bertaux, D., "From the Life-History Approach to the Transformation of Sociological Practice", in D. Bertaux (ed.), *Biography and Society: the Life History Approach in the Social Sciences*, Sage, London, 1982
"Stories as Clues to Sociological Understanding: the Bakers of Paris", in P. Thompson (ed.), *Our Common History: the Transformation of Europe*, Pluto Press, London, 1982
Boyle, E., " 'Linenopolis': the Rise of the Textile Industry", in J.C. Beckett *et al.*, *Belfast: the Making of the City*, Appletree, Belfast, 1983
Budge, I.; O'Leary, C., *Belfast: Approach to Crisis*, Macmillan, London, 1973
Campbell, W., "Down the Shankill", *Ulster Folklife*, 22, 1976
Carnwath, T., *Report to the Special Committee of the Belfast Corporation on the Municipal Health Services of the City*, typescript, Queen's University, Belfast, 24 December 1941
Clarkson, J.D., *Labor and Nationalism in Ireland*, Columbia University Press, New York, 1925
Coe, W., *The Engineering Industry in the North of Ireland*, David and Charles, Newton Abbot, 1969
Communist Party of Ireland, *Outline History*, New Books, Dublin, [1973]
Confidential Document, *For Members of Parliament Only*, n.d. (probably 1935/6, and probably the dossier prepared by the Nationalist Party on which their demand for a British government inquiry into the occurrences of July 1935 was based; available in Linen Hall Library, Belfast)
Coogan, T.P., *The IRA*, Fontana, London, 1980
Cronin, S., *Frank Ryan: the Search for the Republic*, Repsol, Dublin, 1980
Cuthbert, N. *see* Isles, K.S; Cuthbert, N.
Davis, M., *The Struggle for Workers' Unity in Belfast 1930-1935*, unpublished M.Sc., University of California, 1975

Dean of Belfast, " 'Orange Terror': a Rebuttal", *The Bell*, 17 (5), 1944
Deeny, J., "Poverty as a Cause of Ill-health", *Social and Statistical Inquiry Society of Ireland Journal*, 1940
Denzin, N., *The Research Act*, McGraw-Hill, New York, 1970
Derrida, J., *Positions*, Chicago University Press, Chicago, 1980
Devlin, P., *Yes, We Have No Bananas: Outdoor Relief in Belfast, 1920-1939*, Blackstaff, Belfast, 1981
"Documentary Appendix: Principal Documents, July-August, 1935", *Catholic Bulletin*, 25 (9), September 1935
Dohrs, F., "The Linen Industry of Northern Ireland", *The Textile Quarterly*, 2 (2), 1952
Eagleton, T., *Walter Benjamin, or Towards a Revolutionary Criticism*, New Left Books, London, 1981
Farrell, M., *The Poor Law and the Workhouse in Belfast 1838-1938*, Public Record Office of Northern Ireland, 1978
Northern Ireland: the Orange State, Pluto, London, 1980
Foucault, M., *The Archaeology of Knowledge*, Tavistock, London, 1972
"Politics and the Study of Discourse", *Ideology and Consciousness*, 3, 1978
Fraser, R., *Blood of Spain: the Experience of Civil War 1936-1939*, Penguin, Harmondsworth, 1981
Grele, R., "Movement Without Aim: Methodological and Theoretical Problems in Oral History", in R. Grele (ed.), *Envelopes of Sound*, President Publishing, Chicago, 1975
Griffith, K.; O'Grady, T., *Curious Journey: an Oral History of Ireland's Unfinished Revolution*, Hutchinson, London, 1982
Hannington, W., *Ten Lean Years*, Gollancz, London, 1940
Harrison, B., "Oral History and Recent Political History", *Oral History*, 1 (3), 1976
Henige, D., *Oral Historiography*, Longman, London, 1982
Isles, K.S.; Cuthbert, N., *An Economic Survey of Northern Ireland*, HMSO, Belfast, 1957
Jefferson, H., *Viscount Pirrie of Belfast*, Mullan, Belfast, 1948
Johnstone, T.M., *Northern Ireland: the Crisis in Industry*, Johnstone, Belfast, 1930
Kelly, J., "Journalist's Diary: Ten Years Back", *Capuchin Annual*, 1944
Kennedy, D., "Catholics in Northern Ireland, 1926-1939", in F. MacManus (ed.), *The Years of the Great Test*, Mercier, Cork, 1966
Kennedy, H., "Riot at Lancaster Street", *Aquarius*, 5, 1972
Laclau, E., *Politics and Ideology in Marxist Theory*, New Left Books, London, 1977
Laplanche, J.; Leclaire, S., "The Unconscious: a Psychoanalytic Study", *Yale French Studies*, 48, 1966
Larrain, J., *Marxism and Ideology*, Macmillan, London, 1983
Leclaire, S. *see* Laplanche, J.; Leclaire, S.
Lynn, Sir Robert (Chairman), *The Protection and Welfare of the Young and the Treatment of Young Offenders*, HMSO, Belfast, 1938

Macbeath, A., *Fifty Years of Social Work, 1906-1956*, Council of Social Welfare, Belfast, 1956

MacEoin, U., (ed.), *Survivors*, Argenta Publications, Dublin, 1980

Messenger, B., *Picking Up the Linen Threads*, Blackstaff, Belfast, 1980

Methodist Church in Ireland, Belfast District Synod, Temperance and Social Welfare Committee, *Report of a Survey*, 1938

Midgley, H., *Food For Thought*, Northern Ireland Labour Party, Belfast, 1933

Milotte, M., *Communist Politics in Ireland, 1916-1945*, unpublished Ph.D., Queen's University, Belfast, 1977. (Later published as *Communism in Modern Ireland: the Pursuit of the Workers' Republic since 1916*, Gill & Macmillan, Dublin, 1984)

Mort, F. *see* Weedon, C.; Tolson, A.; Mort, F.

Munck, R., "A Divided Working Class: Protestant and Catholic Workers in Northern Ireland", *Labour, Capital and Society*, 13 (1), 1980

"At the Very Doorstep: Irish Labor and the National Question", *Éire-Ireland*, 28 (2), 1983

Murray, S., *The City Mission Story*, Belfast City Mission, Belfast, 1970

Norris, C., *Deconstruction: Theory and Practice,* Methuen, London, 1982

Northern Ireland Council of Social Services, *First Annual Report, July 5th, 1938-March 31st, 1940*, Belfast, 1940

O'Grady, T. *see* Griffith, K.; O'Grady, T.

Okihiro, G., "Oral History and the Writing of Ethnic History: a Reconaissance into Method and Theory", *Oral History Review*, 9, 1981

O'Riordan, M., *Connolly Column*, New Books, Dublin, 1979

Passerini, L., "Work, Ideology and Consensus under Italian Fascism", *History Workshop*, 8, 1979

Pêcheux, M., *Language, Semantics and Ideology*, Macmillan, London, 1982

Popular Memory Group, "Popular Memory: Theory, Politics, Method", in Centre for Contemporary Cultural Studies, *Making Histories*, Hutchinson, London, 1982

Reid, A., "Skilled Workers in the Shipbuilding Industry, 1880-1920: a Labour Aristocracy?" in A. Morgan and B. Purdie (eds.), *Ireland: Divided Nation, Divided Class*, Ink Links, London, 1980

Rolston, B., "The Limits of Trade Unionism", in L. O'Dowd, B. Rolston and M. Tomlinson, *Northern Ireland: Between Civil Rights and Civil War*, CSE Books, London, 1980(a)

"Community Politics", in L. O'Dowd, B. Rolston and M. Tomlinson, *Northern Ireland: Between Civil Rights and Civil War*, CSE Books, London, 1980(b)

Rosaldo, R., "Doing Oral History", *Social Analysis*, 4, 1980

Shea, P., *Voices and the Sound of Drums*, Blackstaff, Belfast, 1981

Socialist Medical Association, Belfast Branch, *Health in Belfast*, Northern Ireland Labour Party, Belfast, *c.* 1945

Thompson, P., (ed.), *Our Common History: the Transformation of Europe*, Pluto, London, 1982

The Voice of the Past: Oral History, Oxford University Press, London, 1978
Tolson, A. *see* Weedon, C.; Tolson, A.; Mort, F.
Walker, G., *The Politics of Frustration: Harry Midgley and the Failure of Labour in Northern Ireland*, Manchester University Press, Manchester, 1985
Weedon, C.; Tolson, A.; Mort, F., "Theories of Language and Subjectivity", in S. Hall *et al* (eds.), *Culture, Media, Language*, Hutchinson, London, 1980
"XQ", *Are You on the North's £2,800,000 Pay Roll?*, Irish News Publications, Belfast, 1932
"XQ", *The Truth About Stormont*, Irish News Publications, Belfast, 1933